Thanks you for sticking with us for our first year of publication!

Inside this special edition, you will find every edition released in 2021, but first, let's get to know each other a little better.

The TalesOfTheGods & Practical Witchcraft magazine was created by Desirée Goulden, owner of TalesOfTheGods.com. TalesOfTheGods.com is a metaphysical networking website dedicated to connecting practitioners and pagans from across paths. It sports a database of online and offline stores and shops, book recommendations for many paths, a social media aspect, forums, articles, and more. When created in 2019 TOTG had the intention of expanding into print as well as a brick and mortar pagan community center.

While TOTG wanted to get into publishing, as it was the creator's background, it was never our first priority. One day, while couch-surfing my (Desirée's) aunt's house after being displaced due to COVID-19, I floated the idea of the magazine to a group I was a mod for. I didn't think it would go anywhere, had a budget of $0, no idea how to publish, and no software to speak of, but I had something more important: community.

The people in the mod chat loved the idea, and I asked if people would be interested in writing. As I was poor, I couldn't pay, but I would split the income equally between everyone who was involved. To my surprise, many people were interested. They liked the idea of a publication bringing together a hodgepodge of occult and religious knowledge, views, and news.

As I sourced the original team from the Practical Witchcraft group, I felt it was only right to include them in the title. Practical Witchcraft is a private FaceBook group dedicated to connecting to practitioners and giving a safe space for knowledge exchange and peer-to-peer help and teaching, rather than the usual meme and drama-filled groups that are known to thrive online.

In a month we organized and created the content for the first edition of the magazine, the Fall 2020 edition. Originally intended to be a twice-yearly release, Brooke (owner of Practical Witchcraft) suggested releasing on days on The Wheel Of The Year. This gave us a predictable release schedule, as well as a basis and theme for each release. In the first editions, you can really see that we had more enthusiasm than know-how. I was just relearning how to design a magazine (something I had done in the past for my mother's company) for the first time in 5 years, with open-source software rather than adobe (re: $0 budget). I was learning how to organize a team and enforce deadlines, as well as teaching myself how to self-publish and market the magazine as best as I could.

Since the first edition up until Yule we have released essentially every other month. Each magazine brings change and more polish and more news and information. Although useful our original publisher, Kindle

Direct Publishing, limited our reach and alienated those who oppose what Amazon stands for. We switched mid-year to Ingram Spark, which had a price tag that came out of my pocket but increased our reach and put us in physical stores like Barns & Noble, and indie shops. This increased our reach enough to cover most of the price of publishing.

Unfortunately, publishing every few months on a team of volunteers led to burnout as well as conflicts around the Yuletide season. As such, we decided to take an edition off. Rather than picking up with the Imbolc edition, we have decided to forgo the archives and create a once early anniversary edition with all the year's content in one book. This allows the team to have 4 months off and provide better content in the future.

I have given all the magazine contributors a forum to fill out to help the readers get to know them a little better, so without further adieu: the contributors.

Dana-Lee Beaudreau

What was the first edition you worked on/ when did you join?

Fall 2020 edition (1st edition)

Tell us about your craft a bit.

I practice as a Christian witch and a Dream Mistress. I've received certification and degrees in various arts over the years including intuitive arts, psychic training, Usui Reiki Master, amongst others. My beginnings in intuitive readings and dream work began in the mid to late 70s. I follow crystal works, spellwork, dream work, psychic and intuitive reading, reiki, herbal work, amongst other arts. I enjoy sharing with, learning from, and supporting my fellow craftspersons both in their journey and in life. Love you all. Blessings.

Do you provide services, own a shop, or teach? If so, tell us about it!

At present I do offer my services in dream interpretation, distance reiki, distance readings, and soul contract revelation. I also will be offering training in Level 1 Usui Reiki in September for a limited number of individuals (please contact me for costs and details). I can be reached at dana.vanes@gmail.com.

> How has your experience been contributing for the magazine? What are your thoughts on the culture of the magazine, the content covered, etc?

This project has been a great experience with a wonderful, caring, and supportive team/family. I appreciated everyone involved, the hard work of our lovely leader, and all the new things I learned over this time. I look forward to continuing my connection with this staff.

> What do you think in regards to pagan and occult publishing in the 2020s? What do you think about the existence of occult and pagan magazines? Should there be more indie publishers, or should publishing be relegated to well known occult/ pagan public figures?

I'm really happy that we have found an accepting forum for our voices. It has been hard to find my place in this divisive world where my whole self is accepted and where I can lend my love and support to others. While the occult is slightly more accepted these days, it still has a long way to go, especially in the face of attacks by those in positions of influence with biases, and ulterior agendas that speak loudest. I pray our craft and our community continues to grow and find support through this media and the freedom we enjoy in being able to make our voices heard.

> How has the internet and online spheres effected your views, practices, and social interactions within paganism and the occult?

While I enjoy our freedom to fairly teach and share our craft with others, I feel the internet has a long way to go. Hate mongers from the religious realm and even those exclusivists in our own art, are still a force to be reckoned with. It is my hope that through learning, teaching, and enlightening each other, we will grow and slowly overcome the prejudices that exist in time.

> **What do you think about the growing acceptance of the metaphysical in main stream media?**

I am glad and encouraged at the sign that we are becoming more acceptable and less feared as people become more aware of how foolish their superstition and entertainment media skewed ideas are.

> **2021 was a tough year for everyone, that being said, what is something good that happened for you? What new things did you start? What did you learn? What do you expect from 2022?**

In 2021, I found my voice. I began to write in earnest. The articles I wrote for the magazine allowed me to stretch my comfort zone as I shared some of what I'd learned in my life and my views. I also began writing my first of a series of fantasy novels which presents the idea that all fairy tales are based in baseless rumours. I also joined a group of online artists who share a variety of creative arts in an online forum. I am hoping that 2022 brings more of the same, a greater readership, and potentially a completion of my first novel.

> **What is something you always get when visiting the local metaphysical shop / witch shop?**

Personally, I'm addicted to buying crystals. Fortunately for me, it's something my family shares a passion for.

What is your favorite content creator for you path? (author, video creator, musician, ect)

My favourite teacher and greatest influence is Catherine Graham of Journey Healers. Not only does she teach in a way that I can understand, but she also continues to learn and grow which inspires her students to do the same.

When kind of content would you like to see more of in media?

I might like to see a bit more history behind the how to in our craft. I also appreciate and enjoy the "news" articles of things that are happening but I'd like to see some where these situations are resolved. While we need to fight for our rights and justice, also giving us a sign of hope so we keep fighting might help.

Is there anything else you would like to add before we finish this?

Most importantly, I want to thank Desiree Goulden for bringing us all together on this project and all her hard work every month. You are a true and gifted heart. I pray your future holds great joy and success. Love you. "Mom"

Desirée Goulden

What was the first edition you worked on/ when did you join?

Fall 2020 edition (1st edition)

Tell us about your craft a bit.

I am a Hellenic Pagan with a background in neo-wicca. (Dianic) My magic practice comes from a mix of ancient Greek magic, chaos magic, and local and familial traditions.

Do you provide services, own a shop, or teach? If so, tell us about it!

I own TalesOfTheGods.com, the TalesOfTheGods & Practical Witchcraft magazine, and a spiritual etsy shop. talesofthegods.com - etsy.com/ca/shop/AzimuthSpirituality

How has your experience been contributing for the magazine? What are your thoughts on the culture of the magazine, the content covered, etc?

As the creator, I do the organization of the project, am in charge of creating the magazine and publishing it, as well as managing contributors, advertisers, and customers. I also contribute to the articles. As such I approve everything that gets published. I have found it very interesting learning from others on paths I don't follow. Every single person I interact with comes from a different walk, with different experiences, with different knowledge.

Some people may have perspectives I either don't completely agree with, or follow deities I do not, and even in articles where I don't believe what is stated, I enjoy learning about what brings fulfillment to others and what is important to them and their path.

The people involved in this project are some of the best people I have met and I adore everyone involved. The contributors have proven time and time again to be of spectacular character and quality and I can not speak highly enough about my colleagues.

This magazine has been a labor of love, and often is paid for out of pocket, but it has been worthwhile and one of the things I am most proud of in my life. I started this while homeless in the depths of the beginnings of the Covid-19 pandemic and it and the people involved have pushed me outside my shell and convinced me to take chances and dive head first into things where usually I stand back and wait and miss opportunities. It and it's team has been my motivation throughout 2021.

> What do you think in regards to pagan and occult publishing in the 2020s? What do you think about the existence of occult and pagan magazines? Should there be more indie publishers, or should publishing be relegated to well known occult/ pagan public figures?

I think we have met a sort of equilibrium in occult publishing. I recall the 90s and the early 2000s and I see a market saturated with people publishing essentially anything and riding the wave of popularity brought to the community via movies like The Craft. For a while, almost anyone and everyone published through publishing houses and direct publishing trying to cash in on the money that followed the growing spiritual communities. As such often times most of what you could find in stores were very... "fluffy" or pushed forward misinformation or white supremacy and colonist content in the guise of "The old ways" or magical knowledge.

Now a days there is more ways to publish yourself no matter your credentials, but we have also collectively have taken a step back and started boycotting people who may be using the occult and pagan community for a quick buck. The availability of google, amazon, and good reads reviews makes it easier to sus out people who may not be all they present to the world and thus have made it a bit harder for these people to be taken seriously.

There is a new wave of indie publishers out there making their mark on the witchy world and bringing new knowledge that may not in the past have had a voice. I think the combination of the cultural shift away from Abrahamic dominance to a more multi-faith society, the internet allowing cross referencing to be easier and connecting communities, and the opening up of the publishing industry has brought the new frontier of the metaphysical sphere.

This is a long way to say: I am optimistic.

> How has the internet and online spheres effected your views, practices, and social interactions within paganism and the occult?

The internet (and in specific the ability to connect to other practitioners on my path that don't live in my area) has brought me out of my solitary practice. It has helped me with self acceptance and finding my own power and worth. It has introduced me to like minded people who have become my family and has drastically improved my view of the world.

> **What do you think about the growing acceptance of the metaphysical in main stream media?**

I think it is overdue. I grew up in a city that was extremely Abrahamic. That is to say the city I grew up in was very Christian and Muslim. As such, my family being atheist, and my being a edge lord goth wiccan at the time, we were not well liked. My teachers told my parents specifically that my family would be treated better if we "found the lord".

I remember getting gifted Silver Raven Wolf's Book Of Shadows (groan, I know. Trust me, I know.) from a friend's mother who lived in a different province. I remember sneaking it into my house, getting caught with it from my parents, being told that I "can't be that stupid". I remember that when people at school found out, I was called a Satanist and my friend's mother stormed into my 5th grade class room, screaming that I was the devil and I was "polluting her daughter with my witchcraft" and moving him to a private Catholic school the next day. I wouldn't see him again until grade 10.

There were no metaphysical shops, and it was the early 2000s so online was... well, when I could get onto the family computer, the online witchy world was lacking. This growing acceptance and normalization of the occult and paganism is something I would defend with my life.

I feel like it is easy to pretend that witchcraft and paganism is accepted when you live in a liberal city and have lived a life where in the internet was just a part of life, and not a privilege you couldn't get until your tweens. As someone who was brought up in a very Abrahamic city, before gay marriage was legal, with no metaphysical shops, and next to no resources, I fee like I as well as many others remember (and some still live in) places and times where being the slightest bit witchy was dangerous.

It is for this reason that I am to push forward the normalization of metaphysical practices and non Abrahamic, pantheistic belief systems.

> 2021 was a tough year for everyone, that being said, what is something good that happened for you? What new things did you start? What did you learn? What do you expect from 2022?

I started the TalesOfTheGods & Practical Witchcraft. I have learned how to connect and lead others and be confident in myself and my presence in the world. I have also opened up to astrology and began to dive into that. I have learned safe past life regression practices, learned more about the ethics and practices regarding my mediumship. As for 2022 I aim to release The Multi-Faith Guild Of Occult Practitioners, a guild that aims to hold online occult spaces to higher standards than what is often found online. It aims to build a platform of inclusion dedicated to seeking out and casting out racism and predatory cult like behaviors in the otherwise not moderated online world.

> What is something you always get when visiting the local metaphysical shop / witch shop?

Incense. Metaphysical shops usually have the best incenses.

What is your favorite content creator for you path? (author, video creator, musician, ect)

@elliemackinroberts on TikTok. while she is not a pagan or witch, she is an Ancient Greek Historian who often interacts with and accepts rather than rejects modern practitioners of Hellenismos.
@selkigirl on TikTok and Spotify has some of my favorite music since Damh The Bard

When kind of content would you like to see more of in media?

I would like to see more traditional Hellenic pagan content that is factual historical practice mixed with the occult, rather than paths who are clearly bread from a combination of reading too much Lore Olympus and texts and listening to western content creators who are buy in large colonizing Greek religion and magical practices and changing them to fit their narrative.

Is there anything else you would like to add before we finish this?

If you are looking to join our team, reach out via TalesOTheGods@gmail.com

Brooke Mirabella

What was the first edition you worked on/ when did you join?

Fall 2020 edition (1st edition)

Tell us about your craft a bit.

Eclectic gray witch and pagan

Do you provide services, own a shop, or teach? If so, tell us about it!

I teach and also provide divination, cleansing and spell work services for those near my area

How has your experience been contributing for the magazine? What are your thoughts on the culture of the magazine, the content covered, etc?

I've really enjoyed contributing to the magazine. A lot of much needed topics are covered by a wide variety of practitioners that are rarely touched on in other publications available.

What do you think in regards to pagan and occult publishing in the 2020s? What do you think about the existence of occult and pagan magazines? Should there be more indie publishers, or should publishing be relegated to well known occult/ pagan public figures?

I think it's important that other publications include practices other than those "most popular" in recent culture as ours does. I also find it extremely important that those who publish, life up voices of BIPOC and LGBTQIA individuals in the practice as ours have.

> How has the internet and online spheres effected your views, practices, and social interactions within paganism and the occult?

It is a humbling experience to learn from others who come from other cultures outside of my own. Being exposed to and willing to sit and learn with those not in your "usual" circle helps develop a well rounded practice.

> What do you think about the growing acceptance of the metaphysical in main stream media?

While I think it is great that these topics are being discussed more widely, white washing other cultures and the spread of appropriation has become a larger issue. The practice of the metaphysical needs to include respect for the origin and use of the practice.

> 2021 was a tough year for everyone, that being said, what is something good that happened for you? What new things did you start? What did you learn? What do you expect from 2022?

I am hopeful for more experiences for my children in the world as a whole, watching them grow and to become more involved in the metaphysical practices around in my area.

What is something you always get when visiting the local metaphysical shop / witch shop?

A new crystal and something new to me I can learn about

What is your favorite content creator for you path? (author, video creator, musician, ect)

Author: Scott Cunningham (although I do not adhere to the Wicca path. There are many, many more creators I highly respect as well)

When kind of content would you like to see more of in media?

Origins of practices, practices outside of Wicca

Is there anything else you would like to add before we finish this?

Thank you for this experience!

Owen Lee Heavenhill

What was the first edition you worked on/ when did you join?

Imbolc (2nd edition)

Tell us about your craft a bit.

Slowly ever evolving is how I would describe it. I've been researching and asking questions that pushed me out of Christianity and into a pagan witch for so long, yet still feel like I've only touched the surface. My craft and altars were actually part of what led me into the witchcraft side. I started with altars after already so many years of research. And then stuck with altars for many years using that for everything. I started with deity work back at the beginning of 2020. Came back to my great grandmother's church after saying I was never going to step foot in church again. (Welcome to sometimes having to directly confront some of your own trauma for ancestor work). I work with death/the dead a lot, and the new growth that follows after.

Do you provide services, own a shop, or teach? If so, tell us about it!

Not yet, and if I do anything, it'll probably be a book, on accident. Or mentorship... But nothing at the moment.

> How has your experience been contributing for the magazine? What are your thoughts on the culture of the magazine, the content covered, etc?

I appreciate that we try and keep a variety and not let things over run it.

> What do you think in regards to pagan and occult publishing in the 2020s? What do you think about the existence of occult and pagan magazines? Should there be more indie publishers, or should publishing be relegated to well known occult/ pagan public figures?

Knowledge is knowledge, you don't have to be well known to actually know what you're talking about and to be able to talk about it well. The issue comes up more when someone relies on their name/an association more than their own research and experience, and just talks out of their ass, because they can.

> How has the internet and online spheres effected your views, practices, and social interactions within paganism and the occult?

It's gotten me more experimentative in general, but especially when it comes to the chaos side of things. Sometimes I'll scroll past something someone did and go that's dumb, but... And it thought bubbles things a little bit. But the internet has always been a fantastic idea generator in my experience anyway, just due to the fact you can get exposed to so much more. That makes you think, and maybe experiment and push past.

What do you think about the growing acceptance of the metaphysical in main stream media?

I'm. Still very unsure. Part of me wants to be hopeful, but there's another part that's just worried about it getting whitewashed and lost in translation. Some of the articles I've seen really do just lessen what it can actually be.

2021 was a tough year for everyone, that being said, what is something good that happened for you? What new things did you start? What did you learn? What do you expect from 2022?

I learned to find myself, resulting in a break up. That break up was one of the best things that happened to me this year. Its been part of the process of unmasking and giving myself the space to just be. And I'm excited to be carrying that through 2022.

What is something you always get when visiting the local metaphysical shop / witch shop?

People visit shops and spend money? I kid, mostly incense and usually some sort of tool that calls out to me. The most recent was a new tarot deck, if virtual counts. In person, it was a pendulum.

What is your favorite content creator for you path? (author, video creator, musician, ect)

.... I don't really actually have one.

When kind of content would you like to see more of in media?

The weird niche rambles people could go on for hours about pertaining to their craft/a tree branch off!

Veronica

What was the first edition you worked on/ when did you join?

Fall 2020 edition (1st edition)

Tell us about your craft a bit.

When I wrote for the first edition I was pretty set on using chaos magic principles in a largely herb-focused practice with a heavy dose of spirit work. At this point in time I've veered more toward energy work using a lot less tools and adopted a framework that's more reflective of late antiquity greek magic (specifically at the turn of widespread christianization.) I find this suits my everyday private life better as well as being loosely a Hellenic pagan in a dominant Christian culture.

Do you provide services, own a shop, or teach? If so, tell us about it!

Not currently! I'm taking an extended break from monetizing my practice while I navigate it's newest twists, tuns, and additions.

How has your experience been contributing for the magazine? What are your thoughts on the culture of the magazine, the content covered, etc?

The overall experience was good! I'm not currently contributing due to prolonged issues in my personal life, but have the utmost respect for Des, a good friend and the founder, as well as fellow current and past contributors.

> What do you think in regards to pagan and occult publishing in the 2020s? What do you think about the existence of occult and pagan magazines? Should there be more indie publishers, or should publishing be relegated to well known occult/ pagan public figures?

I think indie publishers play an important role which is primarily providing access to less openly discussed subjects for larger publishing houses. We've all seen the hundreds of books on Wicca, eclectic witch self care, psychic shielding, and on and on. I had a recent experience at one of Canada's largest occult bookstores where I asked where the rest of the ritual magic section was. The one I found was two single shelves in one bookcase amongst a wall of other sections that focused on paganism, Wicca, and eclectic witchcraft. There was no other section for ritual magic, it was just too hard to find books from large houses that didn't better fit the Venusian witchcraft angle versus the Mercurial ritual/sorcery angle.

> How has the internet and online spheres effected your views, practices, and social interactions within paganism and the occult?

For a long time it made me more vocal in my every day life about being a practitioner. However that flipped about 3 months ago and I've found it easier to keep quiet about it in most areas of life so I'm not debunking tiktok & Tumblr misinformation whenever I mention it to someone I haven't told before.

> What do you think about the growing acceptance of the metaphysical in main stream media?

I think it's never been a good sign for upcoming sociopolitical events and policies. I also think it's always been allowed to be depicted in our modern media forms, and the feeling of acceptance is simply that the depictions are getting more accurate and less coded as shameful or dangerous. The latter also hinges on recent movements for the liberation of POC, specifically folks indigenous to turtle island and black folks descended from slaves in North America (turtle island.)

> 2021 was a tough year for everyone, that being said, what is something good that happened for you? What new things did you start? What did you learn? What do you expect from 2022?

I escaped my mother's medical and financial abuse. I don't expect 2022 to be particularly memorable nor distinct, which is infinitely better than the past few years are unforgettable.

> What is something you always get when visiting the local metaphysical shop / witch shop?

I always get to know the shop keep. Even if I don't end up buying something, I can still make a positive impression and gain a community connection.

> What is your favorite content creator for you path? (author, video creator, musician, ect)

selki girl (none of my friends will be surprised about this including selki.)

When kind of content would you like to see more of in media?

Content that treats oral history as valid and worth preserving. It's just coming into more mainstream acceptance that oral histories are accurate...I'd love to see that be taken further and have the people who keep the oral histories be in charge of how media about said peoples and histories is formed—from research to publication to upkeep of already published materials. This applies from academic spheres all the way to every day news broadcasting.

Is there anything else you would like to add before we finish this?

Strong relationships will always hold more power than any sort of metaphysical ability. Someone with an iron support system will always triumph over a metaphysical adversary. And a bridge you crossed in the distant past will always be stronger than one you burned after using. That is to say, mundane over magic applies to how you seek and keep help, not just if you're suspecting your headache is a warning.

Note from the creator:

The following magazines are the magazines as they were released with no additional editing, additions, or retractions. While everything is always checked before publishing to ensure that it does not promote misinformation, bigotry, or otherwise harmful content, we do not censor personal experience, UPG, and personal religious beliefs.

The opinions presented in this magazine may not represent what TOTG, Practical Witchcraft, or its contributors believe.

There may be ads, content, or items promoted in these magazines that are no longer available or in circulation and we have not gone back to check if the ads run in the TalesOfTheGods & Practical Witchcraft magazine. If a product, person, or item is no longer available, we apologize for the inconvenience.

If you have any thoughts, comments, or wish to write in or join the team contact us at TalesOTheGods@gmail.com or through the contact feature on TalesOfTheGods.com

Please note, due to tech and moving complications, some images have been permanently lost.

Tales Of The Gods
& Practical Witchcraft

Natives smudging and their practice

Lunar 2021 chart, murals and art

Interview With a Romani Witch

Restraining Order Because you're Wiccan? Christian claims religion instills fear

Home-made goods and recipes

Information-and-entertainment for all levels of experience and all paths

Gnosis What is The ins and outs of UPG, SPG and VPG

FALL 2020

TalesOfTheGods
and
Practical Witchcraft
Fall 2020 Magazine

The views expressed in this publication do not necessarily reflect the views of TalesOfTheGods, but of the views of each individual contributor. We strive to have a wide range of views and opinions, and the only ones we turn away are those that can be factually proven to be false, or are harmful to a protected group. This publication supports the GRSM and other minority communities.

Contributors

Desiree Goulden	TalesOfTheGods Owner, Article Contributor, Layout Design, Project Organiser
Neico Anderson	American sales assistant, editor
Dana Beaudreau	Editor, Article Contributor, Christian Witch, Reiki Master, Dream analysis
Brooke Mirabella	Article Contributor, Owner of Practical Witchcraft
Veronica	Article Contributor, Psychic, Medium,

This magazine is a community project aiming to bring information and entertainment to the metaphysical and pagan communities.

Everyone involved in contributing to the articles in this zine, takes an equal portion of the after sale income.

This is a team effort and everyone involved brings their own flavour and expertise to bring you a unique blend of content. When you buy this, you support families, entrepreneurs, and small businesses.

Thank you for supporting us.

Table Of Contents

Lunar Calendar 2021 — Pg 2
Days of the gods — Pg 3
A Hellenic Pagan Wheel Of The Year — Pg 4-5
Interview with a Romani Witch — Pg 8-10
Sigils, the Lady Azimuth method — Pg 12-14
Posters / Altar art — Pg 15-17
Anon's thoughts on Past Life Regression — Pg 18-20
Avoiding cults in the occult — Pg 22-25
A restraining order due to religion — Pg 26-29
A beginner's guide to dream annalysis — Pg 31-32
What is a Christian witch? — Pg 33-34
Homemade goods and magical objects — Pg 36-39
Gnosis or not? — Pg 44-46
Cleansing your home for newbies — Pg 48-49
The overconsumption of crystals in new age — Pg 50-51
On the topic of sage — Pg 52-53

This magazine was originaly intented to be a e-zine to be released twice yearly, but due to increased intrest by our crew and partners we have changed.

This will be sold both physically and digitally and if this issue shows promise, we will be releasing a new issue on every sabbat of the Wheel Of The Year. If you would like to join our team for the next issue, please feel free to contact Desiree through TalesOTheGods@gmail.com or through her other social media profiles.

If you would like to write in to us, send your message to the TalesOfTheGods email. Keep an eye out on TalesOfTheGods.com and Practical Witchcraft for updates on future releases. Thank you to our teams, and thank you to those who have supported this project.

 instagram.com/talesofthegods

 twitter.com/talesofthegods

 facebook.com/groups/665578877692886 (Practical Witchcraft group)

2021 Lunar Calendar

	New Moon	Waxing Crescent	First Quarter	Waxing Gibbous	Full Moon	Waning Gibbous	Last Quarter	Waning Crescent
Jan	13th	14th	20th	22nd	28th	1st / 29th	6th	7th
Feb	11th	12th	19th	20th	27th	1st / 28th	4th	5th
Mar	13th	14th	21st	22nd	28th	1st / 29th	5th	7th
Apr	11th	14th	20th	21st	26th	1st / 28th	4th	5th
May	11th	12th	19th	20th	26th	1st / 27th	3rd	4th
Jun	10th	11th	17th	19th	24th	1st / 25th	2nd	3rd
Jul	9th	11th	17th	18th	23rd	25th	1st / 31st	3rd
Aug	8th	9th	15th	16th	22nd	23rd	30th	1st / 31st
Sept	6th	8th	13th	14th	20th	21st	28th	1st / 30th
Oct	6th	7th	12th	14th	20th	21st	28th	1st / 29th
Nov	4th	5th	11th	12th	19th	20th	27th	1st / 28th
Dec	4th	5th	10th	12th	18th	20th	26th	1st / 28th

Days Of The Gods

Did you know that the 7 day week is thousands of years old? Not only that, but that in many ancient civilizations they named the days after the gods! Here are some of the days dedicated to the gods of the Norse, Greek and Roman pantheons!

Days	Norse	Greek	Roman
Monday Lundi	Mani	Selen	Luna
Teusday Mardi	Tyr	Ares	Mars
Wednesday Mercredi	Odin	Hermes	Mercury
Thursday Jeudi	Thor	Zeus	Jupiter
Friday Vendredi	Freya	Aphrodite	Venus
Saturday Samedi	None	Cronus	Saturn
Sunday Dimanche	Sól	Helios	Sol

The Canadian Hellenic Pagan Wheel Of The Year
By Lady Azimuth

This is part of my personal practice as opposed to the actual Hellenic Hearth Wheel of the Year created by Ὕπατο Συμβούλιο των Ελλήνων Εθνικών (YSEE) This is made to fit into the wheel of the year made popular by Wicca and commonly used by many practitioners, to be able to take part without taking part in the propitiation of Celtic religious practice that the Wheel of the year is taken from. For full information on the way I celebrate these days, head to TalesOfTheGods.com

Yule
Οι γιορτές
Oi giortés
(The Celebrations)
December 20 - 23

Deities celebrated: Hestia & Dionysus
Offerings: Wine, bread, grapes, incense
Activities: Throwing family and friends parties. getting drunk, connect with family and friends you haven't seen in a while. Veil and abstain from 'adult activity' until after the 23rd

Imbolc
Ημέρα βοοειδών
Iméra vooeidón
(Cattle Day)
February 2nd

Deities celebrated: Hermes & Apollo
Offerings: Food offerings of beef or other herd animals
Activities: Play music, play harmless pranks on friends and family, give to charity, make art and write poetry

Ostara
Εαρινή ισημερία
Eariní isimería
Spring Equinox

Deities celebrated: Persephone (primarily) & Hades
Offerings: Pomegranates, roses for Persephone. Mint, coins and hard liquor for Hades
Activities: Plant flowers and herbs. Clean up your garden and house. Burn incense and give attention to Hades as well.

Beltane
Ημέρα φωτιάς
Iméra fotiás
(fire day/ day of fire)
April 30 - May 1

Deities celebrated: Gaia & Ouranos
Offerings: Rocks, crystals, flowers, anything of the earth
Activities: Tell the creation story, pray, give thanks for the creation of the Titans and Gods for without both we would not be here. Celebrate love and birth, get engaged.

Litha
μεσοκαλόκαιρο
mesokalókairo
(midsummer)
Summer Solstice

Deities celebrated: Gaia, Demeter, Persephone
Offerings: Fruit, berries, flowers, seeds, floral incense
Activities: Greet the day with a bonfire. Tend your gardens. This is a day to celebrate fertility and nature in full bloom.

Lughnasadh
ημέρα προβληματισμού
iméra provlimatismoú
(day of reflection)
August 1st

This is a day in the Wheel Of The year that is taken solely from Celtic Pagans, and as such I do not feel comfortable in taking part, as I feel it leads to the appropriation of a religion that was once illegal. Take this time to learn of your own religion, or of the Celtic Pantheon.

Mabon
Φθινοπωρινή αντανάκλαση
Fthinoporiní antanáklasi
(Autumn Reflection)
Autumnal Equinox

Deities celebrated: Phanês & Thanatos
Offerings: Prayers of thanks
Activities: Give thanks for the life you have. This is a thanksgiving day. Contemplate the balance of life and death and the importance of both to the balance of life on earth.

Samhain
Νύχτα του Άδης
Nýchta tou Ádis
(Night of Hades)
October 31st to November 1st

Deities celebrated: Hades
Offerings: Mint, white poplar, coins, alcohol, masculine incense
Activities: While also a Celtic day, this is also the day where the veil is at its thinnest. Honour the lost, give thanks to Hades who cares for our souls after we are gone.

— Laura Del —

Laura Del has her bachelor's degree in radio, television, and film from Rowan University. She is a lover of books, writing and anything fiction. Del currently lives in New Jersey, where she runs her blogging website www.thefictionwriters.net
(About the author from Amazon)

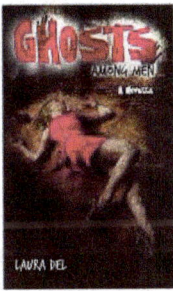

Ghosts Among Men: A Novella (Samantha Davidson Novella)
Laura Del
★★★★½ (32)

| Kindle: | $0.97 |
| Paperback: | $5.99 |

★★★★★ **Ghosts Among Men**
Reviewed in the United States on March 15, 2017
Verified Purchase
Samantha is a private investigator and just so happens to be able to talk to dead people but don't think it makes her job any easier. Well ok maybe it does. I loved Samantha and think she is absolutely bad a**. Great mystery thriller that had me on the edge of my seat through the entire story. I can't wait to find out what kind of craziness Sam gets into next.

★★★★★ **Enjoyable quick read**
Reviewed in the United States on July 5, 2019
Verified Purchase
Fun female lead.
Wish book was longer.
Already added her next book to wish list.
Don't want to read it enough to pay 1.99 (it's also a novella).
Would like to see full-size books in this series.

★★★★★ **Fantastic Urban Fantasy and Mystery**
Reviewed in the United States on August 24, 2016
Verified Purchase
This had better be the beginning of a series because it can't be over. Samantha is funny and smart and such a strong character. The police officers and her office manager were original and added to the picture of a world where Samantha Davidson is so vital. And I need more of it. All of it.
If you are a fan of Sue Grafton or Sookie Stackhouse then you should read this immediately. This is A for Alibi but with ghosts and a far more relatable character.

Samantha Davidson sees ghosts for a living. More specifically, she sees ghosts as a private investigator, working alongside the Chicago Police Department to put away killers and put troubled spirits to rest. When the daughter of one of Chicago's wealthiest families turns up dead, Samantha and her assistant Mark team up with homicide detective Lance MacDowell to get to the bottom of the crime.
Allison Allen is tall, blonde, beautiful–and very much dead. As Samantha interviews the girl, who doesn't remember anything about the circumstances of her own murder, it's clear that there's more going on behind the walls of this manicured home than anyone wants to let on—and that Samantha has her work cut out for her this time.
Juggling her own love life, tracking down troubled spirits, and evading attempts to thwart her investigation keeps Samantha on her toes. Good thing Samantha knows how to keep her eyes open, her wits about her, and her sense of humour.
A paranormal mystery that is both dark and funny, Ghosts Among Men will cause chills to run down your back even while you're laughing out loud at the lovable, strong, and supernaturally sighted private investigator Samantha Davidson.

⭐⭐⭐⭐⭐ **Ghostly Murders**
Reviewed in the United States on March 20, 2017

Samantha Davidson is at it again in the second Ghostly Murders Novellas. I absolutely love this character and the humor that is in these books. I hope there will be many more cases for Samantha and her partner Detective Lance Macdowell.

⭐⭐⭐⭐⭐ **A must read!!**
Reviewed in the United States on February 8, 2017

From page 1 I was hooked!! The style of this novella is fast paced and such a great story! It will leave you wanting more!! Can't wait for the installment!!

⭐⭐⭐⭐⭐ **Five Stars**
Reviewed in the United States on February 8, 2017

Greatest read ever! I love this series and can't wait to read more!

⭐⭐⭐⭐⭐ **Read it, read them all!!!!**
Reviewed in the United States on April 14, 2017

Became hooked on PI Samantha Davidson from Ghosts Among Men and just like that book this one did not disappoint either. Page turner! Can not wait to read another!!! Thanks Laura Del!

Ghostly Murders: A Novella (A Samantha Davidson Novella Book
Laura Del
⭐⭐⭐⭐⭐ (7)

Kindle: $0.97

Paperback: $5.99

Get ready for more ghostly adventures in the second installment of the Samantha Davidson series, Ghostly Murders.
When a body pops up in a suburb of Chicago, PI Samantha Davidson is on the case with her partner in crime, Detective Lance MacDowell. But when the two of them go to investigate, there's a little glitch in their plans. It seems that the Chicago PD has stumbled upon a serial killer's victim. Now they have to work with the FBI, specifically very Special Agent Brennan, who is not a fan of Samantha's methods.
After all, when you can speak to the dead like Samantha can people tend to not believe you, and Brennan is no different.
So with this special agent against her almost every step of the way, and the dead girl not being of much help, Samantha must rely on her keen investigation skills to solve this murder before the killer strikes again.
Can she do it? Or will this monster slip through her fingers and slaughter another victim?
Find out in the suspense thriller that is Ghostly Murders.

Ghosts Among Men

https://www.amazon.com/Ghosts-Among-Men-Samantha-Davidson-ebook/dp/B00Y3597IO

Ghostly Murders

https://www.amazon.com/gp/product/B01N9XJVIV/ref=dbs_a_def_rwt_bibl_vppi_i1

Interview with a Romani Witch

First of all, thank you for taking the time to talk to us. I have followed you for quite some time on TikTok, but for the sake of the reader, please introduce yourself.

Hello! My name is Eurydice Ehra and I'm a Romani Witch also studying Celtic beliefs and practise. I've been practising for almost ten years now and currently study under a Chovani to learn true Romani witchcraft.

There are many questions around Romani practice, but as it is widely accepted as a closed practice we are more interested about your experiences in the wider metaphysical community. As a Romani practitioner, how have the other paths treated you thus far? Have they been accepting or closed minded to you?

Well people certainly aren't welcoming. There's this stereotype surrounding my people that we are essentially con artists who use metaphysical beliefs and practices as a means to trick others. Those who don't believe my people mock theirs tend to have a skewed perspective of our people, and believe that being Roma is something you can simply decide to do for the popularized "g*psy" aesthetic.

Do you find the witch and pagan communities are better or worse with respecting you and your heritage than non practitioners?

I will say that the pagan community is better about respecting my culture, as many practitioners (while remaining ignorant on many stances) do fancy themselves researchers and historians. Often I'll tell a practitioner I'm Romani and the next time we meet they've studied my people and our origins extensively. Sometimes learning wrong things from poor sources, however that is more attempt at understanding us than I've ever seen outside the community.

How do you feel about the relationship between non practitioners and spiritual people? Do you feel confident in saying you're a witch /practitioner in this day and age?

I feel like to an extent it's much easier to talk about it these days. You'll always get the same "clever" comments from some people but it's not often and usually easy to ignore. I sell spells and charms, as well as readings as a source of income and surprisingly I receive little backlash for this. At most the occasional pamphlet advertising Jesus to my apparently damned soul, but that's about it. The most controversy I've experienced has not been in my day to day life but online where everything is controversial.

You are part of one of the largest metaphysical communities in the world through TikTok and by extension WitchTok, how do you feel WitchTok has effected how the world sees practitioners? Has it effected how the world sees the Romani at all?

I have a love-hate relationship with WitchTok, because while I love that the practice has become so easily accessible to anyone with an interest and that connecting with others of your path has become so easy, problems, gossip, harassment, and rampant misinformation spread like wildfire because that's what gets views and likes. It's odd to go from one day seeing people teaching each other parts of their paths, to the next suddenly everyone arguing over whether or not the moon has been/can be hexed by beginner practitioners to the point where I actually saw a genuine news article on that particular event. There's a lot of needless panic and fearmongering. However it's still a wonderful beginner friendly way to be introduced to things, I feel like the comedy and memes spread actually do help to make the community more inviting and also genuinely learn things easier. When it comes to how it views the Romani, it's getting there? People are listening more which is lovely. Still working on it but I think with the information being more available it's easier now.

What got you into making TikTok, and what inspires you to continue?

I initially wanted to help people learn tarot, as I heard from a beginner practitioner that they had a hard time learning by reading. As I've been reading tarot far longer than I've been practising witchcraft, I thought it would be a good idea to read the cards aloud using TikTok to help auditory learners. Honestly I think the friends I've made and the people I've met on TikTok motivate me to continue. I've wanted to stop on several occasions mostly because I'm deaf and have a hard time with the app, but everyone is so excited to share their paths and knowledge it's hard to not want to join in and show off my own.

If you could change one thing about the world, what would it be?

Oh gods how to choose... I could say something broad I suppose I think I'd want to revamp the justice system to be genuine in its pursuit of justice. Probably starting with North America and moving outwards. Perhaps by removing people in power and replacing them with people who have genuine understanding of racial, gender, and disabled inequality. Right now it's hard for anyone to deal with anything including this pandemic because the world we live in simply doesn't allow for people to exist in times of unrest without severe consequences. Having the infrastructure to actually help its people trust that the system will help them without threat of violence, homelessness, traumatisation, etc., would actually be a major step that allows more issues to be resolved in a manner that will face the least resistance.

Thank you for sharing your input, where can readers find you online and do you have anything to say to the readers, before we end this?

I don't have much in the way of an online presence actually! My tiktok is @vaeule-nais though and I'm usually lurking there. My only comment to the readers I think is not to be afraid to ever ask questions and pursue an answer yourself.

@inkwood_tarot @InkwoodJournal

inkwoodtarot.com

Inkwood Tarot - Readings by Cynthia: tarot reader, empath, certified Reiki practitioner and ordained Pagan clergy.

" I offer tarot readings by phone, video call and seasonally in-person at local events, festivals and shops. With over 20 years of tarot study and experience, I love helping people bring harmony, balance and success to their lives. Join me in exploring your ultimate potential!"

To learn more or schedule a reading visit:
http://inkwoodtarot.com

Sigils – The Lady Azimuth Method

This method was taught to me when I first joined the craft. People may have different ways, but this is one of a few ways I make my sigils, and is similar to how I've seen others making theirs.

**A B C D E F G H I
J K L M N O P Q
R S T U V W X Y Z**

Write your intention remove all vowels from your sentence.

I WILL BE SHEILDED FROM NEGATIVITY
👇
WLL B SHLDD FRM NGTVT
👇

After removing all vowles we will remove repeating letters.

WLBSHDFRMNGTV ← this

Combine your remaining letters into one 'sigil' I try to make them fit into a circular image because I can concentrate on it to charge better, but how you do it is up to you.

Charge the sigil, and you're done! →

turns in to

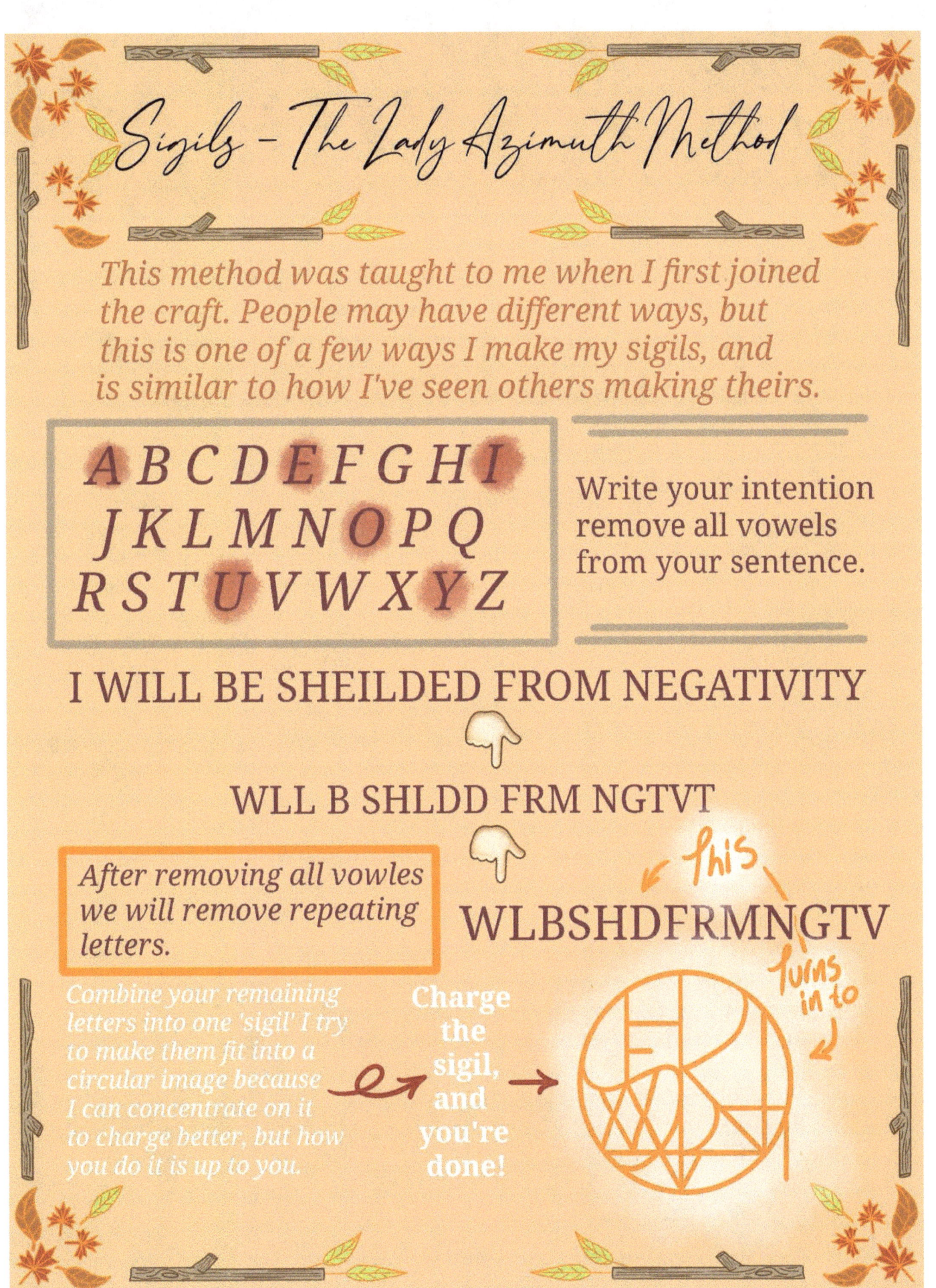

Sigils, how to make and use them for warding your room.

Sigils are a basic form of magic, and one of my favourites. They are something no practitioner can go without knowing (in my own opinion) and come in many shapes and forms.

The word "sigil" comes from the Latin word "sigillum" which translates to "seal" and can be found throughout many magical practices and can be used for a wide range of spells.

I prefer to use them in protections, both to be worn and to protect a space. On the page beside this, you'll find an info-graphic on how to create sigils, the way that I do and if you're new that will give you the basics on how to craft them. There are many ways to make them. Some make them using Theban script, some with numbers and what you do should depend on what feels comfortable for you.

Remember that making sigils means you must be careful with how you word things. You need to know what you want. Try to keep it short and sweet. Don't be afraid of including symbols of protection, including different colours and inks, and really personalize them. Included on this page is a slightly more intricate sigil that includes 4 sigils and a pentacle as a protection for a room or sacred space.

This was a ward I used at my old apartment which I found worked well. I'm going to walk you through how I made them for you to try yourself. This is no longer in use and will not be used again for my apartment and thus is safe for use.

This ward uses a few sentences separated into 4 different sigils, surrounding a pentacle. To make this you need only paper and something to write with (If you're fancy: black paper to help absorb incoming negativity/ energy, and ink or paint of your preference)

Cut your paper into small circles. They have to be big enough to fit the sigil but also small enough to put on windows and doors to your space. You need as many circles as you have entryways to your space.

Your message is:

This space is protected
From negativity
From entities From harm.

Shortened ->

THSPCRD
FRMNGTV
FRMNTS
FRMHR

Construct the sigils as you will, focusing on each part of the message when you craft each corresponding sigil. Keep note of each one. Number each on the same scrap of paper you did the rough work on if you need to.

Draw the pentacle on the circular pieces of paper and then the sigils in order from 1 being at the top, 2 on the right, 3 on the bottom and 4 on the left. Now charge all the warding sigils.

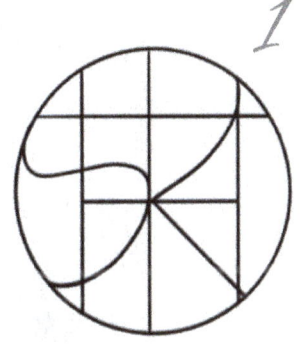
1

2

3

4

Post on every entrance to the space and envision an energy field falling over the walls of the room, connected by the sigils. Smoke, smudge or sound cleanse as you usually would, do not use sage unless you want to weaken your wards. (Try lavender or sandalwood)

These few pages were meant to be printable colouring pages when we were only going to release digitally. We are keeping the full colour versions as free posters / art as we are also releasing physical copies.

palmistry

History

Ancient palmistry

Palmistry is a practice common to many different places on the Eurasian landmass,[1] it has been practised in the cultures of India, Nepal, Tibet, China, Persia, Sumeria, Palestine and Babylonia.

The acupuncturist Yoshiaki Omura describes its roots in Hindu astrology (known in Sanskrit as *jyotish*), Chinese Yijing (*I Ching*), and Roma fortune tellers.[5] Several thousand years ago, the Hindu sage Valmiki is thought to have written a book comprising 567 stanzas, the title of which translates in English as *The Teachings of Valmiki Maharshi on Male Palmistry*.[7][8] From India, the art of palmistry spread to China, Tibet, Egypt, Persia and to other countries in Europe.[6][9]

From India, palmistry progressed to Greece where Anaxagoras practiced it.[7] Aristotle (384–322 B.C.E.) discovered a treatise on the subject of palmistry on an altar of Hermes. Aristotle then presented to Alexander the Great (356–323 B.C.E.), who took great interest in examining the character of his officers by analyzing the lines on their hands.[10]

Palmistry is indirectly referenced in the Book of Job,[1][8] which is dated by scholars as between the 7th and 4th centuries BCE.[11]

During the Middle Ages the art of palmistry was actively suppressed by the Roman Catholic Church as pagan superstition. In Renaissance magic, palmistry (known as "chiromancy") was classified as one of the seven "forbidden arts", along with necromancy, hydromancy, aeromancy, pyromancy, geomancy, and spatulamancy (scapulimancy).

Palmistry consists of the practice of evaluating a person's character or future life by "reading" the palm of that person's hand. Various "lines" ("heart line", "life line", etc.) and "mounts" (or bumps) (chirognomy) purportedly suggest interpretations by their relative sizes, qualities, and intersections. In some traditions, readers also examine characteristics of the fingers, fingernails, fingerprints, and palmar skin patterns (dermatoglyphics), skin texture and color, shape of the palm, and flexibility of the hand.

A reader usually begins by reading the person's dominant hand (the hand he or she writes with or uses most often), which is sometimes considered to represent the conscious mind, whereas the other hand is subconscious). In some traditions of palmistry, the other hand is believed to carry hereditary or family traits or, depending on the palmist's cosmological beliefs, to convey information about past-life or "karmic" conditions.

The basic framework for "classical" palmistry (the most widely taught and practiced tradition) is rooted in Greek mythology. Each area of the palm and fingers is related to a god or goddess, and the features of that area indicate the nature of the corresponding aspect of the subject. For example, the ring finger is associated with the Greek god Apollo; characteristics of the ring finger are tied to the subject's dealings with art, music, aesthetics, fame, wealth, and harmony.

Hand labels:
- Finger of Jupiter
- Finger of Saturn
- Finger of Apollo
- Finger of Mercury
- Girdle of Venus
- Line of heart
- Line of sun
- Line of life
- Line of destiny
- Travel lines
- Line of Mars
- Will
- Logic
- Wrist Bracelets

Spirit Board

Yes   **No**

A B C D E F G H I J K L M
N O P Q R S T U V W X Y Z

0 1 2 3 4 5 6 7 8 9

Goodbye

Why Past Life Regression Shouldn't Be a Trend

(Trigger warning, mention of sexual abuse, loss of a child and suicide).

While the mainstream population in the USA and Canada are becoming more and more comfortable with the idea of spiritualism outside of Christianity, and magic in general, the unfortunate downside to this is that people who do not have any background in the occult are attempting things that require a lot of preparation with no regard for set up or safety.

The most recent, and the subject of this article, is past life regression. Every life has baggage, and most of us have difficulties handling our own current baggage let alone the baggage of a whole different life. Some people who believe in past lives think that the soul has certain lessons they need to learn in each life that affect what will happen in the coming life. These karmic lessons change from life to life and sometimes require the soul to go through great strife in one life or another. TikTok however, doesn't know that this is the case.

Whether through the WitchTok tag or through outside sources, the non occult TikTok audience has found past life regression and jumped into it head on. The result has been waves of young people posting 60 second videos and memes where they talk about the trauma they relived causing a snowball effect. People are posting about some horrible thing that happened in another life, tears falling upon their face. Others watch and want either a tragic or glamorous story of their own to tell to their #spooky followers, and the trend would grow.

The result of this trend is a wave of people giving themselves second hand PTSD from a life they physically have not lived.

So what do you have to know, if you want to do past life regression?

First, you need to separate yourself from these past lives. It's a weird thing to state, as they are by all intents and purposes, you, but you need to realize that they are the past. Nothing that happened can be changed, and although you may regain some memories through the regression, the only thing that you can control is this life. You can't change the past, only influence the future.

Second, shadow work. If you are still dealing with your personal trauma, you should not seek out more. You need to make sure you are in the proper head space to possibly deal with some very dark topics. Your past life ended in some way, and death is not always kind in the act. You also need to take care after the fact. Journal your experience, follow up by grounding and self care. If you are being negatively affected by the experience, do some shadow work and figure out a way to deal with the trauma in a healthy way.

Third and last, understand that you don't need to do this. Past life regression isn't necessary for the majority of people. If you will gain from it and it is an important part of your practice, go for it, but don't go blindly into it. At the risk of being called a gatekeeper, I will say, however, that if you do not have a background in the occult, the proper mental health to do so, and the ability to do proper after-care, do not attempt past life regression. It's not a game to be played with so that you can have content for your TikTok, Tumblr or Twitter. It can leave you hurt (and with PTSD in some cases) if not handled appropriately.

Many people who do it properly still have difficulties with the fall out and how it influences their lives and their views of themselves. So let me share with you my experience. For my privacy and to avoid awkward questions from my non practitioner friends and family, I will be remaining anonymous. I am a God Spouse and have been in the craft since the early 2000s. I'm a medium and am training to be a Hellenic Pagan Priestess.

The nature of my practice is to help heal people dealing with death and loss, and help spirits cross who have become stuck, or to remove particularly hostile entities. As such, I have been moved to do past life regression. The deity I am spouse to (for privacy on both parts I will not be disclosing the name outside those close to me) has been present throughout many of my lives, and they and I have been bonded in many lives, so I had the privilege of being told beforehand that my lives have not been kind to me in nearly any of them. Most of them resulted in my suicide. I had warnings that most if not all experiences I have with past life regression would most likely be negative… many others do not have that sort of warning.

The meditation I took part in was a little over an hour and resulted in the vivid recovery of some integral memories.

My name was Ithaca, I lived in Mycenae, Greece (which was something I had to Google afterwards) I was 19 and stood at the side of the mouth of a river, shrouded in thick forest. I had my hair cut short and wore no veil in masculine clothing. Across the river was the deity I am now spouse to.

Before I go on, as a Hellenic Pagan, I believe that the gods once walked among us, and used to commonly take the form of mortals to fornicate and indulge in humanity, what can I say? Half of the mythology is just Hera being furious with the women Zeus laid with, we wouldn't have Heracles otherwise. Whether this person is or isn't my deity (who confirms it is) isn't up for debate.

They forced themselves upon me. Luckily the meditation forced us forward in time a bit before I had to witness too much of anything, but I did hear things in the transition.

Ithaca returned home to her father, a grain farmer, who berated her for embarrassing him, sneaking out dressed as a man, and that this is why he couldn't marry her off. He took note of the bruises covering her and injuries left from the assault. He accused her of impropriety and wouldn't hear her claims of assault. She knew not who this person was, and assumed they were just a cruel stranger.

Her father exploded with anger and commanded her to do hard farm work for the week, stating, "We know how to get rid of problems like that, one way or another" and forbid her to enter the home for the night, the threat of direct violence in every word. He however failed to work her to miscarriage and she bore the child.

In the next memory, Ithaca sat nursing only a few hours from giving birth. Her father stormed in, pulled the babe from her breast and told her to leave. The child's name was Tidus, which added to the discomfort of this scene. I've never been the motherly kind, however what happened next, had I not been prepared, would not sit well with me. I'm not even sure I'm OK with it now, but at least I wasn't blind sided.

She stumbled out, emotionally numb and barely walking. She ran into the stranger from the river and he demanded where Tidus was. She explained everything that happened, and he stood in furious silence. He sent her to a hut in the woods, telling her he would handle the situation.

When he returned many hours later, he was in a darker mood than Ithaca had last seen him. It was around this time where I almost pulled out of the meditation. He explained that the father had drowned Tidus, and implied that he, in turn, killed the father. He explained his divinity and that he didn't care for her, but lusted after her for her boyish attitude, leading to his stalking her to the river, and if she had never gotten pregnant he likely would have never seen her again.

The meditation brought us farther in time and Ithaca was once again with child. This time she was in the back of a cart being pulled through the streets by a donkey when she began to go into labour. The owner of the cart ordered her off and sped away from her, leaving her in the middle of the street. She was miscarrying.

Someone in the crowd yelled for a healer as Ithaca screamed and gave birth to a gory terror. There are many things I wished to never see, and that was definitely high on the list.

A woman with a pale yellow veil helped her and took her into her house. The memory flashed forward to Ithaca in the woman's house. She thought her saviour was asleep and was in the middle of stealing a length of rope. The woman however was awake and watching her from the other side of the room.

She asked her where she thought she was going and Ithaca burst into hysterics. She explained everything and trudged to a tree on the side of the road outside the woman's house. She explained everything from the river on. She explained how this child was the deity's and how he left mysteriously. How he never cared for her and how she was going to swear revenge on him, how she was going to haunt him for the rest of eternity, how she was binding her soul to his to make him pay for what he did to her.

Then she hung herself. Which was an experience I can't quite explain. In a second everything went black, and I could hear her soul screaming in rage. I fully believe that if Ithaca hadn't swore revenge in the next life, I would not be here, I'd be a wrathful spirit harassing some innocent house somewhere.

I saw everything through her eyes, felt her emotions as well as mine and bore witness to what could almost be considered a classic Greek tragedy.

Now imagine, you're a random 16 year old, trying past life regression with no idea that that may be what's waiting for you. This isn't a trend to be done as a joke, you can be seriously, mentally harmed if you don't know what you're doing and how to properly take care of yourself and separate that life from yours afterwards.

I know I am not Ithaca. I know that that life influenced my soul and life now. I know that it's likely why I have a strong aversion to children, fight for women's rights and pro choice movements, struggle with depression, and struggle with anger management, but I knew that I would likely see what I saw. I can not fathom how children are doing this and coming out OK.

I'm not going to tell you not to do it, I will have to do it a few more times for my practice myself, but I'm asking you to be careful, prepare, and share this with your non practitioner friends if you hear them talking about doing it. Your mental health should be more important than your curiosity.

-Anonymous

Christina & Martin

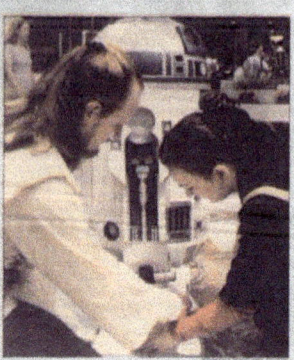
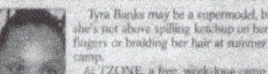

✉ carrhunger@carrhunger.com

📷 www.instagram.com/Carrhunger/

f www.facebook.com/carrhunger/

Meeting at a Dr Who convention in Toronto in 1987, Christina and Martin have, combined, over 62 years experience in the entertainment industry.

Accumulating such titles as Camera, Editing, Tape Operator, Director, Actor, Writer, Costumes, Props Builders, AD, Fight Coordinator, etc and so on... their experiences are broad and diverse BUT they still, to this day, love bringing the joy of building props, education on the industry and the popular process of Cosplay to conventions and events. X-Men, Cody Banks, Total Recall 2070, Scooby Doo, Stargate, Star Trek, FX The Series, EFC, Flash, Arrow, Legends of Tomorrow, are only a few of the productions on their list of experiences.

Stage, Live Performances, Characters at Festivals, add to their range of talents. Come experience their love of sharing knowledge, their skills and stories of their experiences.

How to identify cults within the occult

(Trigger warning: mentions of mental, physical, and sexual abuse)

If being on the internet has taught me anything, it's that it's not all that difficult to form a following. From cults of personality to straight religious cults, the internet has made it easier for people to manipulate people for their personal gain. Luckily the internet has also made it easier to recognize and teach others how to avoid these situations.

The B.I.T.E model was created to help people recognize and avoid mind control and cults. Created by Steven Hassan for the Freedom Of Mind Resource centre, the bite model has been used by many to help get out of toxic situations. I found this through videos made by Telltale Atheist and Jimmy Snow, two very prominent people within the ex Mormon and ex Jehovah's Witnesses communities on YouTube. Whether you are an atheist or not, knowing the B.I.T.E model can be beneficial in protecting yourself.

This will be a simplified breakdown but if you want to have more in-depth information, you can find the full B.I.T.E. model at https://freedomofmind.com/bite-model/

B.I.T.E stands for BBehaviour, Information, Thought, and Emotion control.

Behaviour control covers everything you would think it would. They may control what you eat, when / if you sleep, who you sleep with, who you associate with, how your dress etc.. This wouldn't be an immediate thing. They would start slowly through group indoctrination. The group does this, so you should do it, otherwise, you aren't one of us.
If you failed to do what they wanted or expected of you, they would punish you physically. They would likely physically harm you or make you believe they will, and are not above threatening your life or sexual assault.
If you slip up you will be threatened or harmed and their rules, while they may have begun harmless, now fill you with fear for stumbling.

For example:
Keira and Nora are both part of covens. They both are required to participate in a monthly full moon and monthly new moon ceremony. In this ceremony, they are required to wear white and are allowed to bring one person who isn't in the coven to the meetings if they wish.

Both Keira and Nora work full-time jobs and therefore sometimes they can not stay up late to take part in the meetings and rituals.

Keira's group understands that she is an adult who needs to pay bills and her life comes before the group's meetings. They don't hold it against her and wait until she misses a month or two before commenting and possibly removing her.

Nora's group takes offence to this. If she misses a meeting she is imminently condemned and yelled at. They claim she does not care about the group and that her not appearing for the meetings is disrespecting them, and people who disrespect them get hexed or worse.

Keira feels understood and feels that she can leave the group if she wants to.

Nora is fearful of leaving and expects violence for stepping out of line.

Keira decides to bring her trans friend to a meeting. Her group accepts them both and welcomes her friend with open arms, changing things if need be to make them feel comfortable.

Keira will likely bring her friend again and is happy that she can share her craft with her friend.

Nora brings her trans friend and the friend is handled as an 'other' the entire night. When they go home, the group leaders and some of the group yell at her because they have strict gender roles and expectations.

Nora will not only not bring the person around, the friend will not speak to her because they assume she thinks in the same way as the group. If she begins to question her identity or identify as something other than what the group expects and wants, she will expect violence.

Information control covers the restriction of information that goes against the group. They will distort information to their gain, minimize access to other forms of information, segregate information on the outside versus inside information, and control who knows what. They will encourage members to spy on each other and push cult generated propaganda and info.
If you seek out other sources of information or question the information they are pushing, they will lie or make up info that backs up their position. If they can not control where you get your info or stop you from speaking against their teachings, they may use your confessions or blackmail from other members against you.

Both Keira and Nora's groups have specific books, websites, YouTube videos, and mentors that are used in their practice and that the group is built off of.

Keira brings other books that go against the information that the group swears by. While the group doesn't feel comfortable with the idea that they're wrong, they read the books and possibly grow and change depending on it.

Nora brings other resources and is imminently told that it's not valid and that the group is the only people who know the right way to practice. They push their own propaganda on her and she may even begin to believe it. They will then give her a script and a list of books to give people who tell her that the group is wrong. If she however pushes the fact, then people who know personal secrets about Nora will use it against her.

Keira grows to respect her group and feels that she is equal to them intellectually. She will value the information of the group knowing that they would change if proven they're wrong.

Nora will not bring up other information and will begin to parrot the group rhetoric to anyone who challenges her or the group in the future. If she disagrees with anything, she will likely not say anything for fear of having her personal life put on display.

Thought control is the kind that is the most obvious to outsiders. Thought control isn't about unity, its about conformity. The group reality is the only reality. They decide what is good and evil in the world and enforce it on everyone, within the group and without. They may change one's name and identity to one that aligns with that of the group. They police thoughts and may even attempt to regress the maturity of the members. They teach thought stopping, instil false memories, and promote excessive chanting, meditating, praying, and speaking in tongues.

Keira's group may want their members to have a similar way of thinking but embraces people's individuality. Her emotions are validated and when she has negative thoughts and experiences she is given the proper support and guidance to process them in a non-destructive way. Although they may pray, meditate, or speak in different languages, none is done to control or stop her from walking her own path or experiencing the world outside the group.

Nora's group does not allow any negative thoughts. Speaking of anger, sadness, or feeling of inadequacies are silenced with phrases like "love and light" and then she is informed about how her negative thoughts will stop her from being her higher self. She is denied the right to think for herself or express individualistic traits.

Keira feels free to be herself and think freely.

Nora fears her own thoughts.

Emotional control goes hand in hand with thought control. With emotional control the group in question seeks to manipulate your feelings, deeming some as selfish and evil. They teach emotion stopping techniques, especially around homesickness and anger and self-doubt. Every single problem the person has is their own fault, never the group or the leaders, especially when the group has harmed you. They make you believe you aren't living up to your potential. Whether it's your identity, your accomplishments, or lack thereof, your family not being good enough, your friends aren't good enough, etc..
They will love bomb one minute and claim you are horrible in one way or another the next. They may make a ritual of publicly confessing your mistakes or 'sins' and instill the idea that outside the group there can be no real happiness.

Keira's group understands that she may battle depression and anger due to past trauma. While they do wish to help her process that, they do not belittle her for feeling that way. They may also suggest seeking outside help to better address her personal internal battles.

Nora's group on the other hand tells her that it's her fault that she's feeling this way, that she is the only one to blame for her emotional difficulties and that it is proof that she is somehow deficient. If she would just BE HAPPY she could be her higher self. Anything less is 'lowering her vibrations'. Her problems are her own fault, and her problems make everyone around her look bad.

Keira feels safe to express her emotions freely with little to no repercussions outside the societal norm.

Nora fears her own emotions and expressing them will make her feel as if she or her family and friends will be harmed.

Nora is part of a cult that uses new-age philosophy to negatively manipulate her. With the rise of online forums, we have seen such cults multiply. From a woman claiming she was Medusa made human, to a gray-haired ex-drug addict faux crone, I've seen no less than 5 different cults in as many months arise online, all of which doing immense damage to those who well into them.

Mind control is the way cult leaders gain and keep power. It starts slow and before you know it, you've been trapped in a box where you feel you can never escape. Be vigilant and watch over your friends, anyone can fall into one of these cults, and people who have escaped deal with the scars for years. The occult can give you the freedom and answers you seek in life, but it also is a place where well-meaning people can be manipulated and hurt.

A Restraining Order Due To Religion

While scrolling on TikTok I came across a rather concerning video with a woman claiming her neighbour took out a restraining order on her, because she's Wiccan. This stuck with me because, in the past few years, the world has become a more safe place for Wiccans, Pagans, and the like. While we do catch some flack now and then for our practice and beliefs, it's far better than even 10 years ago, so I was struck by this video.

Of course, I seem to have an issue keeping my nose to myself, so I had to interview her for the magazine. Note that personal information will be withheld, save for her user name.

When talking to shipwreckshark, hereby known as Shark, the first thing you notice is her warm personality. She's completely sociable, easy to talk to, and kind. Shark does not come off as the kind of person to start drama or enjoy conflict.

She lives in Alaska on base, as her husband is in the military. She lives with him and her young son. She is Wiccan and Puerto Rican and is studying to be an EMT with a 4.0 average in school. By all means, she is the ideal American, yet she found herself at the end of a restraining order based on bigotry.

So what happened? What lead to this? Shark and the neighbour originally started as friends but there were warning signs that the neighbour wasn't what she seemed from the start. Now everyone has at least one witch aesthetic thing, and Shark is no different. She had a Ouija board door mat which was the first thing that made the neighbour seemed uneasy about. Shark claims she's had a pride flag on the outside of her house so she was taken by surprise when the mat was a point of contention.

Alaska is a rather conservative state and Shark claims that the state can be rather unfriendly to both the Native and spiritual communities, so she accepted that the neighbour would likely be uncomfortable with her path, but nothing would prepare her for how the neighbour would act.

From the get-go, the neighbour would be uncomfortable around her house if so much as a tarot deck was out, so she began packing the more notable items away if the neighbour was coming over. That being said, she seemed interested, Shark commented about how the neighbour would ask questions about her beliefs, but no matter what she said, the neighbour would comment about how 'scary' it was.

Shark is a Wiccan and doesn't use magic to harm anyone, not that she could if she wanted to, given the Wiccan Rede which states to harm none and preaches the Rule Of Three. It was enough to make Shark uncomfortable and anyone reading can already see some red flags.

She would begin to show some toxic traits as Shark's husband went through a mental health crisis. Shark supported him through it, as a good partner should. The neighbour seemed to take offence to Shark's approach. Shark alleges that through her husband's difficulties the neighbour was urging her to leave him. The neighbour continued to keep trying to push her way into Shark's life and situation and it came to the point where she had to set up boundaries and tell her that she was no longer comfortable with her actions and that they couldn't be friends any more more.

The neighbour took this setting of boundaries personally and began saying that Shark implied that she hexes everyone she doesn't like.

Eventually, Shark's husband's situation improved and she rekindled her friendship with the neighbour. Yule comes and she has the neighbour over and things seemingly go better as the neighbour doesn't comment on her décor (a hung pentacle with antlers and holly). A few weeks later Shark asked her neighbour if she would babysit her son as she had mentioned she had experience babysitting. The neighbour refused to do it in Shark's house as apparently, her house made the neighbour uncomfortable. It was clear she was on her best behaviour on Yule and she didn't plan on continuing to pretend any more.

The neighbour continued to push to have the kid at her house to the point where Shark began to get nervous, which caused the neighbour to take offence and begin her toxic antics again. Shark decided enough was enough and it became clear they could not be friends any more, despite her attempts.

This is where the neighbour becomes unhinged. She seemed to take Shark's setting of boundaries and not putting up with her toxicity as a personal slight and began a campaign of slander against Shark.

A shortened list of the accusations flung against Shark is as follows: tampering with her car in the middle of winter, smoking weed inside the house (note that marijuana is legal in Alaska, and she never had anything on base or smoked on base.), having and holding drugs on base, walking down the stairs in her home and slamming on the connected wall to disturb the neighbour.

Attached are images submitted by Shark. We have permission to share images from the report that she received. All names are censored to protect the identities of people involved

This went on for about a month before Shark confronted her. The neighbour would begin calling the cops on her numerous times. She noted that the neighbour herself had a smell of weed to her and she felt like she was trying to set her up as part of her little vendetta.

They ended up needing to talk to the military housing company because the neighbour ended up filing a complaint. This in itself is aggravating as Shark had filed a complaint against the neighbour when she began this over a month before, but was ignored.

Shark brought up the neighbour's anti-pagan stance and was ignored. The two left with nothing being done.

Two days later, Shark was woken by the police knocking at her door. Given the stress of her life mixed with the fact that her husband was away on training, this triggered a panic attack. She had assumed the police were there to tell her that her husband was hurt. Luckily when he heard about the incident and talked to the police, it was more of a formality than anything.

This neighbour apparently has a history of being somewhat of a Karen and has harassed and made enemies of many of the people she's met in her life.

The police eventually came back when she was calmer and explained why they were there. Shark had a cinnamon broom attached to her fence in her yard. Cinnamon brooms can be used to "sweep away" obstacles or negativity of people that were brought into your home. Seems like exactly the kind of thing a woman in her position would need, frankly.

Attached to the broom was a spell charm protected by a zip-lock bag with the words "Blessed Be" on it to protect from the constant rainstorms they were dealing with. The neighbour called the cops because she got the idea in her head that the bag had her name in it and it was a hex or curse against her.

The neighbour took it upon herself to bring her to court to get a restraining order on her shortly after. This is where things get… tricky. It is no secret that the military is usually pretty conservative, on top of the fact that she lives in a very conservative state, as she mentioned earlier.

Not only was the neighbour awarded the restraining order against Shark, but the judge also said that Shark's "religion can instill fear". The neighbour had a lawyer and Shark, as a mother and student did not so there wasn't a lot she could do aside from just dealing with it.

So to recap: an angry ex-friend who tried to get her [Shark] to leave her husband when he went through a mental health crisis harassed and lied and wasted police and military resources to get back at Shark for not putting up with her toxic and domineering attitude. The military refused to take Shark, the Puerto Rican Wiccan's harassment complaint, yet dealt with the white Christian's complaint quickly despite the obvious lies. Despite the right to religious freedom on which the United States Of America is founded on, a judge looked her in the eyes and told her that because of her religion, people fear her to the point where restraining orders are an appropriate course of action.

It baffles the mind to think about the hypocrisy of this situation. This is not something that would ever happen if we turned the tables. You would not see months of harassment, fake phone calls to the police, and restraining orders because you saw a bible once at your friend's house, and then she hung a cross outside. Why is it that we bend over backward to cater to Christians whenever we can, from removing their kids from sex ed to literally forming the bank and work cycles of the country around their practices and religion but all a non-Christian has to do to get BROUGHT TO ACTUAL COURT is to hang a good luck charm?

Shark is preparing to fight back however, she will be appealing and doing whatever she can to make this right. She is not laying down and taking this crap. She is building her appeal, but no longer feels safe in her own home. Her husband leaves again soon and she doesn't leave the house without her family or friends on video call as now the neighbour has installed cameras focused on her cars to watch her. She fears that the moment her husband leaves, the neighbour will begin again, as she has been doing this when her husband is gone.

I wish there was a resolution to the situation, but unfortunately, this has only just begun. Who knows how long the appeal will take or if she will even win the appeal. Shark makes it very clear that she does not think that this sort of thing would happen in other states, and I'd have to agree.

Fire-Monkey Forge

A hobby turned passion. A passion turned obsession. Creating things by putting them in fire and beating them with a hammer. What's not to like?

The artist featured on this page is self taught medically retired disabled Navy Corpsman. He makes knives for fun and has a passion for very sharp blades.

facebook.com/NoPanicButton/

firemonkeyforge.wixsite.com/mysite

What Dreams May Come
A Beginners Introduction to Dream Analysis

Welcome to Understanding Dreams 101. Lol. OK. I'm here today to demystify the art of dream analysis. I advise anyone to begin with themselves before they try to read anyone else's.

Many people have a hard time remembering their dreams in the first place and to them I say relax. I will suggest a few methods to help you relax your mind and open yourself to your own subconscious later in this article.

The first thing you need to understand is that not all dreams are predictive or valid at all. Your subconscious is like a big garbage collector and your dreams are your mind's way of sorting it out. To truly be able to decipher your dreams and their significance, I recommend that you begin by keeping a dream journal. I'm sure many of you already do. If writing things down is hard for you, try drawing your impressions or insights as soon as you wake up. A dream journal, for the beginner, needs to be kept close at hand for recording before the first impressions fade.

The second thing you need to learn is to sift out the garbage. Did you watch a movie or show, listen to a podcast, read a book or article, speak with or argue with someone, were you anywhere that you may have overheard something that may have ribboned its way into your subconscious? All of these may be important in deciding about an issue you are considering but then again, they may also just be mental noise.

After sifting out the fog and drizzle, take a look at what remains. Pay attention to the environment, the feelings, the lighting, any significant things that feel like they were yelling "look at me!". Pay attention to crystals, colours, animals, numbers. In many dreams we fall to the standard symbols, (stairs, falls, water, death, birth) but these may not always represent what the books insist that they mean. Your own life experiences may influence how you see these things. Are they friend or foe, do you like or hate these things or persons? Write down these symbols and impressions.

It helps to have appropriate resources at your disposal. I keep a book on numerology, a book on spirit animals, a book on colour, a book on herb and plants, and a book on dream symbols on hand for a starting point.

Now on to the analysis of your first dream. After you have sifted out all the junk and listed your key factors, look them up one at a time and write down your general interpretation for each of them separately. These will change according to setting and correlation. At first the whole picture may not make a lot of sense. Sometimes this is because it isn't what we wanted to hear or see. It forces us to take a real look at ourselves without the prejudices we hold on our own persons like shackles. People are
ever changing. Who you were at 14 is 100 miles away from who you know yourself to be at 40.

We need to continue to grow, learn and evolve over our lifetime. Dreams are an inexpensive and convenient tool that we all have access to. Ask your guides to direct you to the more significant or important symbols because sometime others may try to interfere with things we are being told or directed to. I'll explain more about this at some other time but for now this is only a jumping off point.

Improving your ability to remember your dreams. Part of it is just practice but there are a few things you can try to help you improve your recollection.

1	Drink warm tea before bed. Not coffee. Tea, even with caffeine, will sharpen the mind while coffee will just keep you awake. I prefer a fruit, a white, or a chamomile tea.

2	Keep a piece of amethyst or rose quartz under your pillow or sewn into a piece of white cotton with lavender hung over your bed to induce a more soothing or relaxed sleep.

3	Seed you dream. If you have a concern or question, write it down and place it under your pillow before you go to sleep.

While there are other ways and other types of dreams to assist you in training your mind to this library of information, I suggest you begin here. Once again if anyone has any respectful questions, please feel free to contact me at TalesOTheGods@gmail.com. Until next time, sweet dreams.

(TalesOTheGods@gmail.com is not the email of the author of this article. For their own personal privacy they have listed the TalesOfTheGods email. Anything sent to us about this will be directed to the author and they will decide weather to reply through their own email or ours)

What is a Christian Witch?
By Dana-Lee

I remember sitting in church bored out of my mind like any other 13-year-old listening to the wives obey your husband sermon for the 8th time and deciding I'd rather read my Bible for myself. I came across a verse that no one had ever preached on or has since.

> Genesis 6:1-4 " 1 And it came to pass, when men began to multiply on the face of the earth, and daughters were born unto them, 2 That the sons of God saw the daughters of men that they were fair; and they took them wives of all which they chose. 3 And the LORD said, My spirit shall not always strive with man, for that he also is flesh: yet his days shall be an hundred and twenty years. 4 There were giants in the earth in those days; and also after that, when the sons of God came in unto the daughters of men, and they bare children to them, the same became mighty men which were of old, men of renown."

Since then, I've asked many pastors and religious teachers about it and find the answers rather lacking. I don't believe you can take parts of the Bible and ignore them or take other parts to support your own agenda. Sadly, that's what many "Christian" leaders do. For myself, this marked the beginning of my own journey of self discovery. I am what I am, a Christian Witch.

Many of you will argue that the two seem to be an oxymoron. We struggle for our place in the grand scheme of things, walking on eggshells. Often, I will use the term lightworker in place of Christian witch in an attempt to avoid offending anyone on either side of the argument. The term "witch" is often misunderstood thanks to the media and Hollywood take on things. The Christian community closes its mind, eyes and heart to anything reminding them of the roots from which they have grown. So, we hide who we are or suppress our God given gifts, even if we are called to use them for His purpose and plan.So, what is a Christian witch?

Like many of you out there, we are born to our gifts and raised to our craft. We study the old ways. A proper understanding of what a witch is is needed. We are the descendants of the original wisewomen. We practiced medicine and accepted our place in the world. We are open to the magiks that we are gifted with or exposed to from the universe. We are educated and not just to the accepted learnings.

We are multidenominational be that Catholic, Anglican, United, Evangelical Baptist whatever in our upbringing. Many of us struggle with a fear of rejection in the face of the manifesto of each sect. A multidenominational church known as Unity church has arisen where we can all gather with our different ideas and learn from each other and practice our gifts. We believe in the scriptures and even in salvation. We ground ourselves in this faith. And here is where we differ from the media perceived Christian masses. We cringe at being confused or bunched into the idea and stereotypes that exist. We are not the Spanish Inquisition, the Crusades, the Westboro Baptists, the religious terrorists of today or the phony politicians who use religion to gain more votes and control the masses. In studying our scriptures, we follow Christs footsteps. He taught a message of love and acceptance. He practiced healing and learning and call it what it was, magik. We focus our studies in kitchen witchery, dousing, healing, aura reading, spells, crystals, astrology, divination, dreams, reiki, any of the old ways. I have trained for decades under my aunt and others in order to understand how to use my primary gift and to access the tools available to me. (Yes, that includes Tarot Cards, crystals, Augham staves, potions, and candles).

In finding that verse, I felt like a light had turned on. All the theologies presented to me as stories or mythologies were real. Greek, Roman, Egyptian, Asian, all of them now were simply a different understanding of the truth. The giants, the men of renown, the Faye, I believe in them all and attribute them all equally the respect they deserve. Right there I felt like so many things I had learned needed to be questioned and studied further. Here I get a lot of questions. So many people think if you question something you must throw out the entire old idea with the bathwater. I tend to think there is nothing wrong with what I believed other than it was incomplete. I do not feel that I am called to crush the beliefs of others but rather to follow the example of Christ in healing and helping others. I am not here to convert anyone to my way of thinking. I'm here to learn and teach others in the ways of our gifts. I am here to train up my children to be open and accepting and to be true to themselves even in the face of persecution from thosewho should be showing love. I teach them to stand up to the "Christians", the fanatics who like the Pharisees before them attacked Christ and His followers, the uneducated and undereducated to strike out in fear at anything they don't and can't understand. In many ways we are still living in the early days of the witch hunts. Nothing has really changed so us.

So, what is a Christian witch? We practice our gift, learns our craft, believe in more than what the world tells us is possible. We live outside the box. Our Akashic records are open and accessed regularly. We believe in miracles and in all things magical and powerful. We are careful and cautious to ground all our spells and rituals in the God we believe in. We are just like you. Sisters and brothers in the craft. May we continue to learn from each other and of each other in the future, the way it was meant to be.In the future I hope to delve deeper into the correlation and connection between the Bible and the arts.

If anyone has respectful questions or suggestions for future topics, please feel free to forward them to me through TalesOTheGods@gmail.com and I will try to answer them to the best of my ability after further research.

Homemade Goods & Magickal Objects
By Brooke Mirabella

Witches Brew

Witches brew is used to cleanse and bless the home while also bringing in prosperity, abundance, good luck and other options depending on the ingredients used. As a plus, it also makes the home smell delicious as it is simmering. For my brew, I chose and dried the herbs, fruits and ingredients based on what correspondences I wished to see manifest in my home:

New moon water charged with clear quartz to guide new paths and bring vision

Cranberry- love, energy, healing and abundance

Bay Leaves- money, wishes, protection, manifestation, home spells, success and prosperity. As bay leaves are ideal for wish spells, I also chose to write and set an intention on each bay leaf included. For mine, I wrote: "peace", "love", "good health", "money" and "abundance"

Rosemary- cleansing, protection, love and purity

Himalayan Salt- absorbs negative energies and cleanses

Hibiscus- love, passion and divination

Clove- money drawing, love, protection and purification

Cinnamon- money drawing, purification, love and sex magic

Star Anise- love, money, psychic awareness, luck, prosperity, and quiets gossip

Apple- love, prosperity and good luck

Orange peel- energizes both physically and spiritually, brings happiness, joy, luck and money

Rose- love, health, good luck, and protection

Alfalfa- prosperity, abundance, enjoyment and pleasure of life and relationships and protection from poverty

Pomegranate- protection, prosperity, transformation, strength, vision and creativity

It is also an option to write your own chant to bless the brew as well as the home. Focus on each ingredient as you add it to the pot of water, visualizing how each correspondence will present itself in your home and life. When finished adding the ingredients, boil the brew and let it simmer for several hours to cleanse the home and fill the air with good intention. As the brew is simmering, recite your personalized chant to set your intentions.

As an example chant, you could say: "I bless this brew and bless this home. I welcome goodness, abundance, peace and love for each day to come. I cleanse any negative or stale energy residing in this home and replace it with passion, creativity, and prosperity."

Depending on what ingredients you may have chosen, the leftover liquid may be strained, saved and stored to cleanse other objects such as crystals or used in a similar manner as moon water. As the brew has been given intention and purpose, the liquid can aid in future spell work where those properties may be helpful. Be sure to research if it may need to be stored in a particular way to keep from spoiling due to the ingredients chosen in your brew.

Poppets

What is a poppet? Poppets are person-shaped objects which are made to represent a particular individual and used to cast spells upon the person. This could include either aiding or harming the person it is intended for. They have been used throughout history and in many different cultures. A poppet is not inherently good or bad as you may see in movies. Poppets are only the intentions and motives behind them. These magickal objects can be as simple or elaborately made as you would like. However, it has been said that the complexity or the more work put behind the poppet, the stronger the connection is to the goal that is intended. As always, intention and focus in all spells is everything. Poppets can be made from cloth, paper, wood, sticks or even corn husks and can include a variety of materials on them.

It is important to remember that although all Voodoo dolls are poppets, not all poppets are technically Voodoo dolls. Voodoo pertains to the specific practice behind the making of the dolls and is to be respected as it is a religion. The making and using of poppets in general or as a whole however, is not just simply Voodoo and can be made respectfully without the risk of cultural appropriation when research is taken into account.

An example poppet may be for protection of a loved one. In this illustration, it is made of sticks, ribbon, herbs, blessing oil, candle wax and the person's picture. After assembling the sticks into the shape of a person (pictures included for example), an option would be to tie or incorporate a picture or name of the person the poppet is intended for. In this case, the herbs chosen were:

Bay leaves- protection and wishes

Rose- love

Lavender- peace and calm

Blessed Thistle- protection from evil

Mugwort- strength and protection

Angelica Root- protection

Sage- cleansing of evil or bad intentions

Black ribbon and black candle wax were also used to represent the sealing and protection from harm. White ribbon too was utilized symbolizing purity and red candle wax symbolizing love. You may write your own chant to set your intention for the poppet and visualize its purpose manifesting in the person's life.

An example chant may be for this case, "May this poppet protect (insert person's name) from harm, ill will, bad luck and pain. May it represent a white light of goodness surrounding (insert person's name), providing love, blessings and peace in all areas of their life". Now you are ready to charge and use the poppet.

thequirkycupcollective.com.au

📷 instagram.com/thequirkycupcollective

f facebook.com/thequirkycupcollective

P pinterest.ca/quirkycups

$148.00
BUY NOW
CELESTITE CLUSTER

$169.00
BUY NOW
CELESTITE CLUSTER

$67.00
BUY NOW
PURPLE FLUORITE ROUGH

$82.00
BUY NOW
PURPLE FLUORITE ROUGH

frostmothapothecary.com

Frost moth apothecary is a one-woman shop based out of the verdant mountains of Vermont. Norea ritually crafts fragrant potions, incense, and candles designed to evoke archetypes and themes from history, mythology, and religion. She seeks to bring themes of the metaphysical and fantastic to our daily life through scent.

Amber on 18 Oct, 2020

★★★★★

Absolutely wonderful! Smells like stepping into an October forest and finding an abandoned cemetery. I love the earthiness and I love the patchouli!

SAMHAIN | Handmade Perfume Oil | Autumn Fragrance | Halloween Perfume | Fall Fragrance | Witchy Perfume

Lisa on 22 Oct, 2020

★★★★★

This is one of three scents I purchased at the same time. Great packaging, easy to identify the smaller vials (I bought more than one to try). I look forward to re-visiting this shop to check out what other scents will be available in the future.

RITUAL | Handmade Perfume Oil Blend | Gothic Fragrance Oil | Witchy Perfume | Amber and Honey

★★★★★

I was so excited to get my order in the mail! Samhain is probably my favorite scent I have ever owned!

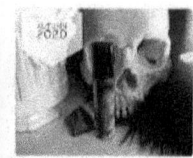

SAMHAIN | Handmade Perfume Oil | Autumn Fragrance | Halloween Perfume | Fall Fragrance | Witchy Perfume

Fashion & Accessories

Now the practice isnt an aesthetic, but it is a guilty pleasure of mine. So here are some accessories that we have come across that we think will spice up your witch aesthetic, while supporting the community.

Moon Phase Pentacle Pendant

$51.60
https://www.moonchild-spiritual-emporium.co.uk/collections/jewellery/products/moon-phase-pentacle-pendant

Goddess Cradle Necklace

$24.07
https://www.moonchild-spiritual-emporium.co.uk/collections/jewellery/products/goddess-cradle-necklace

Futhark Cluster Necklace

$34.40
https://www.moonchild-spiritual-emporium.co.uk/collections/jewellery/products/futhark-cluster-necklace

Sterling silver veles signet ring

$79.95
https://norsespirit.com/collections/viking_rings/products/925-sterling-silver-veles-signet-ring

Leather buckle valknut cuff

$65.95
https://norsespirit.com/collections/viking_bracelets/products/leather-buckle-wrist-wrap-with-metal-valknut-design

Tiger Brooch & Wool Shawl

€59.00
https://celticfusiondesign.com/womens/tiger-brooch-and-shawl-handwoven

TheMotherOfRaven
etsy.com/ca/shop/TheMotherOfRaven

Heather on 14 Aug, 2020

★★★★★

Absolutely beautiful!! The seller had fantastic communication and you can immediately tell she puts her heart into her craft. Shipping was fast and efficient and the item was packed securely with no damage. Can't wait to purchase another piece!

 Skull coffin box

Emmalee Schooler on 23 Aug, 2020

★★★★★

Stunning as always! I ended up putting it with a wreath I made on my door and it looks perfect there! It's never too early to decorate for Halloween!

Gnosis or Not?

The phrase "Personal Gnosis" gets used a lot in today's occult, witchcraft, and pagan communities. With reconstructed or relatively new religions and in some cases magickal frameworks, how could it not? Think to chaos magick, a fairly new framework of practicing magick all about gnosis, or to Hellenism, an almost completely reconstructed religion that is practiced in vastly different ways by vastly different people due to varied myths and presentations of the gods in even modern context. Practices firmly rooted in pop-culture also struggle with gnosis as a whole, as there has never been a magickal and pagan "Cult of Sailor Moon," unlike, say, Hekate. These are the frameworks I am working within, I should disclose. Gnosis is an everyday challenge and reward. When we talk about gnosis in magick and (typically) paganism, we're often talking about one of three types: unverified personal gnosis (UPG), shared personal gnosis (SPG), and verified personal gnosis (VPG.) First, however, how I define gnosis is: the state between believing and knowing, between science and the ethereal, 'knowing' what is inherently life's unknowable.

UPG:

Unverified personal gnosis, or UPG, is often not widely shared or able to be verified through other people's experience nor the recorded canon of the topic at hand. The fact that it is unable to be fact-checked doesn't make it at-the-core untrue; instead it is merely the true unknowable, the extremely personal. Some UPG takes are, to be frank, worrisome. The worrisome gnoses are often what is perceived by others as damaging to one's mental health or magickally dangerous. Such gnoses may include that belladonna is in some cases non-harmful to use in sympathetic magick, or that one was told to do something extremely harmful against someone else by a deity.

SPG:

The problem and beauty of shared personal gnosis is that it takes on a new form and spirit in the zeitgeist of magick and paganism. Shared belief is a hefty lifeforce and becomes its canon in many instances to those who share it. Some shared personal gnoses include: that one can use almost anything in a spell or ritual and that Anubis enjoys fireball as an offering. These become shared servitors and hard to avoid in one's practice as they are popular and what is often stumbled across first in internet searches on paganism and magick.

VPG:

Verified personal gnosis is supported by canonical media forms. Media can include interviews with experts in said field, source material(s), professional analyses of source material, source-period art forms, among other less utilized media styles. Any gnoses supported by canonical media is said to be the most reliable.

The Beginnings of Gnosis:

Pop-culture practices are a mix of (U/S/V) personal gnosis and a general system. Does this sound familiar to what one does in their practice and possibly religion? The system is essentially that one does the types of magick described or shown in whatever piece of media's canon they are following as a (part of their) practice. This is inherently a system of magick, although not canonized in anything but chaos magick, and even then it is fringe. Spirit work with these entities described in the media's canon can also be done, including systemic and often deeply religious paganism-like/adjacent practices, worshipping these spirits as deities and working with them as such if desired. The systems of pop-culture practices are often developed from the discovery of new gnoses within oneself, through research, and through deep devotion and interest to the occult and to the canon(s) one will be/is working within.

The Solidification of Gnosis:

I've mentioned pop-culture practices above, what exactly does that mean and how does one form gnoses in such a fringe magickal system, with many different hairs to split such as: which pop-culture pantheon(s) to work within, how to know if a pop-culture spirit is reaching out, and being in-tune to signs that are fictional but appear in reality. Let's explore Lovecraftian Magick to find this out.

H.P. Lovecraft never intended for his writings to inspire religion, magick, and spiritwork. This does not mean that the Necronomicon was never written. The system of magick described within is completely based upon Lovecraft's writings and gods. Fiction made into reality. The jump between fiction and reality came to be when the marvelous grimoire the Necronomicon was written and brought into magickal canon. Many think of it as some old grimoire to do with necromancy, however it is largely the opposite. The Necronomicon is a completely fabricated piece of magickal history bringing pop-culture magick into the occult canon. Pop-culture magick that is not in disguise from history and lack of looking into it is considereddelusional at times. However, let's define what makes a pop-culture practice and delve into the beginnings of gnoses in individuals and in the occult zeitgeist.

Divides in Gnosis:

Gnoses are formed largely through canons. In the occult's case they come to be through parts of systems of magick's literary canon gaining or losing footing, changing with the tides. We see this in the popular Order of the Golden Dawn's complete system of magick. There is an incredible divide in occult communities at the moment of the validity of its teachings due to its appropriation of Jewish Mysticism/Kabbalah. It does, however, remain as the foundations of the tarot, along with various works by Aleister Crowley. I remember mentioning Crowley to a Jewish Studies professor of mine and them being taken aback that I would pay attention to his teachings. In these interactions, we see gnosis/es take hold and at play.

The popular gnosis around the Order of the Golden Dawn is that, quite frankly, its teachings are genius and quite accessible in the realm of deep western esoteric magickal systems. This gnosis is SPG, unprovable but popular. Other, dividing, gnoses include that it should be avoided, as it is clear appropriation. The popular gnosis surrounding Crowley's teachings is that they work in practice but are dense to read through; again, SPG. The popular and world-separating gnosis around Crowley's history, however, is that he was an awful, disdain-deserving person. The disdain for Crowley is supported by evidence, such as that he once put his own semen in food for guests as an experiment. That's VPG. Examples of my UPGs surrounding these systems and teachings are: Crowley's Book of Lies is impossible to understand as it is nonsensical, and the element of spirit may not need so many ways for which to draw a pentagram (Golden Dawn.)

An Ending Note; Deceiving Oneself With Gnosis:

When a practitioner does not investigate enough into their gnoses, or even realize they have them, they will eventually trick themselves into thinking that said gnoses are categorically correct. I implore you, reader, to figure out your gnoses, investigate opposing and differing views of them, and decide if they were made to serve a purpose -- what is that purpose? If you are not talking to other practitioners and members of your chosen religious views, nor reading opposing or differing and supporting sources, you may fall into this trap.

THREADS OF FATE

thethreadsoffate.com

The Weaver Tarot - Journeyer

$79.00

Threads of Fate Oracle - Rose Edition

$69.00

Cleansing your home for newbies

So you want to cleanse your space and can't use a giant bundle of herbs for whatever reason, well you're in luck. Despite what memes and some more... materialistic people will tell you, you don't actually need to walk around your house with herbs as thick as your arm for 5 hours trying to remove negativity from your house.

There are actually quite a few ways to cleanse your space, and not all of them involve setting things on fire.... regrettably. Now pop culture seems to be in love with this idea of people using giant bundles of sage (usually white for some reason) to cleanse their space. This would be rather like using a nuke to kill a fly. Sage removes all energies, good and bad from your space, and if anything, invites energies to fill the area where everything was 'cleansed'. It's really not something you should be using on the regular and unless you're native you should not be using white sage (especially because there are 699 other species of sage you could be using instead)

So there are two main ways to cleanse your area, one being sound, and the other being smoke. Smoke cleansing is probably the cheapest and easiest to do and probably why most newbies seem to think it's the only way to do it. You can smoke cleanse with either dried herb bundles or with incense. How you go about cleansing your area is up to you. I personally open as many windows and doors as I can, and go from the farthest part of the house and work my way outwards. People debate whether it is necessary to keep the doors open or closed for it to work. For the same reason that the energy never needed an open window or door to get in and it's silly to think they'd need them open to leave. I was taught how to cleanse by native family members and teachers, however, who while smudging (a native practice) they insist on having them open. At the end of the day, it's a matter of preference and culture more than anything.

Follow your senses and the smoke and let it wash over certain areas and items that hold more negativity than others. You don't need much to cleanse a house, one stick of good incense can last up to an hour and if you are using dried herbs, you really don't need much either. You may choose what you wish to say when cleansing, I usually chant something along the lines of "Any negative energy, spirits, or entities, deities that have not been expressly invited in, leave this space. This space is warded by my energy and by love, light and the five elements". What you say is completely up to you and there is no wrong way to do this.

So what can you use to do this? Well like I said, it's incredibly cheap to do this and you can easily consult a book or Google protective herbs and plants, but here are some that popular and easy to buy/grow/find.

Sandalwood is one of my favorites. It is used for meditation, divination, cleansing, and protecting sacred spaces. It also smells beautiful.

Dragon's Blood is also a very useful incense and is used in both protection and banishing.

Frankincense is used in protection and throughout many practices and was even given as a gift to Jesus in the Christian birth of Jesus story.

Mugwort can be used in protection and divination but please do not ingest without researching first.

Rosemary can be used in protection, cleansing, and strength

Pine is useful for healing, protection, fertility, and exorcising and cleansing.

There are far more but these are the basic ones that I use. You can use one or all in a bundle to cleanse your space.

The next option is using sound. This traditionally is done with singing bowls. You go through your home in the same manner as before and run a special wand around the rim and it emits a noise at a certain frequency that clears the area. You can get certain bowls that sing at different frequencies and have different effects.

Some people sing certain songs with magic literally written into them to cleanse. You can jingle bells or jewelry or bang pots and pans together so long as you are good at setting your intentions. Be warned that if you have an entity in your space and you choose this, you may just end up angering it. Frankly, I would avoid this technique if you are inexperienced.

The overconsumption of crystals
in new-age practices

Crystals have become a very prevalent thing within the craft in the past few years. As someone who came into the craft in the early 2000s, I always have had a soft spot for shiny rocks but it is a little strange to see how crystals have become such an integral part of witchcraft.

I have no problems with people who use them in their practice, even I have some that I use. That being said there is somewhat of a problem with the overconsumption of crystals these days. Now I know some of you reading this may be wondering how this is that much of a problem. It's a problem because people are dying to mine these stones, we are mining out gems left and right, and child labor is being used to obtain them.

If you're a reconstructionist pagan, it's unlikely crystals have a very major part in your practice, but if you are of the new-age variety, they may be a very integral part. In the past few years, the popularity of crystals has grown exponentially. As per a video by CNBC (How crystals have become a multi-billion dollar industry) 5 Billion dollars worth of crystals are moved every 3 weeks in the crystal trade, and then the sales of crystals have increased five times over since 2009.

There are whole practices formed around healing people with crystals. From placing them on the head to remove headaches or open your third eye to inserting Yoni eggs into your... cavities, to putting them into water bottles, new-age practitioners in particular.

The obsession goes beyond that, however. Go into any metaphysical store and you will find crystals, big and small. Celebrities will have crystal-encrusted walls, practitioners will have drawers full of them. There are hundreds of memes on the internet of people blowing their paycheques on crystals. Crystals are everywhere, and they aren't going anywhere any time soon.

With the rise in popularity, comes the pressure for people to sell more for less. I have always been more than a little suspicious that I can get 6 fist-sized lineament varieties of quartz for less than $60. People will argue that you can just go out and find quartz but that argument falls short pretty quickly. We are beginning to mine out certain gems completely and as soon as buyers hear even so much as a whisper that a gem is about to be mined out, they flock to buy up what's left so that they might have a rare stone for their collection.

We all know mines can destroy the environment but they can also make or break communities. Madagascar is a major contender as far as the crystal trade is concerned. In an article by The Guardian published on Tuesday, September 17th, 2019, they state that " Gems and precious metals were the country's fastest-growing export in 2017 – up 170% from 2016, to $109m. This island country of 25 million people now stands alongside far larger nations, such as India, Brazil, and China, as a key producer of crystals for the world."

Mining companies all but run the economy there and people live below the $1.90 poverty line. People will send their children into the mine to feed their families. Whether they die in the mines, or they die of starvation, there is one thing at the root of it, the crystal trade. There are people who can go into it better than I can, and The Guardian goes into it better than I can, but we need to take some responsibility. There are some who are calling the crystal trade "The New Blood Diamond" and it's shocking to hear that, and then turn to FaceBook or TikTok to see a middle-class woman clutching fist fulls of crystals from her local metaphysical shop.

So what can we do? Well, I don't think we can really reverse the situation we've made. Those communities who rely on the mines for money will not survive if we just stop buying crystals, but they aren't doing much better with the mines. We need to hold suppliers to a higher standard. If you sell crystals, you need to press for information for where your supplier is getting their crystals (a surprising amount of people don't know what mine they are getting their stones from). We need to pressure the mines to pay their workers a living wage and increase safety measures for their workers. We need to pressure the countries the mines are in to hold them to a higher standard. We need to be willing to pay more for crystals and cut back on the hyper-consumerism regarding crystals.

You can do crystal healing without being overzealous in their use. Nobody needs entire drawers for their crystals, nobody needs to be covered head to toe in crystals to be protected. You don't need to fill your pockets with stones, wear jewelry filled with them, stick them in your water bottle, cover your house in them, stick them inside you, etc. There is a point where it is too much. If materialism isn't a problem for you, the exploitation of children and the poor should be.

On the topic of sage

So if you have been on the internet you may have noticed the totally not at all hostile, very friendly conversation regarding sage.

If you've been practising for a while, you may be tired of hearing it everywhere, nonstop. So I formally apologize for bringing this up. Now, I had had someone who was going to write about this topic, however, life can be hectic these days, and they left the team. This article is specifically for new practitioners and those who don't know what the argument is about.

A summary:

People are using sage, particularly white sage in the attempts to cleanse their area. Native practitioners have been trying to tell non Natives that using sage is an appropriation of their religion and culture. Some Non-Natives have pushed against that, a little too aggressively.

Now to recap what was stated earlier, sage isn't really the herb for 'cleansing' and is rather like killing a fly with a nuke. There are around 700 species of sage one could use and it grows around the world, however, people are fighting tooth and nail about white sage.

So why is it a big deal, and why will people get testy when you broach the subject? Well to put it nicely, the occult has had a bad track record of taking Native practices and claiming them as their own and then throwing a tantrum when they are told their behaviour is wrong.

We did this with dream catchers, spirit animals, smudging, war bonnets being worn as costumes, and now white sage. This seems to have hit a peak when places like Amazon, Walmart, and Sephora, as well as small Etsys that are clearly not owned by Native creators started selling 'cleansing packages'. This resulted in big companies taking a sacred practices from the Natives, and profiting off it. Before anyone argues that this is somehow helping the Natives, I will have to inform you that they don't see a cent of that money.

They have to watch people take their sacred ceremonies (which as a quick reminder, were illegal for many years) and make thousands of dollars off them, while many reserves still do not have basic clean drinking water. They have to live in reservations that we would deem near 3rd world, while our people profit off of the same ceremonies that we tried to kill through the residential school system, the last of which only closed in 1996.

People have pointed this out and people, unfortunately, seemed to not care or pretend that they never knew that. The amount of people I have seen called out for using white sage, claiming they didn't know the situation, getting educated, promising they will change, only for them to turn around and use white sage again and then plea ignorance once again, astounding. It really should not be that difficult a concept to grasp, especially when there are 699 other species of sage they could use instead.

When people refuse to listen, they are informed about the threatened state of white sage. The people fighting to use white sage either claim that that is false or overstated, in spite of the Native groups, conservationists, and herbalists that say otherwise. I suppose we must all fall to the feet of the Google PhDs of the world.

According to unitedplantsavers.org "In June 2018, four people were arrested for the illegal harvest of 400 pounds of white sage in North Etiwanda Preserve in California." and that "It is very difficult when companies make claims of sustainable harvest when we have no accountability within a very secretive trade."

Unfortunately, white sage is not protected in any state within the US and has not been evaluated by the IUCN Red List. In my own opinion, considering the situation in the USA currently, I highly doubt (especially considering that big companies have their hands in the trade) that it is going to become protected any time soon and because of that, people are likely to continue claiming that it is not threatened, simply because the government says so.

I tend to believe the conservationists and the Natives about their own plants, they know what they're talking about and aren't about to look the other way for money. This is aggravating because it shows the cognitive dissonance of the metaphysical community. We live a nature orientated life, but turn a blind eye to the white sage situation because we think we need it to "cleanse and clear our energy", and we respect the spirits and demand people listen to us and validate our culture and religion, but turn and ignore and speak over Native voices who contradict us.

You can buy common sage at the grocery store that doesn't negatively impact people who are trying to revive their culture after generations of attempted cultural genocide.

Help our friend, Neico!

Neico is in trouble! One of the people on our team is in desperate need of help.

Neico is a very skilled tarot and natal chart reader and a very dear friend to everyone on our team. She is a mother of 2 with a 3rd child on the way.

Like many of us, Neico has found herself very affected by COVID. She recently had to travel out of state to get her truck fixed and certified to comply with certain standards as it was inherited from her father after he passed. Unfortunately, her siblings have decided to contest the will and the truck was taken by the courts until they can sort out the will.

This has left her pregnant with no way back home. Her home, mind you, is also on the chopping block as well because of this. As she was just barely getting by and needed to take donations to get the gas to come to get the truck fixed in the first place, it's easy to say that this has effectively left her stranded with her family and 2 dogs.

They have been making the best of the situation by couch surfing in their friend's homes and eventually raised enough donations to get a hotel room, and have been attempting to make it back home. This would be no easy task on a good day, but certainly not in her current situation.

As this is 2020, of course, things can only get worse and the courts tell her that she needs to stay in the state for 90 days so that they can work on the inheritance case. This has all but bound her to her current situation. Should the case go her way (as it seems it will) she will have her house, car back as well as an undisclosed amount of money per month that will help her family survive.

They have half decided and a half been forced to stay in the state and her boyfriend starts his job in a few days, but they will not be paid until around the American Thanks Giving. They are teaming up with a friend to split an apartment but need funds to do so.

Neico gives affordable tarot readings, a year ahead, and business readings, and natal chart readings. Email her at magiciansdivinationgmail.com for prices. Natal chart readings are $50 but the tarot readings can vary depending on your budget.

You can donate to her at: **Paypal.me/magiciansdivination3** or at **https://cash.app/$NicciSativa** and her Venmo is: **@magiciansdivination3**

She would really appreciate any help or business you can give. Help get this family into a safe home for the winter.

Thank you for reading!

Keep an eye out for our next release! We are planning to put out a magazine for every Sabbat of the wheel of the year. For release information and general magazine info, visit TalesOfTheGods.com or the facebook group, Practical Witchcraft at (https://www.facebook.com/groups/665578877692886) This magazine was made with contributions from our teams as well as submissions from the community. If you would like to submit your writing or thoughts, feel free to send them to TalesOTheGods@gmail.com

IMBOLC 2021

FORN SIDR
Being trademarked and taken from the community

THE LAW OF HOSPITALITY
The basics of it for the modern Hellenic Pagan

TOOLS OF THE TRADE
The basic tools you should have for magical workings

ALTARS
Everything you need to know to get started

Tales Of The Gods & Practical Witchcraft

Thank you for reading the TalesOfTheGods & Practical Witchcraft Magazine Imbolc 2021 Edition!

By purchasing this, you are supporting your communities. All contributors take home a equal share of the income for this magazine.

The best way you can support us is by giving us a review on Amazon! Want to join our team or write in anonymously?

E-mail us at TalesOTheGods@gmail.com

Front cover image by Daniel Kainz

https://unsplash.com/photos/xx999OYHdwY

Contributors

Desiree Goulden	TOTG owner and operator, magazine lay out artist, editor, contributor
Dana Beaudreau	Editor, reiki master, contributor
Owen Lee VonBrandt	Medium, contributor, photographer

This eddition is brought to you by a smaller team than our last. By the time of publication, both Neico and Brook will be having their daughters! Welcome to the world, Astraea and Ophelia!

Neico and her family has been hit hard by COVID and as a result have found themselves living out of hotels. If anyone can spare anything, we ask that you donate to her via her CashApp link cash.me/niccisativa or via her CashApp name, $NicciSativa

Table Of Contents

About Imbolc	PAGE 4
Pagan Influence On Cremation	PAGE 6 - 10
Tools Of The Trade	PAGE 12 -16
Help Forn Sidr of America	PAGE 18 - 20
The Law Of Hospitality	PAGE 22 - 24
Cystals, Numbers and Symbols	PAGE 26 - 30
The History and How to of Tasseography	PAGE 32 -35
Altars - Jumping Off Points	PAGE 36 - 38
Altars - Spellwork And Divination	PAGE 39 - 41

Is celebrating its first birthday! In January 2020 TOTG was created! We set out with the intention of connecting the spiritual and metaphysical communities, across paths and practices to bring them to the resources they need. In that one year, we have gone through many changes as we find our footing.

We have began to compile our free shops and resources lists, wrote many articles, created this magazine, began publishing books for practitioners to learn and use on their path.

We hope you stay with us on our journey to serve the community. Look out for our next TalesOfTheGods & Practical Witchcraft magazine, the Ostara edition, and keep an eye out for our online expos and festivals, all at TalesOfTheGods.com!

Don't miss out on our limited edition TalesOfTheGods & Practical Witchcraft Imbolc 2021 sweaters. Only available until May 1st, coupons from TalesOfTheGods.com and the Practical Witchcraft Facebook group applicable.

Hoodie: $44.56 CAD
Fanny Pack: $31.83 CAD

Link for hoodie and fanny pouch: https://teespring.com/talesofthegods-imbolc-magazine?pid=212

Link for leggings and sweat pants: https://teespring.com/totg-banner-pants?pid=641

Leggings: $56.02 CAD
Sweatpants: $63.64 CAD

To celebrate the 1st birthday of TalesOfTheGods.com we have released a new item in our merch shop. Check out our TalesOfTheGods logo themed sweatpants and leggings! Coupons applicable.

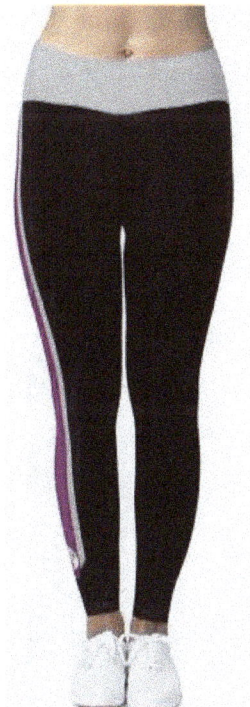   

The TalesOfTheGods Library

Available at TalesOfTheGods.com/merch and TalesOfTheGods.com/magazine

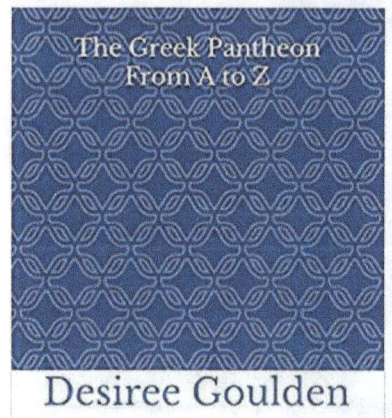

The Greek Pantheon From A to Z. A mini encyclopedia of the Greek gods listing all the major gods, goddesses, nymphs and daimons. Perfect for new Hellenic Pagans, and people who have an interest in the Greek Pantheon. Paperback: $19.18 CAD
Kindle: $6.39 CAD

Meditation Journal. A meditation aid for the recollection of dreams, meditation, and astral travel. Covers set up, prominent symbolism and emotions and is a extremely useful book for recording important spiritual activities. Paperback: $19.18 CAD

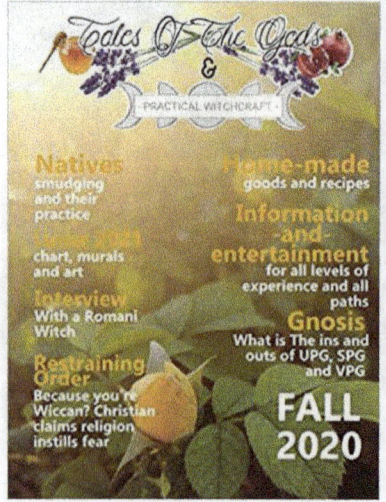

TalesOfTheGods & Practical Witchcraft Fall 2020 edition. The first of the TOTG and Practical Witchcraft magazines. A educational and entertainment magazine for the spiritual and pagan communities across experance and age.
Paperback: $18.27 CAD Kindle: $6.52 CAD

Imbolc

Fire, unlimited stock photo by MariaLoikkii, Jan 4 2016
https://www.deviantart.com/marialoikkii/art/Fire-unlimited-stock-photo-582425597

Imbolc falls on February 1st to 2nd in 2021 and is the second on the Wiccan wheel of the year. It its Gaelic in origin and is sometimes called Brigid's Day.

It celebrates the goddess Brigid and was such a important festival that when the areas that celebrated it were Christianized, they made Brigid into a saint and renamed the festival as St. Brigid's Day.

Imbolc falls on February 1st to 2nd in 2021 and is the second on the Wiccan wheel of the year. It its Gaelic in origin and is sometimes called Brigid's Day. It celebrates the goddess Brigid and was such a important festival that when the areas that celebrated it were Christianized, they made Brigid into a saint and renamed the festival as St. Brigid's Day.

Celtic reconstructionists celebrate the more traditional version of Imbolc that is primarily about Brigid, and Wiccans and Neo-Pagans who celebrate it celebrate the element of fire that it relates to.

 The Underworld Oracle Deck By Desiree Goulden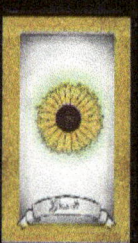

25 Full colour cards

Works with reversed cards

Works with other decks

$23.99 Cad

https://www.thegamecrafter.com/games/the-underworld-oracle-deck

The Pagan Influence On Cremation

In 2014 47% of people within the USA chose cremation over traditional burial, but how many people know that without Pagans, you would most likely not be able to have that option?

While cremation was always around in some form (There are records of burning bodies as funeral processes as far back as Ancient Athens ((1100 BC))) across the world, American Christian grievers were taken aback at the thought of them. American at the time of the first cremation (1876) were very concerned with the preservation of one's self after death and referred to cremation as dehumanizing and disgusting. Caitlin Doughty, Mortician, owner of Clarity Funerals and Cremation of Los Angeles, author, and YouTuber, reports that one of the reviewers of the first cremation called it "Another exemplification of the wickedness of the metropolis" which should give you an idea as to how the general populous thought of cremation.

Cremation wouldn't really shake its stigma and become popular until the 1980's, but if it wasn't for the Theosophical Society Of America, I have my doubts that it ever would be as popular as what it is now. But what is the Theosophical Society and what happened during the first cremation?

The Theosophical Society Of America was formed in 1875 by Helena Petrovna Blavatsky, noblewoman, Colonel Henry Steel Olcott and William Quan Judge, attorneys and 16 others. This religious movement hand amongst its members noblemen and women and influential people of status, including Thomas Edison and William Butler Yeats.

The Society states its beliefs as follows from it's website, https://www.theosophical.org/ "Ever since its founding in 1875, the Theosophical Society has stood for freedom of thought and respect for all people regardless of race, class, caste, sex, or religion. To join the Theosophical Society, you are required to have no specific beliefs. You need only to state your agreement with the Society's Three Objects:

1. To form a nucleus of the universal brotherhood of humanity, without distinction of race, creed, sex, caste, or color.

2. To encourage the comparative study of religion, philosophy, and science.

3. To investigate unexplained laws of nature and the powers latent in humanity."

It draws it's belief system from Vedānta, Mahāyāna Buddhism, Qabbalah, and Sufism and wants to unite Eastern and Western practices to show the commonality of human culture.

Given this rather progressive thinking (particularly for the 1870's) it is easy to see how this group would straddle the line of what was acceptable and what was obscene for the time. It seems people could not come to a conclusion as to what to think of the group as they either loved or hated the idea. None the less, regardless of the public opinion, they made it a goal to push forward with presenting cremation to the western world. A move allowed only by their titles, and class, and money, no doubt.

The first cremation was the cremation of Baron Joseph Henry Louis Charles, Baron de Palm, who died after battling with an illness that effected many of his organs. He left his body and much of his estate to Olcott for his kindness to him in life. He also requested in his will that no clergyman or priest should officiate at his funeral.

His funeral was held as the Masonic Temple in New York on the corner of 23rd Street and 6th Avenue on May 20, 1876. His funeral was a grand spectacle that many "reviewers" showed up to report upon for local news papers. There was roughly 2000 guests for the Baron's funeral. It was due to this media presence that we know what happened during the funerary ceremonies. One of re reporters from The New York Times called the ceremony "a hodge-podge of notions, a mixture of guess-work and jugglery, of elixirs and pentagons, of charms and conjurations"

The ceremonies consisted of "a home-brewed liturgy of Hindu scriptures, passages from Charles Darwin's writings, scraps of spiritualism and transcendentalism, references to fire worship, and invocations of the Nile goddess Isis" and were called "Folly," "farce," "weird," "objectionable," "repulsive," "revolting," "a desecration" "one might have supposed that the company had been assembled to have a good time over roast pig." (via https://www.questia.com/) To the common Christen citizen of the day, this may very well have seemed to be a barbaric display of glee over the death of the Baron. To modern practitioners, this may seem to be a appropriation of many cultures and religions with no real acknowledgement of the fact that if anyone of the cultures of which the Theosophical Society took from tried this, the already abysmal reception would have been far worse.

So they had their ceremony and weather they had wanted the negative press or not, they caught the attention of the United States Of America. Did this allow for them to cremate the body? No. In fact it would be 6 months before the Baron could be cremated. Dr. Francis Julius LeMoyne designed the crematorium that would eventually cremate De Palm.

LeMoyne had the plans for his crematorium for some time, as he began to worry about pollution from the decomposing bodies after traditional burial (a thought process that at the time were unfounded but if he lived today with the commonplace of embalming would have been a valid concern) but was bound by his own money for the project and hindered by protests every step of the way. All while De Palm waited for his body to be tended to.

You can't really blame people at the time for disliking the process. I imagine that this would be extremely macabre to the common folk, especially when you consider that they lost the body of De Palm amongst the cargo on the train carrying him to the crematory. You can't blame them from being struck with fear when he was put into the machine finally and his arm stuck up and apparently raising 3 fingers (it is a normal part of the crematory process for the limbs to curl up and contort as the body burns and the liquid vaporizes out of the body).

Despite the spectacle and outrage, the LeMoyne crematory would continue to cremate bodies after that. It closed in 1901 after cremating 42 bodies, LeMoyne included. His ashes were buried on the property and a headstone stands over them to this day.

As for De Palm, his remains were put into a "Hindu-style urn" and spectators took with them some of his ashes. LeMoyne took some of his bones to keep on his desk and there were rumours that some of the Theosophical Society kept some of De Palm's ashes in snuff boxes which they carried on them, although that may have just been a fanciful rumour.

Since then, cremations became more and more common until today where they account for around half of funerals in America. We may never know if cremation would have become acceptable if it weren't for LeMoyne, De Palm and The Theosophical Society, I for one doubt it would have, but none the less we have them to thank for cremation.

I can't help but to think that one could make a interesting historical comedy based off these events. If you want to know more, head to AskAMortician on YouTube, or watch the connected video beneath this.

It's always interesting to see where Pagan influence lies in modern society, and this shows that we can all make positive change in the world. Even if you're a penniless faux Baron, a strange old man with dreams of burning corpses, or a person who thinks cremation is the only way to stop vampires (listen it was the 1800's it was a valid concern back in the day) never doubt that you as a Pagan can bring about change.

Photo by: Sharon McCutcheon
https://unsplash.com/photos/_L3KpEED4UQ

Neico Anderson
Astrologist and Tarot Reader

Natal chart readings:	$50 USD
Year ahead readings:	$50 USD
General tarot readings:	Donation Based

✉ magiciansdivination@gmail.com

f https://www.facebook.com/magiciansdivination

Mother of 2 with one on the way, Neico has been practising reading tarot cards for 6 years and as been doing astrology for 3. She has nothing but good reviews and is one of the few people that the staff of this magazine go to. She is worth every penny and can work with peoples budget. By far one of the best readers we have known.

Tools of the trade

So you're new and you want to get into magical workings. You may have herd of the terms: athame, wand, etc but what are they, how do you make / acquire them and what do they do?

These things can be easily found in just about any beginner occult / witch book, but if you don't know where to start or look we will give you a run down here. We will be using The Witch's Book Of Magical Ritual by Gavin Frost and Yvonne Frost, Wicca A to Z by Gerina Dunwich, A Grimoire Of Shadows, Witchcraft Paganism & Magic by Ed Fitch, and Solitary Witch by Silver RavenWolf. (Yes I know, groan now about her, but this book has a lot of on hand knowledge and frankly is a good resource for quick look ups on info)

Your basic kit should have a athame, wand, chalice, pentacle incense, and cauldron. Note that while this is suggested to have these items, you can make due without a object or two and replace them with stand ins. This will not go into how to cast a circle, only about the different tools, what they do and how to use them.

Athame: An athame is a dagger with a black hilt that is used to help draw circles. It is a sacred object so despite what one may want to do with the dagger, it is not intended to shed any blood. Not willing nor yours nor a sacrifice's. It represents masculine energy and the element of air.

Ed Finch states that is a strong protection object that grows stronger with each use and the hilt should only be inscribed with a pentacle and the witch's practice name in runes, but I have known others who carve protection sigils and runes in and it depends on your own practice on weather or not you follow that.

Gavin and Yvonne has a very in depth explanation on how to construct your athame by hand, saying that it ought to be made of bronze or aluminum. They state the blade should be 4.675", the tang 3.94", the thickness of the blade 1/8" and the guard 2". They state that you should engrave your ritual name, pentacle, zodiac sign, the double s (for spirit and soul) and the sun and moon on opposing signs.

The Witch's Book Of Magical Ritual is a very excellent book if you are a smith in your free time, but we acknowledge that some people lack the ability or skills or want to hand make it and you can either hire someone to make one for you, or find a stand in. This can be as simple as a butter knife, as long as it represents what you want it to, is consecrated or cleansed depending on your path and never sheds any blood. Many people make their athames out of onyx or other crystals, some being dull blades some being sharp, the symbology and not touching blood being the only things that (from what I've seen) matter.

Candles: This represents the element of fire. Many use them in magical workings but can simply represent fire in a ritual if needed. Although in ancient times candles were made of animal fat and did not have colouring, thus were not overly important in magical practice, in new-age practices candles can be very important and the colour of the candle and how it is anointed can change the effects of ones magic, if you follow that belief.

Candles are useful for fire and wax divination and many use them as offerings for their deities, if they have them.

Cauldron: This is a very useful tool, though a bit pricey depending on the material. It is a iron or pewter pot / cauldron that is very useful for burning offerings, loose incense and more. Having fire safety is critical in the craft and so having one of these is more important than you think as porcelain or glass may crack or explode with prolonged and intense heat. Can be used for brewing potions and the like, this represents all four elements coming together.

Chalice (or bowl): A sacred cup or bowl used in Wiccan rituals and some pagan rituals. Usually silver, it represents the element of water. Part of many Wiccan rituals. It can be a silver goblet, a glass cup, or a silver bowl. Can be plain or ornate, as long as it holds water and is consecrated like your other items in your kit.

Gavin and Yvonne states that it can be a wooden bowl, and emphasize on the hand made aspect weather its from you or another.

Clothing: The clothing you wear while doing workings may differ on your path but it is generally accepted that you should have cloths specifically for rituals or some magical workings. This has spiritual significance but is also important for safety. When working with fire you shouldn't have your hair in your face, or cloths draping into the flames or dangling jewelry that can get in the fire.

Incense: This can be your standard incense sticks from the store, or burning dried herbs. This is important for cleansing a area of negativity. This represents air, as one may assume.

Cauldron: This is a very useful tool, though a bit pricey depending on the material. It is a iron or pewter pot / cauldron that is very useful for burning offerings, loose incense and more. Having fire safety is critical in the craft and so having one of these is more important than you think as porcelain or glass may crack or explode with prolonged and intense heat. Can be used for brewing potions and the like, this represents all four elements coming together.

Pentacle: A very significant symbol in all occult endeavors and many pagan walks. It is a five pointed star contained in the circle. Each of the points represents the elements. (Fire, Water, Earth, Air, and Spirit) In practice you can have your pentacle on wood, wax or metal. This represents the element Earth.

Wand: Represents the element of air or fire depending on the path. Some paths ask your wand to be made of specific material. Ed Fitch says it must be of a willow tree that you asked permission to harvest from and tipped in silver, but depends on the path. I have a few for different workings with different woods and runes on them that help with different things.

Water: This represents... well... water. This can be used for divination but also something you may want to keep on hand to put out small fires if they arise. (Please note that if you are trying to put out any fire where scents or oils were a part of DO NOT PUT WATER ON IT. Smother it with a blanket or towel. Please practice good fire safety.)

There are many more magical items that one may want to use in their craft, but these are the basics that I think the general practitioner should have in their basic kit. Remember that you don't have to spend a lot of money on these, almost everything can be found in and about your house or you can make yourself. Please remember that while Wiccans have a certain way of doing things, not every other magical path follows the same and you should look to your elders and leaders on your path to help guide you in how to craft your tools to fit your practice.

Photo by: Owen Lee VonBrandt

Free shops & services listings

Have a shop or service and want to extend your reach without speding some coin? Contact us! We will set up your shop in our public database including a explination of your business and a landing page to display your wares!

We will post you on our online shops and services for free! Just contact us at our contact page on TalesOfTheGods.com or send us a email at TalesOTheGods@gmail.com or at our social medias! We can be found on Facebook, Twitter, and Instagram!

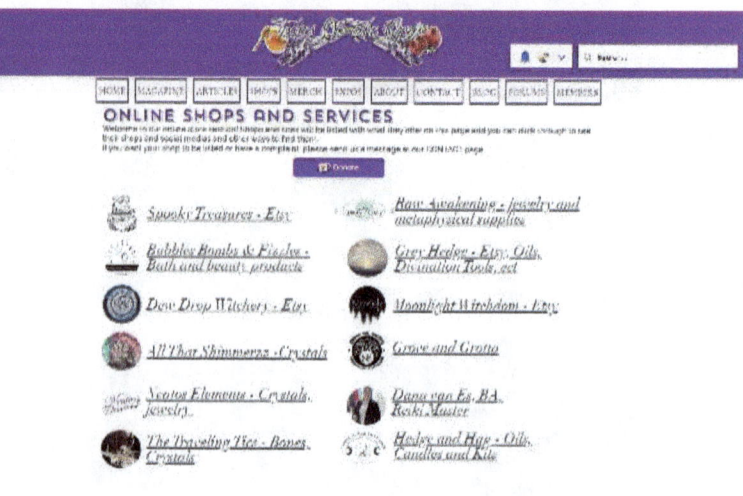

Help Protect Forn Sidr of America

The unfortunate part about being human is that we all experience greed. Everyone wants money and success, however some are more willing to betray their principals to get it.

The Norse Pagans have had a hard go of it in the past hundred years or so. Their religious symbology was stolen and made into hate symbols from Nazi Germany, and then again with the rise of Neo-Nazis and White Supremacists afterwards. You would think that their main battle would be with the White Supremacists who are trying to hijack their religion to enforce their racist ideals, however they are also facing issues from their own people.

The term "Heathen" which is a name for the Norse religious practice was trademarked for commercial clothing items. (You can search the status of this trademark and the applicant as well as the other details on google.) This means that the people who practice the Heathen faiths can no longer refer to themselves as such online or in any commercial or business matter, weather for profit or not, without the person who owns the trademark being able to sue them. I do not need to explain why this is ridiculous.

I wish I could say that this was uncommon, but recently Sage Goddess attempted to trademark the terms "Yule" and "Amatus". Amatus being a Latin word that is a pet name denoting love and being loved, and Yule being... A HOLLIDAY ON THE WHEEL OF THE YEAR THAT HAS BEEN A WIDELY CELEBRATED DAY FOR QUITE SOME TIME.

But now the Norse community is coming under fire once again as the term "Forn Sidr" is now being trademarked. Christopher Fragassi-Bjornson – founder of NORSKK, is attempting to trademark the term for what reason...?

We don't know. Fragssi-Bjornson has allegedly rejected Heathonry and his website is largely about opinion pieces. Despite this, he is attempting to trademark the term across many countries.

The website / group fornsidrofamerica.org has claimed that since he as sent in the forms to trademark Forn Sidr, he has been harassing them relentlessly. I do not know if it has gone through, it seems that it likely hasn't. Witch a search on https://trademarks.justia.com/ it states that the "Opposition is pending" so it seems that the backlash of it has had some impact. It is important to note that "Forn Sidr of America" has been trademarked, though the case is suspended and as it looks to have been filed shortly after the trademark for "Forn Sidr" so it may have been a defensive move to protect Forn Sidr of America preemptively from Fragassi-Bjornson, as it seems likely from my point of view that given how he has harnessed them, as soon as the trademark goes through he will likely attempt to sue Forn Sidr of America.

This is a ridiculous situation and expression of greed and hubris. Forn Sidr means The Old Ways and a quick google of Fragassi-Bjornson comes up with their web page. You are immediately greeted with a hyper masculine page with a notification asking you if you want notifications for their posts where your only options are "Fuck Off" and "Hell Yeah!". Now I (the author, Lady Azimuth) have a bit of an abrasive personality myself so I looked on. He is an author and one of the bits of text from his website talks about "Men, War and the unification of Scandinavia" another red flag but at as some of the best people I know are hyper masculine, I ignored it, and then onward.

The part that made me roll my eyes was from https://ulfheimr.no/ulfhednar and just one of the quotes is " Úlfhéðnar nowadays are still stigmatized. Some of the Úlfhéðnar's traditional skills are seen by western societies as "toxic masculinity", while Úlfhéðnar's spirituality, knowledge, and way of life are often demonized by the church as well as feminized societies."

Now I don't care that people have a "boys club" but what I do care about is this hyper masculine group has the audacity to try to trademark a religious term and pervert it for their malecentric toxic masculinity propaganda, and actively attack people who had already been using it for quite some time as it is (say it with me now) a religious term.

The Forn Sidr of America has asked for people's help. They are asking for donations as they are fighting back. The retainers fee for their lawyers is from 2500 to 3500 to contest this. You can find more information and how to donate at https://fornsidrofamerica.org/blog/

We can not allow Forn Sidr to be trademarked. The Norse community fights every day to reclaim their religious symbology and push out White Supremacists and bigots. Weather Norse or not, we can not allow people to take religious terminology and use it to make profit. This soulless money grabbing along side with the weirdly incel vibes from his website just rubs me and many others the wrong way.

Donate to The Forn Sidr of America and stand up to people like this. This problem is becoming more and more relevant in the digital age and we should work together so that people, no matter the path, can follow their paths without the worry of being sued for just being part of a religion.

Forn Sidr of America is a Universalist and Humanist denomination of Norse Heathenry. We are a 501(c)(3) Church serving North America, providing spiritual services, education, and support for those who seek a compassionate Norse Heathen space. We hold the inherent worth and well-being of all people above any doctrines, creeds, and dogmas. If you like the work of Forn Sidr of America, please consider donating to our cause.

Our practices are done with respect to the indigenous cultures that were here on these lands before us.

Screen shot from the main page of Forn Sidr of America: https://fornsidrofamerica.org/

INTERNATIONAL NEWSLETTER

~Available in Multiple Languages~

THE CORRELLIAN TIMES

~ISSUES RELEASED ON 1st of THE MONTH~

Featuring articles from fellow members & leaders of
the **Correllian Nativist Tradition,** including

Lord Donald Lewis-Highcorrell & Lady Stephanie Neal

First Priest and First Priestess

Learn **MORE** at www.correlliantimes.com

Visit the tradition website at www.correllian.weebly.com

The Law Of Hospitality
Xenia - ξενια

Do not turn away your guests, be it strangers or friends.

Welcome your guest warmly into your house, invite them to stay, show them the house.

Allow to use the bath and change into clean cloths.

Ask how you may help your guest.

Provide them with a good meal, gifts, and aid to reach their next destination if needed.

Do not ask invasive questions until they are clean and have eaten.

Guests may not be a burden to their hosts, do not threaten, harm nor steal from them.

Guests are to provide the hose with stories and news of the wider world and welcome them into their own home in the future.

Follow these rules and honour the gods for Zeus, Xenios, watches over and protects travellers near and far.

The Law Of Hospitality
Xenia - ξενία

The law of hospitality is a very prominent theme within Greek Mythology and it is so prevalent that many people follow most of its tenants to this day in the west without even noticing it.

The law of hospitality is known as Xenia and one of Zeus's epithets is: Zefs, Xǽnios. Xenia means guest friendship and is a very important part of Ancient Greek society. It was not unusual for the gods to disguise themselves and you would never want to insult the gods, unknowingly. More than that, it was a moral obligation. By taking in strangers, travellers and vagabonds, one could rid themselves of miasma.

While we now know that germ theory is correct, we have done away with the theory of miasma, but it still holds a important roll in Hellenismos. Miasma is more than just the possibility of getting sick, it is deeper than that. It is about internal uncleanliness. By following the law of hospitality you could honour the gods and at the same time rid yourself of uncleanliness, as well as get information and stories from the wider world.

In ancient times, getting news of the further world could be difficult so hearing of other cities and tribes through others may have been the only way that a commoner may hear of foreign affairs.

You may be familiar with the Odyssey. When Odysseus was stopped from returning home from the war of Troy, his wife and son, Penelope and Telemachus have to deal with some unwelcome guests. By the law of hospitality they had to welcome the nobles of the city into their halls. The nobles vied for the hand of Penelope after her husband didn't return from war. They would not leave and she and Telemachus could not kick them out of their halls, and it too years for Odysseus to return and join Telemachus to kill them and drive them out.

The Trojan war may have been triggered by the breech of the law as in one of the tellings Paris made off with Helen, thus stealing from his host.

The law of hospitality is the sort of thing that I personally feel should be heeded no matter what you believe in. You shouldn't have to be told to treat people this way and it is a mark of a good person to help people who need it. This is one of the many ways that show that the Hellenic gods just want us to be good to one another, as well and honour them.

Photo by: Hans Reniers
https://unsplash.com/photos/DELDTYAjPrg

Zodiac Wheel

- **Ares** — March 21 – April 19
- **Taurus** — April 20 – May 20
- **Gemini** — May 21 – June 21
- **Cancer** — June 22 – July 22
- **Leo** — July 23 – August 22
- **Virgo** — August 23 – September 22
- **Libra** — September 23 – October 23
- **Scorpio** — October 24 – November 21
- **Sagittarius** — November 22 – December 21
- **Capricorn** — December 22 – January 19
- **Aquarius** — January 20 – Feburary 18
- **Pisces** — Feburary 19 – March 20

Crystals, Numbers, and Symbols

When I first proposed the idea of this article to my chief editor, I was not prepared for things to go in the direction they did. I thought it was all simple straight forward information on healing crystals. It seems I was wrong. However, I ask for your indulgence. Instead, I needed to come at this from the perspective of a Dream Master, having over 30 years in the study, and look at the whole picture and not just the stones. Keep in mind that this is being written from the perspective of a Christian Witch/Light worker and is purely speculative on my part.

I remember once again sitting in church, where my mind tends to wander, and questioning once again what the preacher was discussing at the front. He had decided to preach from a passage found in Revelations.

15 And he that talked with me had a golden reed to measure the city, and the gates thereof, and the wall thereof.

16 And the city lieth foursquare, and the length is as large as the breadth: and he measured the city with the reed, twelve thousand furlongs. The length and the breadth and the height of it are equal.

17 And he measured the wall thereof, an hundred and forty and four cubits, according to the measure of a man, that is, of the angel.
18 And the building of the wall of it was of jasper: and the city was pure gold, like unto clear glass.

19 And the foundations of the wall of the city were garnished with all manner of precious stones. The first foundation was jasper; the second, sapphire; the third, a chalcedony; the fourth, an emerald;

> 20 The fifth, sardonyx; the sixth, sardius; the seventh, chrysolyte; the eighth, beryl; the ninth, a topaz; the tenth, a chrysoprasus; the eleventh, a jacinth; the twelfth, an amethyst.
>
> 21 And the twelve gates were twelve pearls: every several gate was of one pearl: and the street of the city was pure gold, as it were transparent glass.
>
> Revelations 21:15-21

Those of us familiar with the piece, I am referencing John's dream of Heaven. The preacher had decided to use this to spout on about how beautiful Heaven was but all I could think was, this is a dream. Dreams are full of imagery. Rarely, I won't say never, are they a minute-by-minute recounting of what is. I had my Crystal Bible with me, so I took advantage of my run of curiosity and proceeded to look up all the stones that were used to describe the image of Heaven he saw.

Gold, Jasper, Sapphire, Chalcedony, Emerald, Sardonyx, Sardius, Chrysolite, Beryl, Topaz, Chrysoprasus,, Jacinth, Amethyst, and Pearl. Interestingly, these are the same stones mentioned in Ecclesiastes where they describe the breastplate worn by the high priest in the temple. But I digress.

Not just the stones were of interest but also having studied Numerology, I was curious about where the number 12 fit into all this. Heaven is described in measurements of variants of 12, such as 144 cubits, and 12 thousand furlongs. So, I looked up the number 12. I mean there is the obvious being representative of the 12 apostles or the 12 tribes of Israel, but I thought things might go a little deeper.

Finally, there was the imagery of the reed in the angel's hand.

These three things all needed to be looked at more closely, I felt. So here goes.

First, the stones and their meanings according to the Crystal Bible volume 1

- Gold – flexibility on our spiritual path, the search for perfection in all matter

- Jasper – bridge between heave and earth, healing, mental rest and relaxation

- Sapphire – truth, inspiration, intuition, protection, mental stability, wisdom and royalty

- Chalcedony – a joining of three in one, body, mind and spirit

- Emerald – a mature love, empathy, associated with rain and blood

- Sardonyx – earth, said to ward off depression and bad dreams

- Sardius – literally means red stone, ward off bad dreams

- Chrysolite – life and justice

- Beryl – undying youth

- Topaz – truth and forgiveness

- Chrysoprasus – believed to induce a deep meditative state where one becomes one with the spirit (perhaps references to the death of Christ and resurrection)

- Jacinth – spirituality and forgiveness

- Amethyst – love, clarity, leave your past behind you

- Pearl – purity, integrity, life

    I further broke these down into my own understanding. (Keep in mind, I was in church and thinking of how magics work with my own beliefs)

- Gold – spiritual path
- Jasper – bridge between heaven and earth
- Sapphire – truth and protection
- Chalcedony – the holy trinity
- Emerald – love, empathy, associated with blood *
- Sardonyx – earth*
- Sardius – red *
- Chrysolite – life and justice, the payment for human sin
- Beryl – eternal life
- Topaz – forgiveness
- Chrysoprasus – death and resurrection
- Jacinth – spiritual forgiveness
- Amethyst – leave your past behind you
- Pearl – pure life

All of this seemed to echo a reflection of the crucifixion and resurrection that Christians believe to fulfill God's perceived perfect plan for entrance to Heaven, at least as we are taught in Sunday School. So, I thought that might be what he was trying to say. That by His death and the sacrifice of His blood, because He was resurrected, mankind is forgiven and given a permanently clean record, enabling them to enter Heaven. Please keep in mind that I am not preaching or trying to force my beliefs down your throat. My purpose here is to show that crystals, dream imagery and numerology all seem to appear quite freely in the Bible.

It makes me sad how often people try to force a divide between my two beliefs. Magic and religion can coexist if the mind is open. (This being said to encourage the Christian witches and lightworkers not to feel that they are in the wrong. You can be both.)

Next, I looked at the number 12. While I could brush it off as the twelve tribes, apostles, or disciples, I think it means more. According to numerology the number 12 represents the primordial force that makes up all things. It represents space and time and the karmic cycle of existence. It stands for the idea that all life falls under a perfect plan. For me, this read into the message that Christians were being reassured that everything we see, hear, and learn falls under this "perfect plan".

The imagery involved of the angle and the golden reed was more of the same pattern. According to the Islamic Dream Dictionary an angel represents "a greater force that is watching over us" and a golden reed needed to be broken down further. The reed represents the short span of man's life, whereas a golden reed implied an unbreakable span of life. I found those kind of interesting.

Overall, I ask for your indulgence as you read this. These are my own speculations and conjectures and will most likely be easily refutable. I came up with all of this out of my own boredom during a church service that I felt was doing a disservice to the scripture they had chosen. I hope you enjoyed it, if even for just the simple purpose of passing some time.

References
Graham, C. (2013, April). Understanding Your Soul Contract. Understanding Your Soul Contract. Kitchener, ON, Canada: Catherine Graham.
Hall, J. (2005). The Crystal Bible. Blue Ash, OH: Walking Stick Press.
Islamic Dream Interpretation. (2020). Islamic Dream Interpretaion and Dream Dictionary. Retrieved from IslamicDreamInterpretaion.org: IslamicDreamInterpretation.org
The Holy Bible NKJV. (1982). Columbia, USA: Thomas Nelson Inc.

Candles? Candles.

What's one thing that Witches, Pagans, Christians, and middle aged soccer moms have in common? They love candles, scented or otherwise. Here are a selection of our favourite candles, for scents, and rituals!

https://www.soul-terra.com/

Soul Terra
Popular among the online witchy community. Their pyramid candles contain selenite infused wax, essential oils for scent and mystery crystals for you to find inside!

https://thecalmingoasis.com/

The Calming Oasis
Beautifully made candles with crystals hidden inside. With a elegant and sophisticated look and varied scents, this is a beautiful addition to any room.

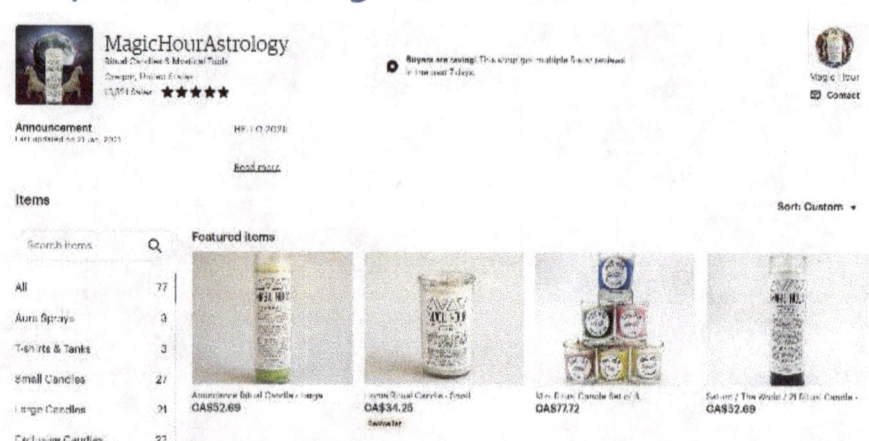

https://www.etsy.com/ca/shop/MagicHourAstrology

Magic Hour Astrology
A verity of skilfully made ritual candles and sprays. Useful and well made, these are a great tool in your craft, no matter what that may be.

The History and How to of Tasseography

What is Tasseography?

Though many of you may already know, for those who don't, Tasseography is the study of reading one's fortune from tea leaves. (Also known as Taseology, and tasseomancy.)

Dating back to ancient Asia, the Middle East, and Ancient Greece, with early studies also using coffee, tasseography has long been a trusted form of fortune readings. Later, in the 1600s, it came to Europe with the introduction of tea from the East. Most commonly, it became recognized as a skill honed by the Romani Gypsies and the parlour psychics. Today, it can be commonly learned by anyone willing to study but only mastered by the gifted.

How to read tea leaves:

Before you begin any reading, be sure to prepare yourself. For some that means a time of meditation. For some that simply requires some time alone listening to your favourite music or reading a book. For some that could mean taking a moment to indulge in a favourite hobby. Whatever you need to set yourself and your environment to the most conducive to opening yourself to the messages you are to receive is ok.

Next you need to prepare your equipment. According to ancient tea ceremonies in Asia, this includes heating your pot and cups for five minutes with hot sterile (boiled to 212o)water.

For a proper tea reading basic equipment you require are:

- A teacup with a handle (any you feel an affinity with. Whether found at a curiosity shop, a market, a fine china shop, or a yard sale, if the cup calls to you, it's meant to be.)

- A matching saucer to catch remaining drips of liquid from the cup

- A teapot. (Be sure not to buy one with an internal sieve to catch the leaves or an external one. You want all the tealeaves who want to speak to pour into the cup.

- A notebook and pen to record your findings
Tea

All about the tea (well not really. Lol)

To be honest there is no hard and fast rule about what type of tea to use. Whatever type you like best, would be my choice. Often a black, white, green, rooibos, or herbal can be used as long as it is a loose leaf, and the pieces are moderately similarly formed. Some small and some larger can make it easier to determine the shapes you are looking at. A chai or matcha is definitely not the kind of tea to use as the milky texture and fine powder makes readings almost impossible. Some readers insist that a tea with flowers or fruit pieces may interfere, but I haven't found so. Be sure to prepare the tea directly in the pot without straining.

Preparing the tea

First prepare the pot and cups with the heated water and let sit for 5 minutes.

Next measure out enough tea for a single reading (two to three cups, about 2 rounded tablespoons of tealeaves to three cups of water (24 to 30 ounces of water))

Then prepare the tea in the pot and stir it three times clockwise and once counter clockwise. Then pour into the cup.

I advise my subject to drink the tea as I feel the contact with the leaves transfers any connections to the leaves. And by drinking the tea from the same pot as the subject, I believe you have created a connection of your own to them.

When the tea is mostly gone, pour out the remaining drops onto the saucer.

The remaining leaves in the cup are now ready to read.

Note: While adding sugar, lemon or honey to the tea will not affect the outcome (drink your tea however you prefer), adding milk or creamer is frowned upon as the milk may cause the tea leaves to clump together altering the reading.

Unlike other forms of readings, tea reading can be done on yourself without any negative repercussions. This is a great way to get the hang of reading before you attempt to do readings for others.

Common Symbols (A beginner's guide)

This is far from a comprehensive list of common symbols and I recommend that if you decide to pursue this study further you find a good book of recognized symbols and their meanings but here is a list of the 20 most recognized.

Acorn: good luck or good news
Apple: success in school or business
Butterfly: fickleness or indecision
Grass: prosperity
Ape: caution, someone near you means you ill
Letters: influence from a person or location
Anchor: clear – good luck, unclear – bad luck
Aircraft: bad news
Heart: good things to come

Dagger: help from a friend
Cross: trouble, delay, or death
Moon: happiness, success, prosperity
Ring: marriage
Spade: hard work and wisdom
Skull: concentration and creativity
Club: new challenges/ danger
Eagle: strength, power, dignity
Trident: use your power well in order to empower others
Wolf: positive in nature, you can overcome whatever lies before you
Wheel: a need for discipline in order to reach your goals

References

Aunty Flo. (2020). Tea Leaf Dictionary. Retrieved from AuntyFlo: www.auntyflo.com
Brigitte. (2013). The Art of Reading Tea Leaves. Retrieved from Tea Answers: https://www.teaanswers.com/tea-leaf-reading-2/page/2/
unknown. (2011). Common Meanings and Symbols Found in Tea Leaf Reading. Retrieved from Best Online Psychics: www.bestonlinepsychics.net/psychic-info/tea-leaf-readings/

-Altars By Owen-
Jumping Off Points

Have you ever stopped to think about what was your real, true actual jumping off point into the craft, and how did it sculpt your practice? I have, a lot actually. I was raised christian, I grew up in the church, so the idea of an altar was not uncommon. However, when you're raised predominantly Methodist, the altar is simple. It's simply a sacred place to go to pray. In a pagan/witchcraft path, the altar is still a similar enough concept, a sacred working space, that, when you introduce the concept of a prayer altar so to speak, it really does start opening up the doors to acceptance of other things. Let's set the scene, it's about five years after I graduated high school and first started looking into other paths besides Christianity and I've already realized that I'm an Omnitheist. The groundwork is already there for the slow realization that, the christian path wasn't for me.

Photo by: Owen Lee VonBrandt

So, when I went on a trip to visit my dad, who is a witch, naturally, I gravitated towards his altar and wanted to know, everything. It was a crash course in altars that forever changed how I worked. It was, in essence, the window crack that led to the doors being thrown open.

My dad used altars as a form of prayer, so how he described it to me was choosing elements and pieces for the altar that resonated with what he was trying to express or convey. He explained the basics of an altar and what was typically included, and then told me that, sometimes you just don't need all of it.

I was fascinated. I watched him make a few during that trip, and then, finally, on one of the last days, I put together my own, with his help. It was such a profound moment that felt so underrated at the time. It forever changed everything though. When I got home from my trip, I went through my own things and compiled together my own altar set up and started doing prayer altars myself.

I still said I was a christian at the time though, and I was using the altars as a way to pray, so, how did I end up a pagan witch? Remember when I called it a jumping off point for me? The more that I did the altars, the more that I found myself looking up the meanings and properties so I could start enhancing my intentions even more. The altars eventually started turning into outlets for my intentions, which later turned into me calling it what it was, spellwork.

I ended up buying some books, electronically, because I was still in the broom closet at the time. I started out small, and just started adding things to my altars, starting with moon water and crystals. Eventually adding in things like, burning intentions written on paper.

As I started to put more and more direct intention into my altars, I started to notice that oh hey, "I put the intention out there for a little bit more money so I can have a little more stability, and, wait a minute..... I got a raise 2 weeks later."

The dots started connecting.

I started asking questions sometimes instead of intentions, and I started watching the altars. The differences were subtle, you'd suddenly look over and a crystal would be shifted an inch or two, or the card had fallen over. Now, all of a sudden, you're also analyzing did the cat knock that over, or, is that my answer? And then two weeks later, "Oh.... That was my answer. Should have known, definite no."

And then, I was sitting in church one day, and just, realized, "Oh.... I'm not...."

It's now five years later and I still use altars for, well, just about everything in my craft.

Photo by: Owen Lee VonBrandt

-Altars By Owen-
Altars As Spellwork And Divination

Divination and spellwork as possible uses for altars might seem a little strange, but it's really not. If we assume a basic working knowledge of altars, the elements, associations, etc, then we can work with that and our intention to put the question out there, or the spellwork. Not to be cheesy with the phrase, but, this is one of the cases of, you have to know the rules to break the rules.

So, how does one start with this? Let's break down the basic steps I follow any time I set up an altar for a specific purpose first. I very first make sure the altar space is clean and ready for my working. I find music that correlates or resonates to set the mood as I start thinking on the intent. I also light incense, I usually pull whatever calls out, but pulling specifically to enhance is always a good bet.

And then I just start building. Well, yes, but, I'm also considering what my question or my intent for the spellwork is and what I can do to enhance it. So, important things to bring in would be associated elements or any elements you may wish to invoke. You can do this through objects, crystals, rocks, minerals, herbs, etc, associated with them. If you work with the elements, you can also call them in as you build it. Other things to consider are practical elements to the question or the spellwork.

Photo by: Owen Lee VonBrandt

Also, if you work with any deities and are bringing them in, make sure they're represented. Candles are always good, but adding in representation through crystals, herbs, objects are always good too.

A couple of examples of different objects that I've used in my altars are: a roll of film, old birthday cards, various antique glasses, a rubber ducky, sunflowers on a pumpkin from a dear friends wedding, dice, coins, cauldron to burn loose incense, etc.

So, how does actually building it work? I've always pulled everything I was drawn to out first, and then candles first, bigger/bulkier things next, it's really just a matter of just setting it up in a way that feels right. Trust your intuition at all times. If you feel like you need to put something back and grab something else, then, you should probably do that.

Now that it's built, what next? actually usually take a photo of it, especially if it was a spell for someone else or a question. When I take the picture of a spell, I try and infuse a little bit of my original intent into the picture, so when I send the picture of it to them, it can continue working for them.... Really however long they keep it charged, or until it's done it's job. I usually use my dslr, so, as I'm focusing, I'm gathering my intent up and picturing it infusing with lens as the camera captures. If you're using a cell phone, the most important step really is to just take the moment to gather up and visualize, so however you need to take the moment to do that and you'll be good. I've even paused after focusing when I've needed longer moments.

Photo by: Owen Lee VonBrandt

Photo by: Owen Lee VonBrandt

I take the pictures of the question simply so I can look back on changes to get a feel for what my answer might be. I have had things shift, I have had things fall over. On this one, again, trusting your intuition is big here. Look at the specific objects that were affected, did one specific candle burn oddly faster than it normally does? If herbs or crystals shifted, look at the associations.

With spell work, things to consider are how long do you want it to go on for and will you need to refresh and recharge them? I have had some spell work altars go on for multiple days. What this looks like is, replenishing water, relighting, or adding new candles, new incense, etc, as you can or need to while refocusing on the original intent. I have also modified them as they went on as I needed to if I need to refocus my intent a little bit. An example would be a healing spell originally done right before a surgery, I don't know about you, but I don't like to do more than just send my good vibes and well wishes for a safe procedure out there. But, after the surgery, I can change that to healing vibes as I refresh it while they recover.

Again, it's really just about knowing the building blocks, and then just playing.

Photo by: Owen Lee VonBrandt

Ostara

Akashic Records
A simpified explanation

Witch Culture
A look into those saying that people shouldn't dress as witches

Meta Angel Theory
A brief explanation

Witchy Hair?
How to combine your craft and your hairstyling!

Pagan Poetry
Presented by Owen Lee VonBrandt

Tales Of The Gods & - PRACTICAL WITCHCRAFT -

Thank You

By buying this magazine, you support small business owners and small creators!

TalesOfTheGods aims to connect the metaphysical and spiritual communities.

We would like to thank Owen Lee VonBrandt, who has stepped up to provide the cover photo and will do so for future editions.

Everything in this magazine belongs to the contributor who submits it. That which is not belongs to the original creators who will be credited under the photo.

If you would like to write in anonymously, or join our team for the next edition feel free to send a email to TalesOTheGods@gmail.com

TalesOfTheGods, March 2021

facebook.com/groups/665578877692886

Contributors

Desirée Goulden	Owner, layout design, contributor
Brooke Mirabella	Practical Witchctaft owner
Owen Lee VonBrandt	Contributor, photographer
Dana Beaudreau	Contributor

The TalesOfTheGods & Practical Witchcraft magazine is a community project. Our roster of contributors is constantly shifting. Everyone who works on the magazine takes home an equal take of the income from the sales of this magazine.

We aim to bring education and entertainment to people of all levels of experience and paths. If you have a point of view that you would like to share with the world, feel free to reach out to join us. We are currently looking for people of colour to join us. Whether you are a teacher, or just interested in taking part, we have a place for you.

Have a shop or product you want to share with the world? Contact us and we will run a free full page ad for you in the next edition! We release on every day of the wheel of the year, so it's easy to follow release dates!

We would like to thank those who have sent Neico donations! They are on their way back home with their family, and have welcomed a baby girl into the world!

Contents

About Ostara	PAGE 2
Witch Culture?	PAGE 4
Akashic Records Simplified	PAGE 8
Witchy Hair	PAGE 12
Spring Poem	PAGE 16
A Ostara Haiku	PAGE 18
Meta Angel Therapy Explained	PAGE 20

 **The Underworld Oracle Deck By Desiree Goulden**

25 Full colour cards

Works with reversed cards

Works with other decks

$23.99 Cad

https://www.thegamecrafter.com/games/the-underworld-oracle-deck

Ostara

Ostara is the 3rd on the Wheel Of The Year and marks the spring equinox. Ostara takes from the celebration of the Anglo-Saxon Goddess Ostara, or Esotre. Some say this is the time Persephone comes from the Underworld to help Demeter bring summer to the living world.

Christians celebrate Ester around this time, and throughout cultures this is a time of celebrating rebirth. The symbols for this day on the wheel of the year is the hare and the egg, and the colours for this day are soft greens, soft blues and yellows.

To celebrate you can begin planting your garden if your climate allows. You can clean and decorate your house (it's spring cleaning season soon anyway). You can take a walk through your local nature trail and clean any rubbish that you come across to honor the earth. You can chose to make up a special alter for the nature or fertility goddess of your choice. You can even decorate eggs like you would with your Christian family and friends.

Neico Anderson
Astrologist and Tarot Reader

Natal chart readings:	$50 USD
Year ahead readings:	$50 USD
General tarot readings:	Donation Based

✉ magiciansdivination@gmail.com

f https://www.facebook.com/magiciansdivination

Mother of 2 with one on the way, Neico has been practising reading tarot cards for 6 years and as been doing astrology for 3. She has nothing but good reviews and is one of the few people that the staff of this magazine go to. She is worth every penny and can work with peoples budget. By far one of the best readers we have known.

Witch Culture?

"My culture is not your costume". This is a phrase many people are familiar with.

While the phrase has been floating around online since the 2000s, but gained popularity after 2011 when The University Of Denver created a photo campaign against people wearing cultural costumes as Halloween costumes.

This was a movement that was needed. People for years were dressing up in outfits for Halloween that at best, were a tone deaf appropriation of traditional garb, and at worst were an outright mockery of culture. This movement went lengths to stop harmful caricatures of races and nationalities as a joke told by people who will never deal with the fallout, and are often the ones who attack the people they are dressing as.

I start here to underline the fact that this movement was about minorities in the west who constantly deal with harassment, violence, and not having equal representation in the media and government.

This is why I was dumbstruck when I came across numerous articles about self proclaimed Witches saying that "My culture is not your costume, stop dressing as witches for Halloween."

Originally I saw this on Buzzfeed, which is... well... its Buzzfeed, but then I saw a article on Huffington Post. Of course I Googled the headline and found dozens of articles claiming that Witches and Pagans are saying this.

This is a problem.

This is a problem because there is no witch culture. This is a problem because Pagans are not all inherently Witches, and as the word "witch" was not a word that had any honor until very recently in history.

My major problem with this is that the people who are out here saying this are not POC practitioners. They are not people who deal with marginalization or oppression, no matter how much they may want to claim they do.

We must all acknowledge that the vast majority of people calling themselves "Witches" rather than say "Practitioner" or "Scourer" or the like, are white. These people are more often than not, middle class white women who are more into the aesthetic of Witchcraft than hardcore occultism. These are people who can log on to Facebook and TikTok and post memes and aesthetically Witchy content and then leave it online and go back to their PTA, HOA, and book clubs with no repercussions.

This being said, there are people who are vilified and looked down on for practicing magick. There's a reason that if you say the word 'Voodoo' around the common folk, they will react with fear. There's a reason that POC women where largely the ones that were accused of Witchcraft back when Witch hunts and burnings were a thing. There's a reason why the Christians tried to remove all versions of magick in the cultures they conquered. That reason is that they hated them and wanted them gone, and they achieved that through bloodshed.

There are still places today where people who are accused of Witchcraft are hurt. There are metaphysical shops that have their windows bashed in constantly. There are people who are attacked by fundamentalists of many religions and what do they look like?

People.

Witches look like people from many backgrounds. Witches have no one uniform 'culture' save that which has been mad online in the last 15 years. They don't look like green skinned, boil covered, pointed hat wearing, hunched over, hags. Witch as a title and identity is completely optional, and some would argue that it is actually somewhat of an insult.

To say that Witchcraft is a culture is false.

You chose to call yourself that. You can chose to be called any number of other things to get the point across that you practice magick. This is not the same as minorities who don't choose to be who they are. They don't choose to be Black, or Asian, or Hispanic, or Jewish. They can't just log off of Facebook to avoid conflict and harassment, it is a daily struggle they deal with.

You chose to call yourself that. You can chose to be called any number of other things to get the point across that you practice magick. This is not the same as minorities who don't choose to be who they are. They don't choose to be Black, or Asian, or Hispanic, or Jewish. They can't just log off of Facebook to avoid conflict and harassment, it is a daily struggle they deal with.

You can not in good faith say that people dressing as a Witch is harmful against you. A Witch in the way the general public sees it is not real. We do not ride brooms and turn princes into toads. The only 'culture' this is emulating is that of children's story books. You aren't the Wicked Witch Of The West, you're Brenda from Tennessee. Sit down and drink your Starbucks, it's not that deep and these articles are just embarrassing.

- Desirée Goulden

Simply Magical Audio!

Want something magical to listen to? Here are a selection of some of out favourite practicioner made podcast and music! From good jams to great podcasts, these creators give hours of education and art!

The Guide Your Soul podcast is a new podcast with great potential! Mary Fellows talks about anything and everything through a spiritualist point of view.

She is a respected healer and spiritual teacher who you should keep your eye on.

A great podcast lead by two experienced practitioners. You will always learn something new from this podcast and is great to listen to throughout your day.

Grab some tea and curl up with your favourite knitted blanket and give this a listen!

Selki Girl brings the nostalgic vibes of the 2000s with a hint of magic. Her album "For The Profane" gained some traction with some scandalous tales of it causing one to astral project. People seemed to make up tall tales about this album and from listening to it, it's not hard to see why. While it wont make you astral project, it is a experience that shouldn't be missed!

An oldie but a goody. Some of my favourite songs from my teen years where written by him.

This bard weaves magic in his words and story telling and music and will forever be an adored musician in the Pagan world.

Akashic Records Simplified

Imagine a library stretching as far as the eye can see filled with books, scrolls, and ancient parchments holding all the knowledge in the universe. Be it known or unknown, it is all there at your fingertips. This is exactly what the Akashic Records are. These are the databanks of all information that you will or have acquired in this, past, or future lives on your path. But then again maybe this all seems a little too simple.

In our lives we learn and we grow. Through all history this is the one constant. Always is, was and will be. In every one of your past lives and in each of your future incarnations you acquire new skills, strengthen old skills, and start building footsteps into other interests. Your Akashic Record holds all this information ready for you to use at any time. Each person's Akashic Records is as unique as the individual who wields them.
(Another school of thought is that we are not limited to our own records and but that we can access any information in the universe after more experience... if sufficient responsibility has been displayed.)
To access your records, you should first clear your aura, your chakra, and your chi. Find a comfortable place to sit or lay down and allow your mind to open to a clearing meditation. **Then repeat the following incantation 3x.**

**I now ask the Masters, Teachers, and Loved Ones of me to Channel through me, out of whatever realms, to say whatever they wish.
I ask that the Masters, Teachers, and Loved Ones will speak the truth and only the truth, for mu highest good and the highest good of everyone else around. Thank you.**

At this point feel free to ask your guides whichever questions you have. A notebook and pencil are always handy to keep around to record what comes to mind. When you are done, the following incantation will help you to close your records. **Simply repeat it 3x.**

Closing the records is advisable to keep others out of your collection. It may be a tool that can be used against you in the future.

I would like to thank the Masters, Teachers, and Loved Ones for providing me with insight and clarity.

Not everyone feels the need to close their records as they may need to access them more frequently than others. But if you are new to this practice, closing them and protecting or shielding them is advisable. Because even you may not be aware of all that is in that library.

To navigate your records, imagine yourself walking up and down the aisles of books and manuscripts. For others it may be easier to imagine yourself pulling up a browser and typing in what you are looking for. There literally is no one right way to search, whatever feels right to you and most comfortable is exactly what you should allow yourself as you discover all that the universe and your spirit have in storage for you.

There are some risks and problems that may occur in accessing your records too frequently so ensure that you have prepared your protections properly. Malicious spirits may play tricks with your library by hiding bits and pieces, setting traps, and mixing things up. If this occurs, take the time to try to clean and sort your files from time to time through meditation.

To be honest, the Akashic Records are not supposed to be entered into without permission. They are protected by your ancestors and guides. Try to keep a good relationship with them and be respectful.

For your own safety and good, it would be advisable to avoid using your Akashic Records if you are in poor health or in a difficult emotional or psychological state. Your bindings and protections will be weak. Also, you may find yourself asking spiteful or illogical questions and offending your guides and the ancestors who guard them.

On a final point, "Yes!", you can access the Akashic Records of others if they ask for help. There are stipulations and skill requirements however. You need to be gifted as an empath or a psychic to gain access to their doorway. Only they can safely give you the key. Manners exist everywhere, so please remember to ask permission first.

Whether you are new to the Records or have been using them for a long time, may they serve you well. Blessed be.

– Dana Beaudreau

Laura Dell

Laura Del has her bachelor's degree in radio, television, and film from Rowan University. She is a lover of books, writing and anything fiction. Del currently lives in New Jersey, where she runs her blogging website www.thefictionwriters.net
(About the author from Amazon)

Ghosts Among Men: A Novella (Samantha Davidson Novella)
Laura Del
★★★★½ (32)

Kindle: $0.97
Paperback: $5.99

★★★★★ **Ghosts Among Men**
Reviewed in the United States on March 15, 2017
Verified Purchase

Samantha is a private investigator and just so happens to be able to talk to dead people but don't think it makes her job any easier. Well ok maybe it does. I loved Samantha and think she is absolutely bad a**. Great mystery thriller that had me on the edge of my seat through the entire story. I can't wait to find out what kind of craziness Sam gets into next.

★★★★★ **Enjoyable quick read**
Reviewed in the United States on July 5, 2019
Verified Purchase

Fun female lead.
Wish book was longer.
Already added her next book to wish list.
Don't want to read it enough to pay 1.99 (it's also a novella).
Would like to see full-size books in this series.

★★★★★ **Fantastic Urban Fantasy and Mystery**
Reviewed in the United States on August 24, 2016
Verified Purchase

This had better be the beginning of a series because it can't be over. Samantha is funny and smart and such a strong character. The police officers and her office manager were original and added to the picture of a world where Samantha Davidson is so vital. And I need more of it. All of it.

If you are a fan of Sue Grafton or Sookie Stackhouse then you should read this immediately. This is A for Alibi but with ghosts and a far more relatable character.

Samantha Davidson sees ghosts for a living. More specifically, she sees ghosts as a private investigator, working alongside the Chicago Police Department to put away killers and put troubled spirits to rest. When the daughter of one of Chicago's wealthiest families turns up dead, Samantha and her assistant Mark team up with homicide detective Lance MacDowell to get to the bottom of the crime.
Allison Allen is tall, blonde, beautiful--and very much dead. As Samantha interviews the girl, who doesn't remember anything about the circumstances of her own murder, it's clear that there's more going on behind the walls of this manicured home than anyone wants to let on—and that Samantha has her work cut out for her this time.
Juggling her own love life, tracking down troubled spirits, and evading attempts to thwart her investigation keeps Samantha on her toes. Good thing Samantha knows how to keep her eyes open, her wits about her, and her sense of humor.
A paranormal mystery that is both dark and funny, Ghosts Among Men will cause chills to run down your back even while you're laughing out loud at the lovable, strong, and supernaturally sighted private investigator Samantha Davidson.

Ghostly Murders: A Novella (A Samantha Davidson Novella Book

Laura Del

★★★★★ (7)

Kindle: $0.97

Paperback: $5.99

★★★★★ **Ghostly Murders**
Reviewed in the United States on March 20, 2017
Samantha Davidson is at it again in the second Ghostly Murders Novellas. I absolutely love this character and the humor that is in these books. I hope there will be many more cases for Samantha and her partner Detective Lance Macdowell.

★★★★★ **A must read!!**
Reviewed in the United States on February 8, 2017
From page 1 I was hooked!! The style of this novella is fast paced and such a great story! It will leave you wanting more!! Can't wait for the installment!!

★★★★★ **Five Stars**
Reviewed in the United States on February 8, 2017
Greatest read ever! I love this series and can't wait to read more!

★★★★★ **Read it, read them all!!!!**
Reviewed in the United States on April 14, 2017
Became hooked on PI Samantha Davidson from Ghosts Among Men and just like that book this one did not disappoint either. Page turner! Can not wait to read another!!! Thanks Laura Del!

Get ready for more ghostly adventures in the second installment of the Samantha Davidson series, Ghostly Murders.
When a body pops up in a suburb of Chicago, PI Samantha Davidson is on the case with her partner in crime, Detective Lance MacDowell. But when the two of them go to investigate, there's a little glitch in their plans. It seems that the Chicago PD has stumbled upon a serial killer's victim. Now they have to work with the FBI, specifically very Special Agent Brennan, who is not a fan of Samantha's methods.
After all, when you can speak to the dead like Samantha can people tend to not believe you, and Brennan is no different.
So with this special agent against her almost every step of the way, and the dead girl not being of much help, Samantha must rely on her keen investigation skills to solve this murder before the killer strikes again.
Can she do it? Or will this monster slip through her fingers and slaughter another victim?
Find out in the suspense thriller that is Ghostly Murders.

Ghosts Among Men

https://www.amazon.com/Ghosts-Among-Men-Samantha-Davidson-ebook/dp/B00Y3597IO

Ghostly Murders

https://www.amazon.com/gp/product/B01N9XJVIV/ref=dbs_a_def_rwt_bibl_vppi_i1

Witchy Hair

In my real life, I'm a hair stylist, and for me one of the interesting things has been this sort of intersection so to speak with witchy things and hair. It's hard to explain, but more than ever I understand that hair really can, and does hold power, it doesn't have to be a particular length, you can keep it shaved and still benefit from some of this, or never cut and benefit. Whatever cut and color that you decide is the cut and color for you, you know that one, that makes you feel super powerful? That's the one. Now, imagine you could take care of your hair so it's as healthy as it can be, but also do some personal protection, or some healing? Well, that's probably possible.

Let's start by first taking a look at the some of the top oils for hair in general, most common being: lavender, tea tree, jojoba oil, argan oil, sandals wood, cedarwood, peppermint, and rosemary.

A quick run down of metaphysical properties are: lavender (calming and healing), tea tree (cleansing and protection), jojoba oil (emotional protection), sandal wood (healing and purification), cedarwood (healing and protection), peppermint (cleansing, healing, and protection), and rosemary (protection, healing, and cleansing).

I don't know if you noticed a trend there?

Now, before we begin, lets talk about these oils specifically in regards to hair. Some of these oils are carrier oils (jojoba oil, argan oil), so these are going to help pack a moisture punch. Argan oil is also a pretty good natural heat protection, very good for deep conditioning. The reason for this is that argan oil is actually both a lipid and a lubricant, two very essential things that are needed for your hair. Jojoba oil is rich in nutrients and minerals that help to nourish hair, it helps strengthen hair, it can help soothe a dry scalp.

The rest are essential oils, meaning they need to be mixed into some sort of carrier medium. You can mix all of your chosen oils, carrier or not, into shampoo/conditioner, or mix your chosen essential oils in with your chosen carrier oil/oil blend. I would say use essential oils about maybe max twice a week.

Lavender is really good at helping keep up a healthy scalp, it helps stimulate blood flow which in turn helps stimulate hair growth. Tea tree oil can help soothe an itchy scalp, can help with dandruff, it can help prevent excess oil production, and once again helps stimulate the scalp in ways that help promote growth. Sandal wood can help treat dandruff, help stop excess oil production, helps with split ends. Cedarwood is another common one for scalp stimulation and hair growth, and can also help with dandruff. Peppermint scalp stimulation and hair growth. Rosemary once again, helps with scalp stimulation/blood floor for hair growth and can also help for dry itchy scalps.

If you're going for a more cleansing, stimulating mix your chosen blend into shampoo, and then follow up with a moisture, protection focused blend.

- Owen Lee VonBrandt

New TOTG Merch!

We have new additions to the TalesOfTheGods.com merch page!

This is a back and white illustration of Achilles and Patroclus with a rainbow background and a inscription that reads: "No dude, they were totally just really good friends!" -Very Smart People.

Buy at https://tales-of-the-gods-2.creator-spring.com/listing/achilles-and-patroclus-being-b

$44.17 $6.20 $31.54

Lovely Leather Journals

Want to start your BOS? Do you just like good stationary? Take a look at these beautiful leather journals we've found!

JUMBO THREE GRACES LEATHER JOURNAL

$76

https://www.jennibick.com/collections/leather-journals/products/jumbo-three-graces-leather-journal

LEATHER BOUND HARDCOVER JOURNAL WITH LINED PAGES

$87.50

https://www.jennibick.com/collections/leather-journals/products/leather-bound-hardcover-journal-with-lined-pages?variant=4549080963

600 Pages Large Tree Of Life Journal

$63.75

https://www.etsy.com/ca/listing/939547602/600-pages-large-tree-of-life

Spring Poem

I used to imagine spring almost as if it were a perputalant child,
All talk, and when there is action,
You best be prepared.
The coming of spring though,
The first signs,
That magical scent of air,
That while, yes, the same as yesterday,
Somehow it's just different,
Breathes a little better.

With children though,
Any reprieve you get,
Never actually gives respite.
It's just a delay in the cycle,
Which can be true of spring too.
Yet,
There's certain inevitabilities that come with spring.
Like the first scent of air,
The birds chirping as it lilts through your window in the morning,
The sun starting to soak the ground and wake everything up.
Moments of true peace,
That while, maybe, they were there before,
They just, weren't quite the same.

Spring is more than that rebellious teenager,
Peace that's almost a little too,
Sneaking out,
They'll just do,
Whatever they want,
With no regard.
But, let us not also forget,
The love of a teenager,
It ebbs, its flows, it soars, it crashes,
But it always persists.

No, spring is really more the teenage lovers,
Grounded,
So, both have to sneak in ways to see the other,
Sneaking out after curfew,
Sending letters maybe.

Or perhaps,
Spring is the daughter,
Free spirited, with no cares to be tied down,
Clinging to an escape,
A place of belonging,
Somewhere she can just be.
Sneaking in those visits to the one place really just,
Can be.

— Owen Lee VonBrandt

Ostara, the spring,
Renewal, hope, and rejoice,
Winter will be gone.

— Owen Lee VonBrandt

The TalesOfTheGods Meditation Journal is now only $10 cad! This is a very useful tool to help in the recollection and analysis of your dreams, meditations and astral travails!

Available at: TalesOfTheGods.com/merch

Meta Angel Therapy Explained

This article is not intended to teach you how to perform this perfectly but rather to explain what Meta Angel Therapy is and how it works. It is an overview. If this seems appealing to you, I suggest that you search out a certified instructor for a full course training.

To simplify things for your understanding, Meta Angel Therapy can be explained by comparing it to hypnotherapy, reiki, psychic surgery, and intuitive healing all rolled into one. It is a hands-on treatment for individuals who are struggling with symptoms from psychosomatic ailments. This is never to be used in place of or before a physical medical answer has been thoroughly investigated.

Many of us internalize our responses to what is going on around us. Stress, anxiety, anger, fear, joy, sorrow, love, all have an impact on our physical body and can create or manifest ailments that are physical or psychological in nature. The physical ailments can be treated by a medical doctor and a medical doctor should always be consulted first. But sometimes we experience symptoms that have nothing to do with any illness our body is navigating. When this happens, counselling is the first bastion of help we should search out. As an empath, a gifted, a lightworker, or a witch, we are innately capable of assisting people or even ourselves in dealing with these symptoms. We can help the patient or even ourselves to reach healing more quickly by working in conjunction with counseling and other health practitioners.

Basically, the first thing you are taught in learning this skill is to tell your client to consult with their regular doctor first to rule out any physical medical condition first. Meta Angel Therapy is designed to assist the client/patient with psychosomatic conditions and illnesses. It uses a cooperation of guided meditation, reiki, psychic surgery, active empathy, and crystals.

The Tools

Like any good surgeon knows, a doctor is only as good as his tools. This practice requires a calm quiet environment, some soft soothing music, gently scented candles or incense, a scalpel made of Blue Kyanite, a suturing stone shaped kind of like a needle made of Green Amethyst, and an antiseptic stone. (We tend to prefer a clear crystal ball about 2" in size made of Clear Quartz).

Blue Kyanite is used to cut. It opens the throat chakra, encourages communication and self-expression. It is used to cut through fears and blockages and help find the truth.

Green Amethyst (also known as Prasiolite) creates a connection to your higher self so using it to reconnect the metaphysical wound is good for strong binding.

Clear Quartz is known as the master healer. It amplifies energy and thought and enhances your psychic abilities. It helps with concentration and unlocks memory. It is also believed to stimulate the immune system bringing the body into balance. This makes it the perfect antiseptic.

As a lightworker and practitioner, it is important to remember to prepare your tools, workroom, and self before beginning a session.

The Healing Chamber, as it is called is prepared with a cleansing. There are many methods to perform a cleansing. Some smudge with White Sage. Some practitioners use a cleansing spell or prayer. Some begin with a cleaning and candle burning.

The room is then set up with your table (a massage bed or chair), a chair at the head and foot for your comfort, a towel for you to wipe your hands on as you will frequently need to wipe the psychic smudge and muck off. A typical session can take anywhere from half an hour to 2 hours or so depending on how much mucky energy is bugging down the body. For the comfort of the client (or yourself) soft music, candles or incense, and healing or keyed crystals may be set up around the room.

To prepare your tools remember to keep them sterilized between uses. Soak them in a Dragon's Blood elixir, Holy Water, or Mineral Water (whichever is most comfortable for you) and leave out to dry for 24 hours to soak up the moon and sun energy. If you do not have enough time between patients, you can create a quick recharge of your crystals by putting them in the freezer for half an hour. However, do not forget that this is not a cure all solution and the crystals will need to be thoroughly cleansed and charged correctly at least every week if they are being used every day.

To prepare yourself you need to prepare your own karma. Ensure that your own chakra are in alignment. Like any other practitioner of mental or spiritual health, you will need to have your own health maintained through reiki, meditation, prayer, and self-cleansing. You may also want to keep a bowl of salt close at hand or cold salt water to remove any sticky negative energy that clings to your hands during a session.

How To

After you have ensured that your room, equipment, and self are properly cleansed, take the time to discuss what is going on with them in order to help them release whatever is causing them these afflictions. I like to start with a cup of tea and a chat to put them at ease. Then I request the client to lay on their back on the table.

Begin by placing your hands wrist together with palms facing out. Then set your fingers on their forehead and your thumbs against their crown chakra.

Repeat these words three times.

(Guides) I ask for you to come to me today and release from me, (or the person you are treating) ____ (energies wanting to be released) from my ancestral body, from my cellular body, from my emotional body, from my mental body, from my physical body, from my spiritual body, from my karmic body, from my ethereal body, from my causal body, in all times and places, and in all directions. Please fill this with unconditional love and seal this with silver and gold.

(when practicing on a patient instead of yourself, replace "my" with "their")

Then count backwards from 100 out loud.

In silence, slowly work your way around them down the left side and up the right. Spend the time to let your empathy and psychic ability to feel the movements and moments as you explore their body and their mind. Be sure not to speak as you this may interfere with what is being revealed to you. As you practice, you may feel moved to place other crystals on locations that call for them. Crystals know what is needed and where they are needed. This looks a lot like a reiki session with few different movements. When the energy calls, stop and remove the dark energy clogging the areas that it reveals itself in. When you reach the stomach, move your

hands in a clockwise followed by counter clockwise motion. A lot of ailments gather here. At each extremity (fingers, feet, heart, and knees) perform a pulling motion to free up any blockages. At all times keep your hands 1" to 2" above the body. At each site, cut using the kyanite, pull and cleanse until the energy comes out clear, throw the smudge into a psychic garbage can (Note: be sure to empty the trash after each session. We do not want the negative energy escaping into your home or your self.) Stitch up the incision with the amethyst. Then roll the quartz over the site as an antiseptic. Once you have finished your session, remember to thank your guides, etc. and close the session. Invite your client to return to a calm, hopefully, healthier start.

Usually after a session, I will offer my client a small snack, fruit, cheese, cookies, tea, or juice, to replenish their energy as a session can be very tiring. Another thing I do is place the space crystals that the session called for into a small bag for them to take with them. These crystals found their way to this person in order to shield them from returning negative chi.

I know I have not covered everything, and you may have questions. So, I will revisit this topic again at a later date in order to clarify and extrapolate on the foundation I have tried to lay here.

– Dana Beaudreau

INTERNATIONAL NEWSLETTER

~Available in Multiple Languages~

THE CORRELLIAN TIMES

~ISSUES RELEASED ON 1st of THE MONTH~

Featuring articles from fellow members & leaders of
the **Correllian Nativist Tradition**, including

Lord Donald Lewis-Highcorrell & Lady Stephanie Neal

First Priest and First Priestess

Learn **MORE** at www.correlliantimes.com

Visit the tradition website at www.correllian.weebly.com

Photo Credits
Front Cover: Owen Lee VonBrandt
Page 2: Taisiia Shestopal
Page 4: Paige Cody, Kayla Maurais
Page 6: Bee Felten Leidel Bose
Page 8: Anna Hunko
Page 12: Shari Sirotnak
Page 13: Guilherme Petri
Page 16, 17: Owen Lee VonBrandt
Page 21: Dana Beaudreau

This edition of the TalesOfTheGods & Practical Witchcraft magazine is dedicated to Hermes and Dana, Brook and Owen. You all, this magazine would not be possible.

This is also dedicated to tacos and cheesy 90s and early 2000s music.

Tales Of The Gods & Practical Witchcraft

The Laws Of Attraction
A letter of observation by Dana

Saying Good-Bye
A death witch sends off a beloved family memeber

Panera Bread
And their religious intolerance

And More...
Inside the 4th edition of the TalesOfTheGods & Practical Witchcraft magazine

Beltane 2021

Thank You

By buying this magazine, you support small business owners and small creators!

TalesOfTheGods aims to connect the metaphysical and spiritual communities.

Cover Photo - Vadim Sadovski.

Everything in this magazine belongs to the contributor who submits it. That which is not belongs to the original creators who will be credited under the photo.

If you would like to write in anonymously, or join our team for the next edition feel free to send a email to TalesOTheGods@gmail.com

TalesOfTheGods, March 2021

TalesOfTheGods.com

- PRACTICAL WITCHCRAFT -

facebook.com/groups/665578877692886

Contributors

Desirée Goulden	Owner, layout design, contributor
Brooke Mirabella	Practical Witchctaft owner
Owen Lee VonBrandt	Contributor, photographer
Dana Beaudreau	Contributor

The TalesOfTheGods & Practical Witchcraft magazine is a community project. Our roster of contributors is constantly shifting. Everyone who works on the magazine takes home an equal take of the income from the sales of this magazine.

We aim to bring education and entertainment to people of all levels of experience and paths. If you have a point of view that you would like to share with the world, feel free to reach out to join us. We are currently looking for people of colour to join us. Whether you are a teacher, or just interested in taking part, we have a place for you.

Have a shop or product you want to share with the world? Contact us and we will run a free full page ad for you in the next edition! We release on every day of the wheel of the year, so it's easy to follow release dates!

Contents

About Beltane	PAGE 2
The Laws Of Attraction	PAGE 4
Saying Good-Bye	PAGE 6
Panera Bread's Little Pagan Problem	PAGE 10
Blind Vision Boards	PAGE 16
Separating Spirituality And Life	PAGE 20
The Internet And The Craft	PAGE 24

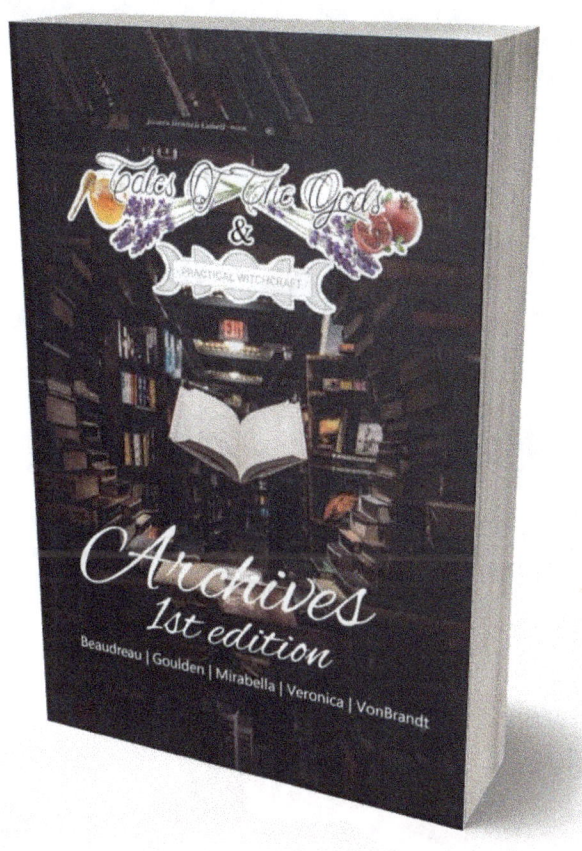

Want to read the articles of the magazine, but have visual setbacks with the magazine format? Want to read without having the budget to buy every magazine?
The Archives are all of our articles in plain text format for your bookcase or digital collection!
Published every 3 magazine editions this has a plethora of knowledge and entertainment!
31 articles, 201 pages of content, all for an affordable price! ($20 cad)
https://www.talesofthegods.com/magazine

Beltane

Beltane is the 4th day on the Wheel Of The Year and represents life and the beginning of summer. It can be celebrated with bonfires, handfasting, and celebrating the divine feminine and fertility.

The colours that represent Beltane are: green, red, silver.

The symbols of Beltane are: chalices, may baskets, honey, oats, milk, antlers, pomegranates, peaches.

TOTG Merch!

We have new additions to the TalesOfTheGods.com merch page!

This is a back and white illustration of Achilles and Patroclus with a rainbow background and a inscription that reads: "No dude, they were totally just really good friends!" -Very Smart People.

Buy at https://tales-of-the-gods-2.creator-spring.com/listing/achilles-and-patroclus-being-b

$44.17 $6.20 $31.54

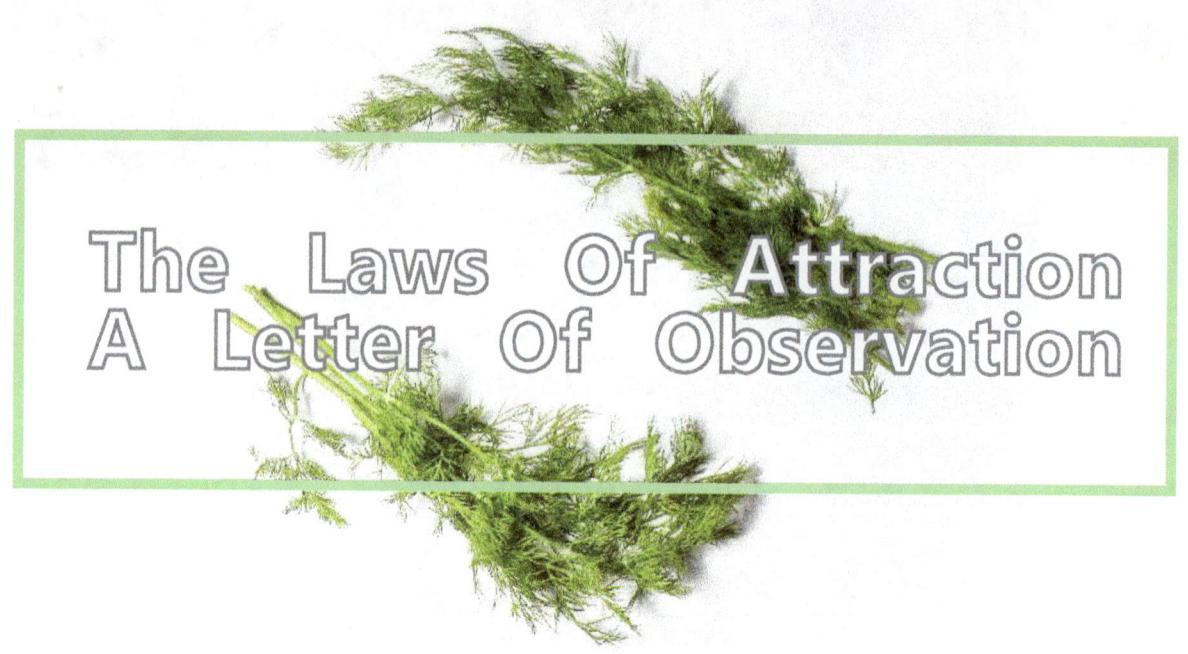

The Laws Of Attraction
A Letter Of Observation

Whether it's tenfold, tit for tat or basic karma, you get what you deserve. In this world there exists one basic universal truth, eventually, you get what you deserve.

A number of years ago a book was released onto the market (The Secret by Rhonda Byrne) promising people that all they had to do was send their wishes out into the universe and they could have whatever they wanted. However today it's a little more evident that things are not as simple as that. If all we had to do was snap our fingers, we would never have to work. Unfortunately, life is a little more complicated than that thanks to things like chi, prayer, karma, and basic physics, the world turns in one direction and life travels in a single line likewise. Even if you have lived multiple lives, you still need to start before you can finish. The laws of attraction actually effect a lot more energy than that. Be it Buddhism, Christianity, or any other theology.

Do you live your life expecting a return for your every action? Do you treat others as you wish to be treated? Do you give out expecting to ward against what may return? I could spit out a lot of cliches that you would recognize but it all wraps up into a simple "there will be butterfly wings involved".

I want to write about things like "do unto others as you would have done onto you". I want to talk about things like "as above so below". I want to speak about theologies that promise great rewards for obedience. I want to explore the idea that we as gifted understand that we have the ability to manifest what we desire. However, in all these instances, we understand that in the end there will be returns and costs. If we want a larger life, we need to put in the work. If we want a better health or a cure for someone else, there is a necessary return we need to promise, put out, or pay up as proof of our sincerity. I will not discourage you from pursuing whatever you wish to receive from the universe. I will, however, warn you to guard against your thoughts and your practices. And most of all remember that the primary law in the Laws of Attraction is that everything has a cost.

- Dana Beaudreau

 *The Underworld Oracle Deck By Desiree Goulden*

25 Full colour cards

Works with reversed cards

Works with other decks

$23.99 Cad

https://www.thegamecrafter.com/games/the-underworld-oracle-deck

INTERNATIONAL NEWSLETTER

~Available in Multiple Languages~

THE CORRELLIAN TIMES

~ISSUES RELEASED ON 1st of THE MONTH~

Featuring articles from fellow members & leaders of
the **Correllian Nativist Tradition**, including

Lord Donald Lewis-Highcorrell & Lady Stephanie Neal

First Priest and First Priestess

Learn **MORE** at www.correlliantimes.com

Visit the tradition website at www.correllian.weebly.com

Saying Good-Bye

    With bated breath, I walked into the studio room that was my Nanna's (my great grandmothers) in her assisted living. After having accepted the fact that I was probably never going to get to say good bye to her in person, moving back, getting some time with her, the great joke of it all was covid almost making it so I didn't get to tell her. I knew though, she was holding on so I could. She would have for as long as she could have. I also knew though, that she was going to be gone when I left the room. As, part of my job, part of why I was there, wasn't just to say goodbye, but to send her on.

    I didn't really get much time for preparation the day of. I was at work when I got the call. I'd done some mental and spiritual preparation as we all knew, the time was coming. As everyone does though, I had held on to the false hope I was going to have more time.

    As I walked in, it took everything I had to not lose it. She always held so much power in her daily presence, and to feel her actively slipping away... Was, hard. To hold all of it together as best as I could.

And to have to hold it together and to not be able to say all of the things that I wanted to tell her because my mother was there.

This wasn't going to be my first time passing someone over. I did it for her sister when I was eight, that's another story for another day though. So, I knew some of what to expect, the heart break, the anguish as you watch their body suffer after their soul has let go.

As I approached her bed, I took in a breath, holding back the tears.

This was it.

When I left, she was going to be gone. And I just wanted to be able to sit and take the moment and breath all of it in and just enjoy the last moment with her.

I knelt down, and covid regulations be damned, I hugged her and cried on her and just, laid. I had had an entire ritual planned to have her let go, but my mother ended up nixing that, so instead. It was silently in my mind.

And then when I left, she was gone. We wouldn't actually get to be able to bury her ashes for another five months. One of the things they don't tell you about dealing with death during covid is how long the death certificate actually takes. And then how long it can take to be able to have the burial.

All of that boils down to, when I left after she passed, my job was not done. Her grave already had its marker, and had been for years. She was going to be buried next to her husband and near her son. Her grave stone marker had always been there. So, before we finally laid her ashes to rest, I cleaned up and cleansed and blessed her gravestone. With no rosemary, because she didn't like rosemary.

I tailored and made my cleansing water/oil mixture based on what I wanted to pull from from her own energy, from mine, from my memories of her. So, for me, one of the biggest ingredients that I used were roses. She was known for her roses, so it acted as a tie to her.

When I cleansed and blessed her gravestone a week before, I focused my intentions on getting rid of any lingering negativity/anything unwanted, and amping up the positives so her ashes had the best final resting place that was possible. I also charged a rose to be buried with her.

The day of the funeral, I woke up and prepared for my day by doing a quick meditation session with her as I was getting ready.

It's been hard, death is hard, even when you know to expect it and that its coming. But, I know, she appreciated the work I put into the space for her ashes, and it brought me the comfort that I needed.

- Owen Lee VonBrandt

Free shops & services listings

Have a shop or service and want to extend your reach without speding some coin? Contact us! We will set up your shop in our public database including a explination of your business and a landing page to display your wares!

We will post you on our online shops and services for free! Just contact us at our contact page on TalesOfTheGods.com or send us a email at TalesOTheGods@gmail.com or at our social medias! We can be found on Facebook, Twitter, and Instagram!

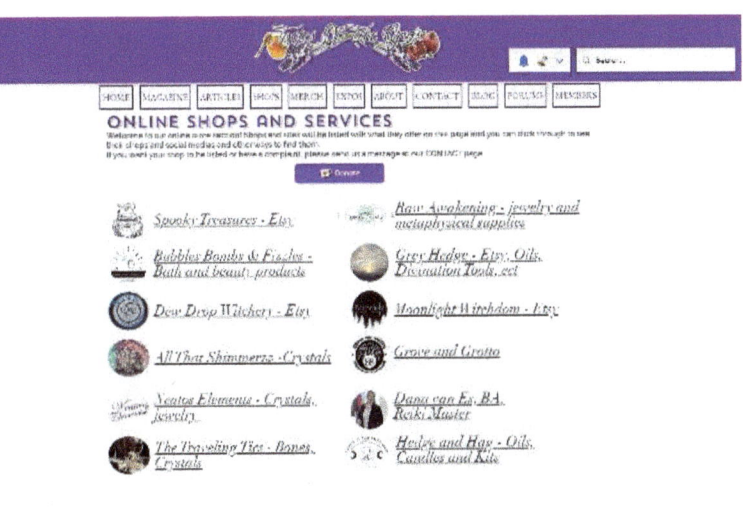

In our first edition we covered a woman who was being sued because she is Pagan and her neighbor said that her "religion instilled fear". Now, we see another Pagan lawsuit but this time it's the Pagan that's suing.

On March 25th Hemant Metha (The owner of the Friendly Atheist blog on Patheos.com) posted an article that caught the attention of the wider Pagan community. He covered the story of Tammy McCoy.

Tammy McCoy and her husband were employees of Panera Bread in Pennsylvania. Now when you hear that a Pagan is suing her business place for discrimination, what do you think? I thought that maybe she wasn't given certain days off, or was told to take off a pentacle or something minor like that. That is unfortunately not the case. In 2019 Tammy and her husband lost both their jobs at Panera Bread specifically and only because they are Pagan.

So what's the story?

Tammy like most of us kept to herself about her religion. She didn't want to lose her job or get into arguments with anyone because of her religion and decided it was better not to mention it at all. This worked for her for a time until one day at lunch she was talking with the Manager and Assistant Manager when the conversation was pushed on her. The Manager (Lori Dubs) and the Assistant Manager (Kerri Show) asked Tammy directly what her religion was. Tammy replied with "Pagan". If it was a open conversation already involving religion and she was asked directly, why shouldn't she? Lori and Kerri were talking about their religion. It's not like she went out of her way to broach the topic. Lori directly asked her and it was 2019 so why shouldn't she respond truthfully?

Her reply got the following response: You know you'll burn in hell, right? To which Kerri agreed and played along.

Tammy decided to leave it be. We all know that you can't really argue with people like this. They will always believe what they want to believe and there's little point in trying to change them. Though she dropped it and didn't continue the conversation, things only got worse for her.

Tammy and her husband started noticing their hours dropping and they started getting sent home early and their hours weren't matching up to their pay. She tried to ask what was going on and was told that "Until you find God, you wont get your hours." The pay discrepancies where never fixed.

Tammy tried to get transferred to a different store and was denied because they were "probably going to get rid of her soon anyway". According to Hemant they even went out of her way to tell her directly to hand in a letter of resignation. When she asked why, she was told "because I don't like you."

Now this seems like a pretty easy call to HR, but when she tried to get the number for HR she was told: If you call HR, you will be fired on the spot.

This seems almost cartoonishly ridiculous. It is like these women are living out their Christian High School drama cheerleader dreams, but in real world adult life.

When Tammy did eventually get the number for HR, her calls were ignored or she couldn't get through despite trying numerous times. It seems that Lori made sure that HR wouldn't take her calls as she even went out of her way to ask her how calling HR was going for her.

The Post-Gazzette even claims that a District Manager visited the store and Tammy reported the situation to them, but was told that the others were "Just joking around." Last time I checked, telling someone they are going to hell for being Pagan, cutting their hours, stealing their hours and telling them directly that they won't get them back until they "find God" is not joking. It's not even remotely funny.

This came to a head when Tammy and her husband were both fired. It's worth mentioning that all this transpired between Tammi, Lori, and Kerri and that Tammy's husband had nothing to do with it.

Now Tammy is suing Panera Bread for religious discrimination. You would think that Panera Bread would be on their best behavior so that its an he said she said situation... you's be wrong though. They took their bullshit to Twitter. One day after Hemant Metha posted his article and people started taking notice of the situation, they posted a tweet of "pepperoni flatbread" circled by candles and the caption "Shh.... we're manifesting."

This post remains up as of the writing of this article over a month later. They are almost rubbing our noses in it. Now unfortunately we know little about this situation beyond this. The case has not yet gone to court, Panera Bread still has the post up on twitter and they are just ignoring the masses of people commenting on their BS on twitter and we are left without closure.

This is a sobering reminder that even though things are leagues better for Pagans in the west, the institution of the USA and Canada are still overwhelmingly Christian. This shouldn't happen. There are laws to prevent this from happening and to defend people's right to religion... so long as that religion is Christian. The unfortunate part of this is that the majority of us keep our religion quiet because we fear this. In this day and age there are still people being refused jobs, fired, or sued because of their religion and it is ridiculous.

This is ridiculous because the same kinds of people who try to not serve the GRSM on the basis of "freedom of religion" don't care about freedom of religion if it's a religion that isn't their own. This kind of hypocrisy plagues nearly all non Christians and I can only hope Tammy wins her case because this behaviour is not acceptable. This is not how civilized people behave.

This is not High School, this isn't your congregation so I fully expect Christians to keep their religion to themselves, as everyone else does. Not everything needs to be about them all the time. It's 2021 this BS needs to stop. It's time to boycott Panera Bread.

— Desirée Goulden

@inkwood_tarot @InkwoodJournal

inkwoodtarot.com

Inkwood Tarot - Readings by Cynthia: tarot reader, empath, certified Reiki practitioner and ordained Pagan clergy.

" I offer tarot readings by phone, video call and seasonally in-person at local events, festivals and shops. With over 20 years of tarot study and experience, I love helping people bring harmony, balance and success to their lives. Join me in exploring your ultimate potential!"

To learn more or schedule a reading visit:
http://inkwoodtarot.com

Blind Vision Boards (Exercise Your Gifts)

Just like you need to eat right and exercise to keep your body fit and healthy, you also need to exercise your gifts to keep them from eroding and fading over time. Whether you are a psychic, an empath, an intuitive, or simply magic, you need to exercise your gifts to keep them sharp and help them to grow. Blind Vision Boards are an easy-to-use tool to help you train up and practice opening your psychic portals.

Purpose:

The purpose of a vision board is to help you set goals and motivate yourself to reach them. The purpose of a blind vision board is to strengthen your intuition, help you visualize your path, and understand your calling. It also serves to improve communication between you and your ruling guide. Generally, I will redo this exercise once a month and on special days such as that of a new moon or a full moon, during the solstices, on a birthday or on New Year's Eve. The reasoning behind doing this over and over is to understand that our paths may change over time based on the experiences we meet in life.

What You Need:

- Glue stick
- Scissors
- Highlighters and pens
- A variety of old magazines
- Cardstock
- Music (preferably without lyrics to avoid being influenced by outside voices)
- Crystals, candles, incense, and other objects that you find helpful in your travels
- A blindfold or scarf h

How to Build Your Board:

1) Key into your subconscious using meditation. Preferably, meditate or pray for guidance for 5 to 10 minutes. Allow the music to guide your thoughts and your words.

2) Prepare your space. For some this includes lighting candles or incense. For others this means placing sigils or crystals around your space.

3) Setting your other tools aside, place the magazines in front of you in a pile and cover your eyes with the scarf or blindfold.

4) Allow yourself a fair amount of time (I let the music play over three or four "songs")

5) Turning the pages of the magazine, you will tear out the pages you feel directed to tear out and place them side up or side down off to the side of your pile of magazines. This is important because the side you -

-place upright is the location of the word or image you are being led to.

6) At the end of the time, remove your blindfold and set aside the pile of magazines for another time.

7) Using the pen or highlighter, mark the locations you feel you are supposed to take note of.

8) Carefully cut out the images or words

9) Arrange these cuttings on the piece of cardstock and glue them into place.

10) Ask your god(s)/guides/ancestors to show you any messages you are being sent. (Note: I keep a journal of the messages I am sent) Any clear key words feel free to write them onto your vision board to help you understand any particular groupings or unusual stand alones.

Place your vision board into a prominent place where you can see it easily to keep you focussed.

Repeat as often as needed. Frequent communication with those who are guiding us is especially important to avoid misusing or forgetting to use our gifts for the purpose to which they were intended.

— Dana Beaudreau

Christina & Martin

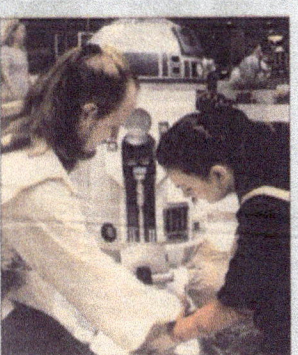

✉ carrhunger@carrhunger.com

📷 www.instagram.com/Carrhunger/

f www.facebook.com/carrhunger/

Meeting at a Dr Who convention in Toronto in 1987, Christina and Martin have, combined, over 62 years experience in the entertainment industry.
Accumulating such titles as Camera, Editing, Tape Operator, Director, Actor, Writer, Costumes, Props Builders, AD, Fight Coordinator, etc and so on... their experiences are broad and diverse BUT they still, to this day, love bringing the joy of building props, education on the industry and the popular process of Cosplay to conventions and events. X-Men, Cody Banks, Total Recall 2070, Scooby Doo, Stargate, Star Trek, FX The Series, EFC, Flash, Arrow, Legends of Tomorrow, are only a few of the productions on their list of experiences.
Stage, Live Performances, Characters at Festivals, add to their range of talents. Come experience their love of sharing knowledge, their skills and stories of their experiences.

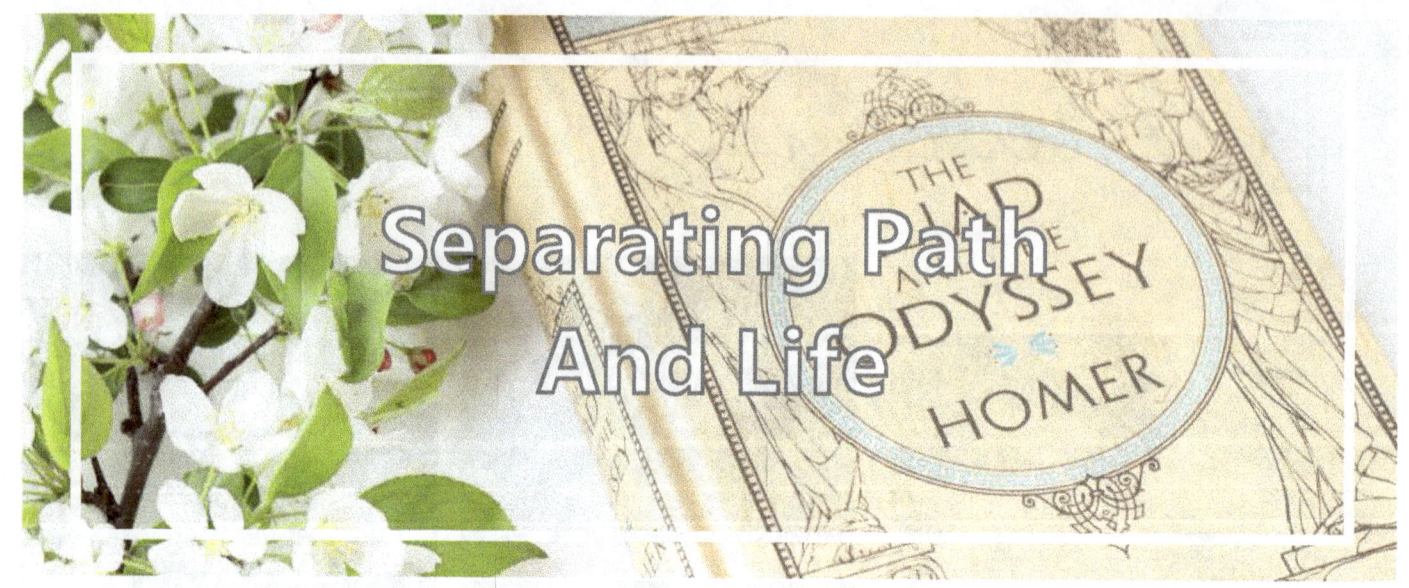

Separating Path And Life

COVID-19 has put many of us out of the public eye for a long time now. It's been over a year of either being unemployed or working from home and as such, we have not had to put our practice or religion on the back burner for a while. This is something that many people online have brought up.

There are worries that people are starting to lose the ability to not be completely enveloped by their spirituality. We are seeing a new generation of young Practitioners begin their paths during COVID, and we are seeing more and more people working from home who are filling their days with WitchTok and spiritual FaceBook groups and locking themselves into their own little comfortable echo chambers.

Myself and others have mentioned that because of this we are seeing people show concerning signs of fanaticism online. People are trying to throw hexes at each other over FaceBook statuses and TikTok videos. We have people surrounding themselves completely with only witchy people and are lashing out harder at non witches. I have seen people make the majority of their content shit talking Christians and their God, while turning around and making it seem as if they are personally going to the mall and are best friends with their own Gods.

I have seen people push other people out of witchy communities and send hoards of people after their businesses and Etsy shops because they disagree with "Shifters". As this goes on they are leaving a long trail of videos, statuses, and ways for future and current employers to use to get rid of them.

It is an unfortunate fact that employers will look at your social medias and will fire you over them. Combine this with the people who hate Pagans and the like and you have more than enough reason to get yourself fired. The worst part is, if you fight back they can point to your hundreds of videos and online statements where you are being combative and threatening to hurt people to use in a defense if it gets taken to court.

Normal people constantly have to watch what they post online, and they aren't part of a group that people dislike. I am not saying that we need to be fearful in our day to day life. What I am saying is that we need to be careful and we need to be able to have a personality aside from the craft.

I run a metaphysical website and magazine. By all means I should be able to be completely engulfed by my spirituality but that's just not realistic. I still have non Pagan friends and family who don't want to hear about who hexed who and what God I am working with. I still have to go to the grocery store and make nice with people who glare at my pentacle. I still have to be able to look family members in the face who either think I am crazy, or a devil worshiper.

Real life does not allow for us to be %100 spiritual all the time. Even if we did, we need to understand that

that's not desirable in a person. We all know a bible thumper who makes their entire life about Jesus and God. We all know how it is to try to speak to them about normal things like love, death, or work only to be met with some hollow "God will take care of everything" comment.

I am seeing many become the Pagan / Wiccan version of that without realizing while criticizing those same people. The difference is that Christian Beccy won't get fired for being Christian (unless shes a bigot and even then it's unlikely depending the area). Christian Beccy won't be screamed at that she's going to hell on a constant basis, and she won't have her hours cut until she "Finds XYZ God"

We will.

We need to remember that in all things there must be balance. Your life can not be all magick all Pagan all the time. This is a reminder to check yourself. Speak to someone who isn't part of your path. This is to protect yourself, but also to ensure that in general you're not annoying to be around.

- Desirée Goulden

Candles? Candles.

What's one thing that Witches, Pagans, Christians, and middle aged soccer moms have in common? They love candles, scented or otherwise. Here are a selection of our favourite candles, for scents, and rituals!

https://www.soul-terra.com/

Soul Terra
Popular among the online witchy community. Their pyramid candles contain selenite infused wax, essential oils for scent and mystery crystals for you to find inside!

https://thecalmingoasis.com/

The Calming Oasis
Beautifully made candles with crystals hidden inside. With a elegant and sophisticated look and varied scents, this is a beautiful addition to any room.

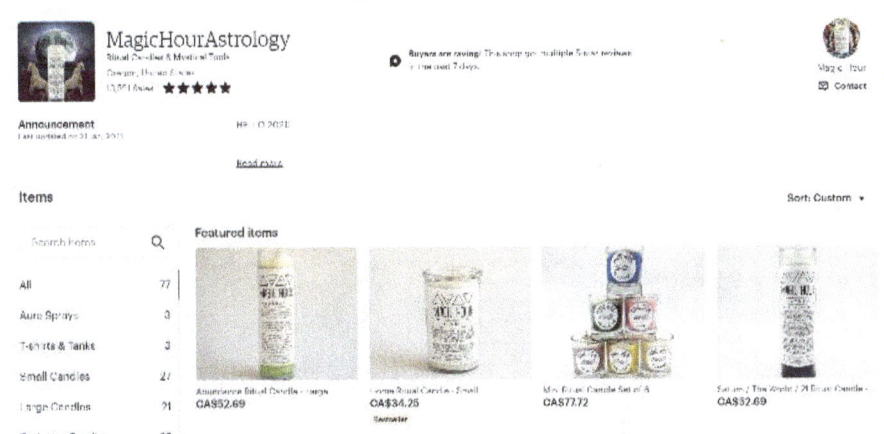

https://www.etsy.com/ca/shop/MagicHourAstrology

Magic Hour Astrology
A verity of skilfully made ritual candles and sprays. Useful and well made, these are a great tool in your craft, no matter what that may be.

The Internet & The Craft

It's no secret that the internet has had major influence in the past 20 years on the craft and Paganism, but is that a good thing?

I came up in the craft in the early 2000s in a very atheist household. Those who weren't atheist were Christian of some sort, to the point where apparently some cousin of mine was the first female pastor or priest of some denomination of Christianity. It's safe to say that I had 2 options: be Christian or be Atheist. I ended up being both in my childhood but found that neither suited me.

I can recall smuggling in my Solitary Witch book by Silver RavenWolf (ugh I know, and I agree, but back then where I lived you took what you could get.) into my house only to be caught and openly mocked and made to feel stupid because "Harry Potter isn't real, you can't be that f***ing stupid." None the less, I continued to study as I fancied myself a Wiccan back then. I remember how hard it was to find books and content back then in a city that didn't have metaphysical shops and the majority of people Christian or Muslim.

I remember the sheer glee when I was gifted books from Witches and Wiccans from estranged family members and parents from friends from more religiously liberal cities. It was a path I was determined to take one way or another and that involved looking around, talking to people from other cities and smuggling in books into my house to study in secret. I remember as a dyslexic child how much work went into doing that. I remember not having people around me to teach, and the only circle in the area being cultish and not safe for underage people.

I recall the effort and work that went into learning, practicing, coming to grips with not being able to have a community and having to find truth, and accepting myself and deconstructing the fear of Hell on one side and being branded as stupid and not believing in science on the other.

I didn't join the wider Witching community until Tumblr around 2014 and even then, I never had much of a taste for the people and mindsets found there. Then came COVID-19 and I got a hold of TikTok and by extension WitchTok and it became clear that being a "Solitary Witch" was starting to die out among the younger generations. It helped that WitchTok sports the largest amount of new and seasoned Witches, Occultists, Pagans, and Spiritualists that the world has ever seen.

The massive amounts of users and viewpoints has both pushed me away and drawn me back in constantly. I have to admit in my own opinion that it has come as a detriment to the general study of the Occult and Witchcraft as the short form videos lack the time to give nuance and really gives rise to false information and cult leaders.

That being said, there are many (myself included) who can wade through the bullshit to find good people and form a community where they couldn't find one before.

On one side, I have seen Elders hate online communities because there is no vetting of information, people can claim to be whoever they want to be and assign titles they have not earned. I have seen Elders claim that online communities have lead to people not having respect and actively saying that Elders deserve no respect. I've seen Elders claim that people make things up and put it on the internet as fact (this is something I agree with completely.)

On the other I have seen people of all ages (Elders included) who say that online platforms are good starting points for people to explore their spirituality and magick. They say (and I agree to a point) that this is spreading knowledge that people would likely never find in their life and it is the only way for many to get a foot hold in a belief system that they find comfortable. They say that the online sphere is the next logical step from paper publications that allows people who can't afford books to find mentors and information that they wouldn't be able to otherwise.

There is logic on both sides that I agree with, though these two different opinions often come into conflict. Ironically, usually on FaceBook... in metaphysical groups. I personally believe that the internet is the next frontier of the spiritual and occult worlds. I think that while the internet allows for people to spread misinformation, it absolutely allows for people to form communities that they couldn't in their area. I can say personally that WitchTok gave me the confidence needed to start TalesOfTheGods.com.

I've made life long friends from there and waded through the sea of drama and Fluffy Bunny / Baby Witch stuff to find some really experienced and interesting creators.

I wanted to hear people's opinions on this so I opened up a questionnaire on Google Forums for people to share their thoughts on how the internet has influenced them. Here are the questions and the 5 responses we've gotten so far!

> How has the internet influenced your craft?
>
> We want to know how the online world has influenced your craft and / or path / religion. We have come in to a new age of information and now more than ever practitioners are gathering and forming communities online.
> This information will be used in upcoming editions of the TalesOfTheGods & Practical Witchcraft magazine and online articles.
>
> How has it positively influenced your practice / path / religion?

Anon 1 — It's allowed me to connect with folks that have a similar approach (and a similar sense of humor!) about spiritual/mythological ideas.

Gaius — Access to more academic sources which helps reduce misinformation and "fluff".

Anon 2 — Connecting with people all over who share similar ideologies and belief structures.

Mary Fellowes I found wonderful people and a lot of encouragement to pursue the path/practice. Generally didn't feel alone, had engaging conversations about the world and found great friends.

Jim TwoSnakes When my path began there was no internet. I was forced to try and tease information out of the highly biased books from my school library. Later when I could drive there were still no sources nearby, so I would send away for catalogs which I could order books from, which was my introduction to Dion Fortune and Draja Mickaharic. The internet became available to me after I graduated high school, so like many people just getting access to it was challenging. But when I gained it, it opened up a world of information. Over the years I have been able to meet practitioners of various paths, and gain a lot of understanding about closed practices and the nuances of some of the schools of thought.

The internet has changed our perception of communication, I think this is even reflected in our interaction with the Gods. In the old myths it was rare for anyone to communicate with the Gods, but this is something many polytheists will report commonly now. I think the internet is in part responsible for this, because communication and the involvement of others into our personal lives has not only become common and quick, it is expected. So too do we now expect the Gods to "check in", and the internet allows for communities and friends to validate this UPG.

How has it positively influenced your practice/path / religion?

Anon 1 — It's mostly a free-for all of misinformation and infighting amongst perceived in-groups over silly ideological differences (some of which make NO sense and illustrate a lack of research and thoroughness on the part of... basically everyone involved)

Gaius — Spending more time dealing with misinformation and arguing with folks than actually practicing.

Anon 2 — It has increased access to trolls and extremists of all kinds as well as popularity fishbowls of misinformation and interpersonal drama

Mary Fellowes — For some time I ended up in a cult-like mindset and belief system that is still affecting me and my mental health now. I got swooped into a lot of toxicity and ungrounded spirituality that had nothing to do and also bypassed the real life issues.

Jim TwoSnakes — There sadly is a lot of bad information along with the good. While this is not new, as people such as Crowley for example, hid good knowledge within misleading information, the internet allows this bad information to evolve at an alarming pace. And the old adage that a lie repeated enough it becomes truth is in full display. The same bad information is replicated on countless sites giving it the perception of authenticity.

Jim TwoSnakes Another aspect I think is negative is that much of the aspects of craft and have become performative. While I am not naïve enough to think this is new, theatrics has always been important and had a place, the persuasive aspects of social media and video have created a competitive atmosphere where it is better to have the proper image and perception than actual skill. Financial and social rewards will flow from the proper "vibe" with youth and beauty being mistaken for knowledge and wisdom.

What do you think is needed for the betterment of the online communities?

Anon 1 More precision + better ways of framing and defining terms + people figuring out how to move on from the fact that human history is constantly problematic ESPECIALLY with regard to religion

Gaius We're over socialized to be honest. We claim everyone is "valid" but really there is just a lot of bullshit. A lot people play acting that they're oracles or personally talked to Zeus. We need to firmly dispel that crap. We have to take ourselves seriously at times and not allow peoples delusions dominate our spaces.

Anon 2 Adequate moderation of hateful behavior, fostering genuine accountability in the communities

Mary Fellowes I would say "curation" but it's physically impossible. Majority of the issues I experienced exist in other communities as well. Changing the whole educational system, helping people to think critically and actively dismantling-

Mary Fellowes -white supremacy (that affect spiritual communities of any kind) will change everything for the best.

Jim TwoSnakes More face to face meetings. It is way to easy to attack people from a place of anonymity.

We also need a better way to police or at least shame and denounce predators and hate groups in our various communities.

I think the common consensus from these replies and from people I have spoken to personally is that while the internet offers a wealth of knowledge, it also needs massive oversight to stop false info and toxicity. People want less cult like mentality and less popularity contests and less cliques but honestly in my opinion, if you get more than 10 people in one place that's going to happen whether we like it or not.

It is clear that we as a community across beliefs need to work on self policing. I understand that that may feel like organized religion and people dislike that, but I honestly think that the only problem with organized religion is when people use it to harm others. We need to build a community across paths and work together to put forward the betterment of Pagans and Practitioners of all kinds. We need to find balance between the old ways and the new ways to build a more healthy and robust Occult and Spiritual community.

- Desirée Goulden

Photo credits

Owen Lee VonBrandt Page: II, III, 2

Vadim Sadovski Page: COVER

Ren Gillard Page: 4

Scott Rodgerson Page: 6

Pedro Da Silva Page: 10

AbsolutVision Page: 16

J Kelly Brito Page: 20

Nathan Dumlao Page: 24

Litha 2021

Pride In The Craft
LGBTQIA2S+ spaces and contributions in witchcraft

Tarot Decks
How to make and sell them for FREE.99

Cartomancy
How to divine using a standard deck of playing cards

And More...
Inside the 5th edition of the TalesOfTheGods & Practical Witchcraft magazine!

Thank You

By buying this magazine, you support small business owners and small creators!

TalesOfTheGods aims to connect the metaphysical and spiritual communities.

Cover Photo - Jason Leung.

Everything in this magazine belongs to the contributor who submits it. That which is not belongs to the original creators who will be credited under the photo.

If you would like to write in anonymously, or join our team for the next edition feel free to send a email to TalesOTheGods@gmail.com

TalesOfTheGods, March 2021

TalesOfTheGods.com

- PRACTICAL WITCHCRAFT -

facebook.com/groups/665578877692886

Contributors

Desirée Goulden	Owner, layout design, contributor
Brooke Mirabella	Practical Witchctaft owner
Dana Lee Beaudreau	Founding member, Contributor

The TalesOfTheGods & Practical Witchcraft magazine is a community project. Our roster of contributors is constantly shifting. Everyone who works on the magazine takes home an equal take of the income from the sales of this magazine.

We aim to bring education and entertainment to people of all levels of experience and paths. If you have a point of view that you would like to share with the world, feel free to reach out to join us. We are currently looking for people of colour to join us. Whether you are a teacher, or just interested in taking part, we have a place for you.

Have a shop or product you want to share with the world? Contact us and we will run a free full page ad for you in the next edition! We release on every day of the wheel of the year, so it's easy to follow release dates!

Contents

About Litha	PAGE 2
Pride & The Craft	PAGE 4
Soul-Terra Family Drama	PAGE 8
Cartomancy	PAGE 14
A Reading In Cartomancy	PAGE 20
Hermaphroditus	PAGE 24
Create & Sell Tarot Decks For $0	PAGE 28
Modern Terminology In Antiquity	PAGE 38

Want to read the articles of the magazine, but have visual setbacks with the magazine format? Want to read without having the budget to buy every magazine? The Archives are all of our articles in plain text format for your bookcase or digital collection!
Published every 3 magazine editions this has a plethora of knowledge and entertainment!
31 articles, 201 pages of content, all for an affordable price! ($20 cad)
https://www.talesofthegods.com/magazine

Litha

The summer solstice, the longest day & shortest night of the year. Litha is also called Midsummer and is the 4th day on the Wiccan Wheel Of The Year

The element celebrated here is fire, and celebrate the warmth of the sun. From here the days get shorter and shorter leading to Yule. This is the time to celebrate Sun Gods, and the Wiccan's take this time to celebrate The Horned God. You can decorate your alter in summer colours and with flowers, herbs, and fruits. Any rituals you do during the day should fall at noon when the sun is at its highest point.

 *The Underworld Oracle Deck By Desiree Goulden*

25 Full colour cards

Works with reversed cards

Works with other decks

$23.99 Cad

https://www.thegamecrafter.com/games/the-underworld-oracle-deck

Pride & The Craft

It's pride month and almost all of the content creators for TalesOfTheGods & Practical Witchcraft are part of the GRSM (gender, romantic, sexual minorities) and are celebrating! It's this time of year that I am reminded of just how many of us are in the Pagan, Occult and otherwise Witchy world.

Witchcraft and the GRSM has gone hand in hand for a long time. Wicca has been an accepted religion since 1986 in the United States of America and for (as long as I have known) have been major players in gay and lesbian marriages. The Satanic Temple (though not a Witchy organization by default) has fought tooth and nail for GRSM rights and are major supporters for equal rights.

While every path has it's own opinions on many things, most have been particularly welcoming to the GRSM. There are even some strictly GRSM paths such as The Minoan's, The Fellowship Of The Phoenix, and The Radical Faeries. There are also many GRSM small covens organizing online on Discord and offline all the time, and the number of inclusive spaces is always growing!

If you're looking to get into some queer witchy books, here are a few for you to check out!

Gay Witchcraft: Empowering the Tribe
Christopher Penczak

Power & Magic: The Queer Witch Comics Anthology
An Anthology by 17 women

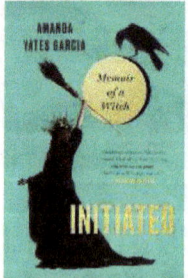
Initiated: Memoir of a Witch
Amanda Yates García - One of the best queer debuts of 2019

Queer Magic: LGBT+ Spirituality and Culture from Around the World, Tomás Prower

Queering Your Craft: Witchcraft from the Margins
Cassandra Snow

We love our GRSM / LGBTQIA2S+ family and would love to hear who your favourite GRSM creators are! You can email TalesOTheGods@gmail.com or answer anonymously on our Google Forum here: forms.gle/pmxH8Cvrk8nb7rfP9

- Desirée Goulden

Jim Two Snakes
Spiritual Advisor

 jimtwosnakes.net

 facebook.com/jimtwosnakes

 instagram.com/jimtwosnakes

 patreon.com/spiritualdad

Many people think the term Spirituality is about religion, but it doesn't have to be. In fact I think most people are Spiritual no matter if they are religious or not! Spirituality is about understanding and exploring your higher purpose, your interconnectedness to all of creation, and living authentically. It is my goal to help you feel inspired and fulfilled.

I do this by asking questions, giving suggestions, and then helping develop ways of marking progress and providing accountability. You don't have to believe the same way I, or anyone else, does. The coaching is centered around your needs and beliefs. I can't do the work for you, but I can help you with motivation and seeing things from a new perspective. Contact me now to schedule a free 15 minute initial consultation.

CONSULTATION PACKAGE

A call, a game plan, and a follow up.
One initial hour long call via Zoom, Skype or Discord
A recording of the call you can refer back to later
20 minute follow up / accountability call two weeks later

$150

TAROT READING

Divination to help guide you.
1-3 questions, submitted by email
Photos, a written report, and an audio report of your reading sent via email
48 hour turn around

$60

FIRE CEREMONY

A POWERFUL ceremony of change performed on your behalf.

You will receive instructions how to prepare for the ceremony
I will conduct the Fire Ceremony at an arranged time
You will receive a video of your ceremony, and any insights I have

$60

A POWERFUL ceremony of change performed in person for you or a group.
For individuals or groups up to ten
I will bring all needed supplies, teach you about the history of the Q'ero and the ceremony, how to participate, and then perform the ceremony
Please contact us about larger groups and gatherings

$250

SPIRITUAL CLEANSINGS

Removal of heavy energy and negativity.
For individuals, homes, or businesses.
I will bring all needed supplies.
Home cleansings can include help sorting and tidying
Rates will vary depending on number of people and/or size of house or business. Contact us for more information

The Best Value For Jim's Services visit
www.jimtwosnakes.net or
www.patreon.com/spiritualdad for more
information

Soul-Terra Family Drama
*All claims are alleged

If you are in the metaphysical spheres in general, whether online or off, you have likely heard of Soul Terra Candles.

They've been around since about 2015 and took the world by storm with their zodiac based, fragranced candles. Each of them hold within them a number of crystals. The large pyramid shaped candles sell for roughly $50 and burn for about 88 hours according to their website: soul-terra.com

Ran by husband and wife, Daniele and Will, they employed a small team and were riding high in the eyes of their customers. They sold out fast, and had a cult like following, but within the last year things began to change for them.

People were reporting that their 88+ hour candles were burning out quicker, one person even claimed that it had burnt down completely in only 4 hours. From my own circles of friends, people were reporting that there was a decrease not only in quality, but the number of crystals in the candles (which are what validates the high price point of the candles in the first place.)

`It was a curious case, and one of the reasons why I never purchased one of the candles myself, but I chocked it up to the corporation getting bigger and greedier over time. These things tend to happen to businesses as they succeed.

It seems that that wasn't exactly the case however.

While scrolling on TikTok as we often do during COVID, I came across a creator called highoffroyalty who was talking about Daniele's (the co-owner) TikTok being hacked and a Go-Fund-Me for her situation. Intrigued, I dug a little deeper.

It seems there was trouble in paradise.

Will and Daniele were dealing with some marital troubles. Now we can not claim to know what exactly went on in their personal lives, and it would be disrespectful to do so, so here is what we do know from what little is available publicly online.

Daniele and Will split up. There may have been tension from her struggle with her bipolar disorder, and there were comments in the Soul-Terra official YouTube page videos that she came into conflict with some of her workers.

Harley 2 weeks ago
Hi I'm an ex employee and I'm not going to stand for the shit Daniele is spewing. I left the company because Daniele tried to force me to do a livestream (which was not my responsibility) the same day my cat died and then tried to FIRE ME FOR IT when I told her mentally I wasn't well enough to do it. Will is the one who tried to save my job because he knew I was a good employee who loved my job and he comforted me when I was on the verge of a panic attack. Daniele forced me to take a week off unpaid. By the time I came back I asked to speak solely to will because he was the only one I felt comfortable talking to. Daniele bullied black and disabled employees and I wasn't going to stand for her toxicity anymore. If you all want to support that woman's choices go ahead but there's a reason the employees stand by Will.
Show less

👍 1 👎   REPLY

In the workplace it is not that uncommon to butt heads with your coworkers and superiors so while I want to believe this comment but I cant. Given the numerous comments on TikTok and YouTube stating that they were deleting any comment that wasn't singing Will and Soul Terra's praises, it seems more like the Daniele critical commentators are damage control.

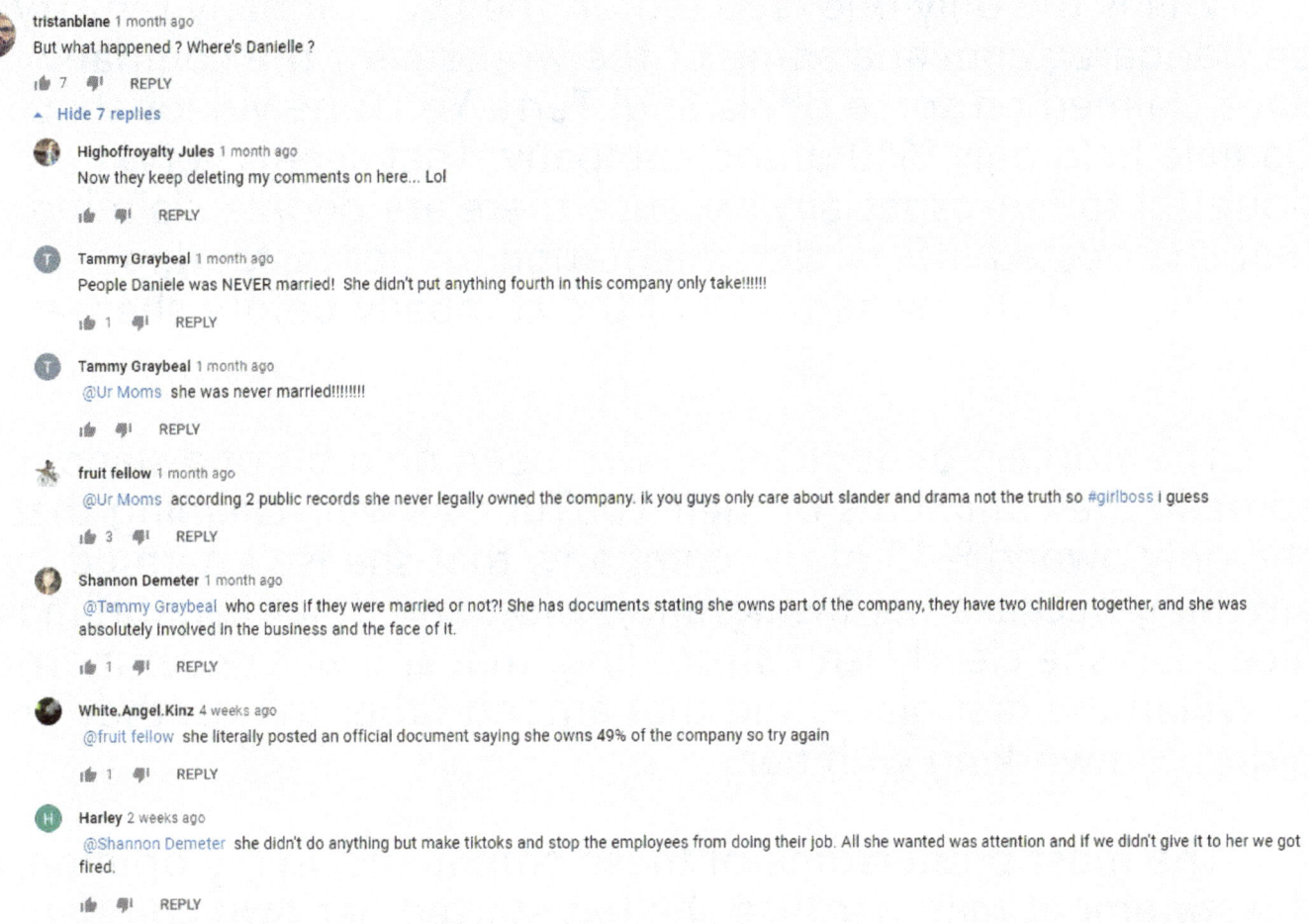

But what were they trying to control? Their image.

Soul Terra's image has been sullied because Daniele separated from Will and in retaliation, he hacked and changed all the information for many of her and Soul Terra's social media accounts and completely blocked her out of their joint bank accounts.

You can imagine how that would affect a now single mother of 2.

This is where things get tricky. You see, you can't just boot out your co-owner from their company just because you're a little butt hurt that you were divorced / left. That's just not how that legally works. But how much do they own of the company?

Will is the only one credited on the LLC company registry on floridareg.com and some of the workers for the company have claimed on some of his Soul Terra YouTube videos that Daniele held only %10 of the company. That seems very doubtful to me, especially because there are people claiming that she posted official documentation on her Instagram showing that she owned %49 of the company before she went private.

The workers of Soul Terra have been on a bit of a slander spree in the comments of their YouTube as well, claiming that she only owned %10 of the company, that she isn't harmed by anything because her Instagram is nice, and if her Instagram is nice then she clearly isn't struggling, that she was never married to Will in the first place, and that among other things, they just didn't like working with her.

The most bothersome of these comments, in my opinion, is the statement that: because she has started her own company since, that she should just be okay with everything and that she is just starting drama.

Daniele has been able to start her own, new version of Soul Terra called Selaluz Candles. She has done this with her past experience of running Soul Terra, on top of a Go-Fund-Me campaign that was started for her on top of her loyal fan base of Soul Terra customers who are tired of the declining quality of Soul Terra on top of the toxic situation Will put her into.

If you would like to support her you can visit her Go-Fund-Me here: https://gofund.me/aeeb9678

They have gotten $1,787 of their $19,999 goal, and if you want something for your money, you can buy from Selaluz Candles here: selaluzcandles.com

Selaluz Candles burn for over 65 hours, use %100 natural waxes, with hemp wicks, and natural oils. They sell candles, wax melts, tarot tarts (wax melts with 3 tarot cards within), and so much more.

This is a wonderful new start and a return to quality crystal containing candles. Hopefully this is a new start for Daniele as well.

There is little we know about the ins and outs of the situation that lead to her leaving Soul Terra. Will posted on the Soul Terra TikTok account that a video would be coming soon explaining everything, but posted nothing but restock videos, and a "The Journey of Soul Terra" video since then (A meet the team esque video with some less than engaging poetry at the beginning and end). The "The Journey of Soul Terra" video has been the source of the screen shots here. It is clear Will wants to silence the people defending Daniele, and if he is not telling his workers to slander her, he is at the very least raising their voices and silencing everyone else's.

This seems like a terribly toxic situation and we can only hope that Daniele can grow Selaluz Candles and build the bright new future she deserves. As far as my opinion on this, I do not support abusers and I am not going to waste $50 on a candle that burns out in 4 hours.

- Desirée Goulden

The Future, Regrettably
Coming Fall 2021

The debut urban fantasy novel from Desirée Goulden, prequel to the Aurora Garroway series.

Julian is a man with nothing but a name. Woken from a coma and thrust into a war he does not want to fight, he is the body guard and right hand man of a tyrannical cult leader, Rose. Escape is futile and attempts cause innocent people to be killed to keep him in line. With death as the only escape, he becomes reckless in battle, hoping to be cut down and finally escape the life he is trapped in.

Rose notices and offers him a boon: stay in line and do as she says and he will be able to visit the future in his dreams. He will be able to live a comfortable life and see why the Conduit Hierarchy's war is just, and how it will better the world.

Will this be enough to pacify Julian? Or will this motivate him to tear down the organization that seeks to control him, and find the truth?

Cartomancy
An Introduction to Reading a Standard Deck

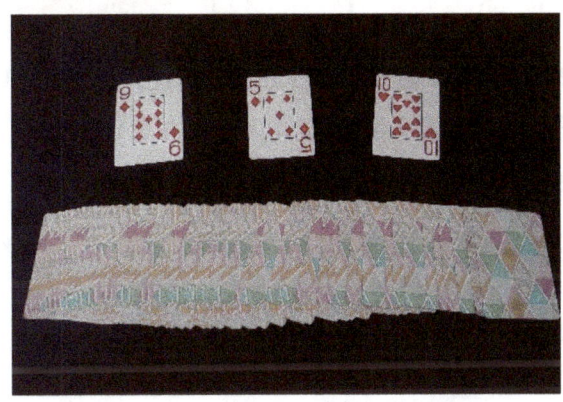

Many of you are familiar with intuitive readings through Tarot, Oracle, Spirit cards, or Runes. This is a brief explanation and introduction to Cartomancy or reading the Standard Deck.

What you will need

- An ordinary deck of cards
- A coin or token to mark subject's avatar.
- A glass of water or a cup of herbal tea (no milk or sugar added)

Sounds fairly simple. Right? And it can be. But there are a few instructions that are common sense. The same kind that you would apply to any reading.

1. Never allow your deck to be used to play games with. It taints the connection. If your deck is used to play Solitaire or Old Maid, I'm sorry to say, you will need to buy a new one.

2. A deck needs to be made of paper not plastic or other materials. This has to do with being in contact with the pure elements.

3. A deck should be prepared before its first use. You can do this through a cleansing in salt or in moonlight, or by wiping it down with purified or holy water. This is to remove residual energy from anyone who may have handled your deck ahead of time.

4. Be sure that the deck you have chosen includes a Joker card. All 54 cards are necessary in a reading. Some people tend to throw out the Joker out of habit, however, the Joker holds a lot of influence over the other cards.

The Suits

Hearts – hearts tends to deal in issues and concepts regarding relationships and emotions.

Clubs – clubs focusses on financial matters, career and business influences, and assets that a person holds.

Diamonds – diamonds delves into the practical things in everyday life.

Spades – spades reveals the troubles, obstacles, and problems one might face in everyday life.

If you keep these basics in mind, you will find learning to read the cards becomes very simple. Even when you have yet to learn the meaning of each individual card, the overall message can be easily discerned.

> There are, however, some basic card combinations which alter the meaning of the original cards. Depending on the spread, these pairings may be anywhere in a line, but they must be in the same line or box to mean the following things...

-An Ace of diamonds and a five of diamonds are believed to indicate the purchase of a new home.

-The three of diamonds with the six of diamonds point to learning and exams or tests.

-The nine of diamonds with the ten of diamonds suggest some kind of travel over water.

-The two of diamonds and the three of hearts mean there will be an offer of marriage or the romantic equivalent.

-The two of diamonds with the five of clubs means a working partnership is involved.

-The ten of clubs with the nine of clubs is considered to represent a lump sum of money as a settlement.

-The ten of clubs with the six of clubs implies the taking out of a loan.

-The eight of spades and the nine of spades together mean there is a health concern involved.

-Two aces of any suit show the patching up of a quarrel.

-Two twos of any suit indicate a parting.

The Different Types of Spreads

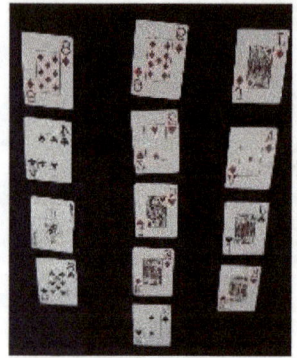

The One Year Spread. Working from left to right the cards are placed from the bottom to the top with the 13th card placed over the center column at the top. Card number one represents the month you are in not the first calendar month. Begin reading from here. The 13th card indicates the overall aspect of the year and adds a little more depth.

The Mini Spread can be used two ways. Spring, Summer, Autumn and Winter or Practical, Financial, Emotional and Problems. This one uses an avatar in order to see where your focus is.

Known as the G*psy Spread, this reading covers the past, present, and future beginning from the bottom and working its way up. This one also uses an avatar to see where your anchor is.

Referred to as the Tarot spread, this reading begins in the center and then spirals out. North, east, south, west. It is used to indicate where a person is at in the immediate and points out how to resolve the issue that is tying them in place.

General Spread is a little different. The deck is cut in two and then each of these decks are cut in two again. An avatar has been selected ahead of time and the pile with the avatar is the one to be read. If the avatar appears on the end of a row, draw one or two more cards to fence it in. There is no set number of cards which you will be reading from in this spread.

*Editors note: Outdated term. Censored to respect our Romani / Traveller readers.

How to Read the Cards

1. Shuffle the cards thoroughly.

2. With the avatar cards facing down, have your subject select an avatar and then replace these cards back into the deck. Reshuffle the cards thoroughly.

3. Ask your subject to select thirteen cards or in the case of a general reading to cut the deck twice.

4. Remove the remaining cards to the side.

5. Keeping the cards in order, place them on the table according to the spread.

6. For the first while you will need to look up the meanings of the cards as they appear on the table. There are several reliable sites online. Eventually, you will have them all generally memorized.

7. Note down any pairings and the placement of the designated avatar.

8. Try to read the cards around the avatar or significator first.

A Few Brief Sidenotes

-Cards can also be used to read for yes or no questions as a clarifier. Red means yes and Black means no. When you are starting out, often you many find that the overall reading doesn't fit together. When this occurs, yes or no questions can sometimes make things a little clearer.

-Always try to clear your psychic palate between readings. A drink of clear ice water or a cup of herbal tea sooth any uncomfortable messages or undercurrents away.

-Treat your cards with respect. Common sense. Do not put them on sticky or dirty surfaces. Do not mistreat them. Do not leave them lying around where anyone can pick them up and play with them. Usually, keeping a cloth handy to place down on any surface to keep them from picking up strange energies or interference. (Many cartomancers keep this cloth wrapped around the deck to shield it from outside elements.)

-When reading for a client, be objective and be responsible. Do not try to read something if it isn't clear to you. Be honest let them know that at this time things are not clear. Perhaps they need to ask questions first or reshuffle the deck.

-It is also an accepted rule that the topic of death will not be addressed in the cards by the reader or the client. If you suspect something is leaning that way, it is best to keep it to yourself and your personal notes.

-Always keep a notebook and pen handy. Write everything down.

If Cartomancy looks like something you might find interesting, I recommend that you read up on it further. Good luck and have fun.

— Dana Lee Beaudreau

A Sample Reading in Cartomancy

Subject A has kindly permitted me to do a sample reading to demonstrate how a basic beginner level reading is performed. The cards have been shuffled, an avatar has been selected based on random assignment from the universe, the cards have been lain out with a G*psy layout. This format examines the past, present and future.

Note: the future is not always intended to be predictive but rather is a useful tool in helping the individual ascertain how to proceed with a decision that they are trying to make. In these instances, the future cards are used to point out more details, influencers, or outside factors which may be tools available at hand to assist in this decision. It's like looking at the situation through a telescope or microscope depending on whether you are being influenced by things external or internal to yourself.

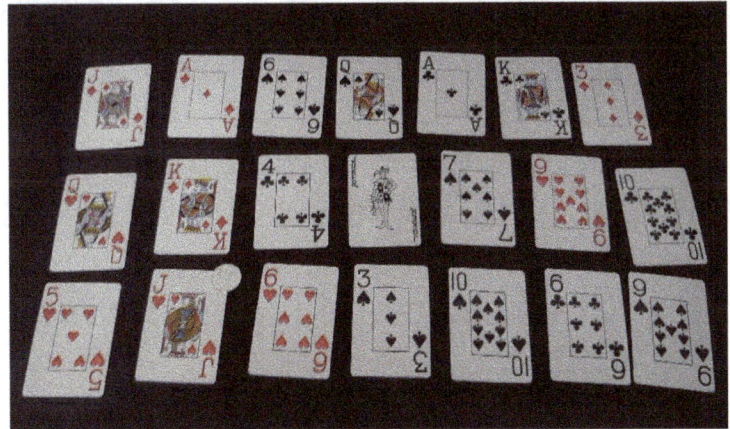

The avatar was selected randomly from the cards face down on the table. In this case the card that presented itself was the Jack of Hearts. The Jack of Heart represents an individual who is emotionally insecure due to past hurts within a relationship. They are good with words and tend to talk or work with words a lot in their life. They need to move around, and change is particularly important to them.

Staying still tends to make them feel very agitated, anxious, or insecure. They have been forced to grow up too quickly. They presentment in the avatar in the lower row indicates that this individual may be ruled by their past. For the sake of showing the avatar in the reading, I tend to put a marker on the card, such as a coin.

When doing a g*psy reading, always start with the individual's past, then the present, and end with the future line. When possible, ask the subject to think of they question or concern as they shuffle the cards and cut the deck. If you are doing a distance reading, ask them if they have any concerns before you shuffle and cut the deck on their behalf.

And so we begin.

Based on the cards on the table, Subject A has needed been very focussed on relationships in their past. They tended to put the needs of their partner before their own. They have been emotionally insecure and have been hurt in past relationships both physically and emotionally. In all honesty, it appears as though they were living in an almost doormat situation in their past relationships. They have been caught in a love triangle. This interfered with their life choices and blocked their creativity. All these factors have contributed to a current struggle with depression and a lack of forward movement in their emotional life. They struggled with money as well. Overall, there was a lot of overthinking and worry leading to depression.

At present, there is an affectionate mother figure and a single minded, workaholic father figure influencing their present decisions. The father figure has difficulty showing emotions and the mother figure is someone shy and possessive. Subject A is struggling with a lack of trust caused by past trauma.

*Editors note: Outdated term. Censored to respect our Romani / Traveller readers.

There is a warning that this individual needs to be cautious with their possessions. They are hiding many things from other, secrets and intentions but be careful for these secrets may interfere with their abilities or may cause some of their abilities to be wasted. Revelations are occurring and they are discovering things about themselves that they may not be all too comfortable with. Many of their fears are groundless and I advise them to take a good look at their surroundings and consider both sides of things instead of jumping in right away. They need to avoid emotional games if they expect to find a stable relationship. It is also advised that they use caution these days as there will be more money coming in for a while.

Finally, be careful of a charming individual. They are intelligent and attractive, but they are also very immature and bore easily. Subject A is facing new beginning, goals, and challenges. Try not to get derailed. With boredom, necessary boredom, comes a lack of focus. Documents may be lost or overlooked. Also, there is a female narcissist effecting their future. Stand strong. With summer comes an increase in income but this is only temporary so be careful in managing their money. There is also a warning of a male who uses money to flaunt what he doesn't really have. He is highly superficial, mean and gets meaner. Caution of a possible abuse situation. Significant to notice is that Subject A becomes a stronger individual in the future. Their future holds much promise if they find the time to carry out certain actions that they may have been avoiding before. In particular, there is a call to search out further education. Note: education does not require one to go to college or university though it also does not preclude it. Life lessons, interest classes, books or lectures may all contribute to this search for knowledge. What is seen here is a presence of education and learning leading to adaptation to change and new ideas.

- Dana Lee Beaudreau

TOTG Merch!

We have new additions to the TalesOfTheGods.com merch page!

This is a back and white illustration of Achilles and Patroclus with a rainbow background and a inscription that reads: "No dude, they were totally just really good friends!" -Very Smart People.

Buy at **https://tales-of-the-gods-2.creator-spring.com/listing/achilles-and-patroclus-being-b**

$44.17 $6.20 $31.54

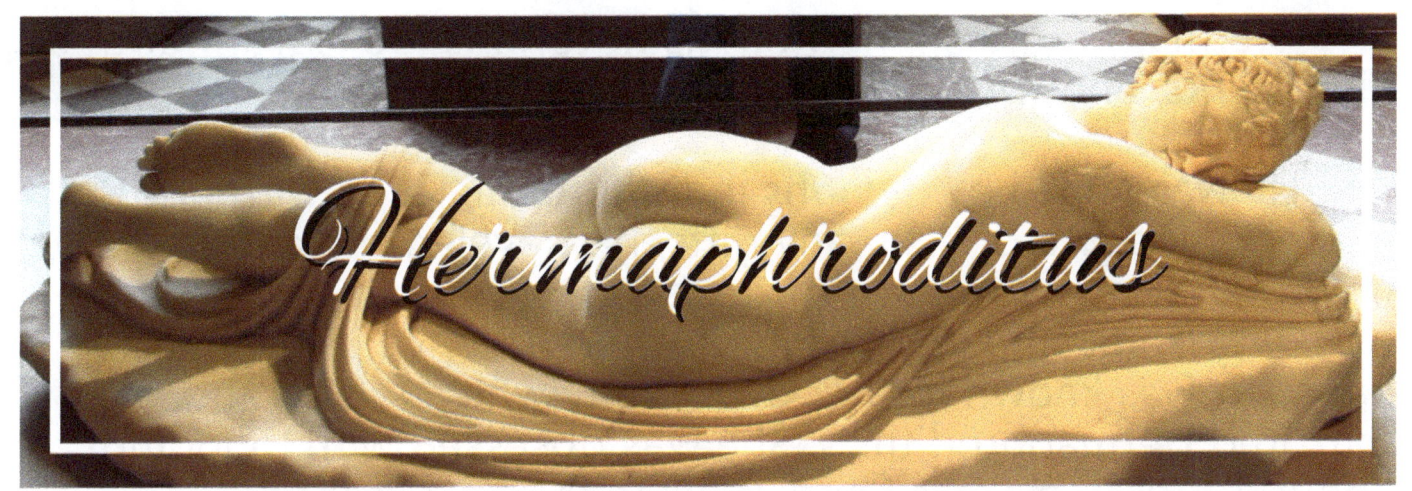

Hermaphroditus

It often times can be hard to find representation within the gods for marginalized identities. How many times have we herd dude-bros say "Trans people didn't exist in the past" "Intersex people aren't a thing" and more? While right in a sense (these terms are modern inventions to explain situations that have existed for time in memoriam) you can't just erase a large part of society that has always existed, even if they wouldn't call themselves by those labels.

People will claim that there were no gay people in history, ignoring that the term wasn't around back then and it was common place to have a wife and a male lover, and boys having same sex relationships was a corner stone of growing up in Ancient Greece. Hell, we have the term "lesbian" and "sapphic" specifically because of Sappho of Lesbos.

We have have just as much evidence that intersex people and trans people existed in antiquity because of the story of the Greek God, Hermaphroditus .

So who is Hermaphroditus ? I know, the name sounds like a very out of date term for intersex, but that is because the name is directly derived from Hermaphroditus.

Hermaphrodites is the son of Aphrodite (Goddess of sexual love and feminine beauty) and Hermes (Psychopomp, messenger, God of manliness as well as male fertility).

Hermaphroditus inherited his notorious looks from both of his parents, and was as charming socially as his father.

He was raised by nymphs in mount Ida. Filled with pride and ego because of his many gifts, he traveled the ancient world. After many months of traveling he found himself tired and dirty and came upon a pond where the nymph Salmakis. Salmakis was known for her own vanity which in a strange way mirrored Hermaphroditus's. She was obsessed with lounging about, grooming herself and relaxing in the pond.

When she laid eyes on Hermaphroditus as he bathed, she became obsessed with him. She attempted to seduce him... to save the less than savory details... and he refused. She asked the Gods as she embraced him to make it so that they were never apart. The Gods granted her wish and combined she and Hermaphroditus's bodies.

Hermaphroditus was transformed to have both sets of genitalia. The poet Ovid told him to be a tragic figure, but if anyone knows me, Ovid is on a short list of historical figures I would throw hands with. He is rather notoriously terrible both at relaying the myths accurately, and making things up to suit a very anti woman and Greek views. (See his odd fan fiction version of Medusa that has become popular).

According to Theoi.com Hermaphroditus is among the love gods (Erots) and is the God of effeminates and Hermaphrodites (Old term, replaced by the more politically correct "Intersex"), androgynous people.

It was said that in a rage over the transformation he cursed the pond so that any who enter its waters would be transformed like he was. Now it is unknown how the ancient peoples would have regarded him. Someone born intersex could be considered bad luck, but considering he was also a Erot who knows how the Hellens would have thought of him.

Rearguardless of how they would have seen him, it was proof that intersex and trans gender people existed in some form back then. It was proof that no matter ones opinion of them, they had a place in divinity. People now-a-days see Hermaphroditus as a icon of gender-queer peoples and is becoming more and more celebrated within the GRSM community.

Gender and sexuality is always a tricky subject when looking back on history, but in Pride month we take the time to celebrate gender and sexuality throughout time. We celebrate Hermaphroditus, Erot, God of Intersex, Trans-Gender and Androgynous People.

- Desirée Goulden

Tales Of The Gods

Free shops & services listings

Have a shop or service and want to extend your reach without speding some coin? Contact us! We will set up your shop in our public database including a explination of your business and a landing page to display your wares!

We will post you on our online shops and services for free! Just contact us at our contact page on TalesOfTheGods.com or send us a email at TalesOTheGods@gmail.com or at our social medias! We can be found on Facebook, Twitter, and Instagram!

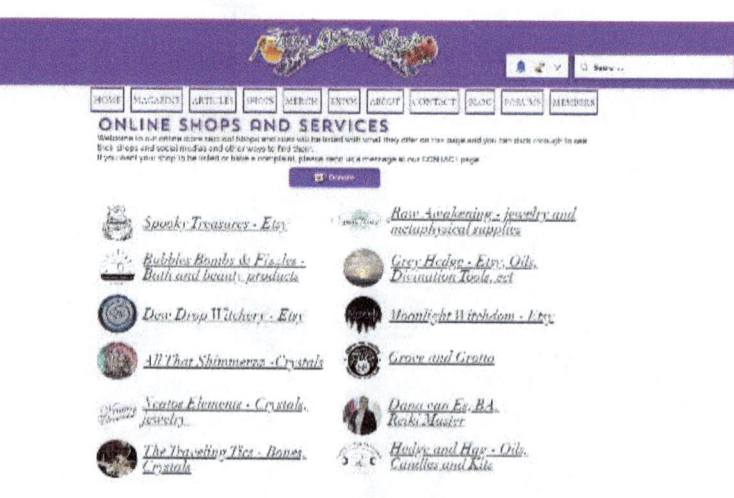

Want To Create & Sell Tarot Decks?
Here's How With A Budget of $0

Practitioners are often creative people and with the internet many have been able to turn that creativity into product and cash. Unfortunately it almost always takes money to make money and these days people don't often have extra to throw at their passion project.

Luckily Go-Fund-Me and Kickstarter have made it easier to get the funding you need for your projects! That is... if you have the time, reach and money to advertise the thing that is supposed to get you money in the first place... and then you have to wait to gain funding... then go through manufacturers, publishing houses, shipping, more advertising, creating a webpage for your product to sell the product (which usually costs money itself) and that's not going to guarantee it is going to actually sell after all that.

With all that, it can seem a little hopeless if you are one person working out of a small apartment on a budget of $0 to create anything. This is a problem that has come up constantly with the Tarot crowd. For years I have seen people asking how to produce and sell Tarot decks and it seems everyone immediately suggests publishing houses and... not much else. Let's explore a more realistic way of creating a custom tarot deck and selling it, for people who don't have ample time, money, or reach.

Here are the programs and websites you'll need to know:

- TheGameCrafter.com
- GIMP
- Autodesk SketchBook Free
- Wix.com
- FaceBook.com
- Twitter.com
- TikTok.com / TikTok App
- TalesOfTheGods.com

We are going to break this down into 3 sections. Design, creation, online presence.

Design

The first thing you need to start with is your design. The Tarot have specific symbology they include that lend to the meaning of your cards, and I assume that if you're making a deck that you're already aware of them. That being said, I encourage visiting a few websites or reading any books you have on hand and jotting down the symbology for each card. Remember, while symbology is important, this is your deck and you should make it as unique as you can. People aren't going to buy a carbon copy of every other deck out there. (Also, you want to avoid looking too much like other decks to avoid legal trouble.)

Find a theme for your deck, find a style, and keep it throughout the deck. While Tarot is about the readings many people value a good looking deck. The more attractive and eye catching the deck, the more likely people will view it when it is finally put online.

Creation

So you've got your theme down pat and want to actually make the deck. Now is where it gets tricky. Using this method, you will be using TheGameCrafter.com so before you begin anything go make an account.

After you make an account click on the menu bar across the scree, the second from the right.

Click MAKE -> GAMES -> Scroll down to "Add a game" and name your deck. Then click +Create game.

On the following screen, on the left, click +Add custom component.

Type Tarot into the search bar and select what add-ons you want in your deck. Select Tarot Deck and it will redirect you to the card addition page. You should name the deck here, then navigate to the left to the Templates section. Select PNG and download the card template.

Organization is everything so make sure to make a folder in your photos folder titled the same as your deck. Move the PNG template to there, make sure you don't delete it. Create 3 folders:

Major Arcana
Minor Arcana
Source Files.

Now you need to figure out what program you are going to use.

If you don't want to or can't draw digitally, you can hand draw your cards. After you draw, paint, or otherwise illustrate the cards you can either scan them, or using a GOOD QUAILTY PHONE CAMERA or photography camera, take a picture of them. If you are doing this, make sure you are in a well light aria, and your shadow does not fall over the cards. Ensure that you are taking the photo head on so the perspective of the cards are not altered.

From here download GIMP from gimp.org. GIMP is a free PhotoShop alternative that I have personally been using since they moved their payment plans from a one time purchase to a monthly fee of entirely too much dollars and ridiculous cents.

Use the Template as a base layer on GIMP to help position your photo where it needs to be. After it fits within the constraints, now is time for the editing. You're going to have to get very comfortable with GIMP, Google, and YouTube to learn how to use GIMP and tune the image so that it doesn't just look like someone copy and pasted a low rez image onto the cards.

If you are going to work digitally, I swore by Autodesk SketchBook which has mobile options. I created the entirety of the Underworld Oracle Deck on SketchBook mobile. You can download it from Google Play and on PC at autodesk.com/products/sketchbook/overview

Create a image layer using the template PNG. Create your frame if you are going to have a frame in every card and export the frame template as its own template PNG. Use that template and design the cards within it.in mass afterwards. (It just takes a very long time if you do).

If you don't want to or can't draw digitally, you can hand draw your cards. After you draw, paint, or otherwise illustrate the cards you can either scan them, or using a GOOD QUAILTY PHONE CAMERA or photography camera, take a picture of them. If you are doing this, make sure you are in a well light aria, and your shadow does not fall over the cards. Ensure that you are taking the photo head on so the perspective of the cards are not altered.

From here download GIMP from gimp.org. GIMP is a free PhotoShop alternative that I have personally been using since they moved their payment plans from a one time purchase to a monthly fee of entirely too much dollars and ridiculous cents.

Use the Template as a base layer on GIMP to help position your photo where it needs to be. After it fits within the constraints, now is time for the editing. You're going to have to get very comfortable with GIMP, Google, and YouTube to learn how to use GIMP and tune the image so that it doesn't just look like someone copy and pasted a low rez image onto the cards.

If you are going to work digitally, I swore by Autodesk SketchBook which has mobile options. I created the entirety of the Underworld Oracle Deck on SketchBook mobile. You can download it from Google Play and on PC at autodesk.com/products/sketchbook/overview

Create a image layer using the template PNG. Create your frame if you are going to have a frame in every card and export the frame template as its own template PNG. Use that template and design the cards within it.

For every finished card, save the file into the Source Files file and export the finished card into the respective Major or Minor Arcana files.

You will also have to design a backing for the cards, which you only have to design one of.

I suggest that after you finish every card you upload it before beginning the next, but you can also chose to upload in mass afterwards. (It just takes a very long time if you do)

To upload your cards, you will have to go to the Tarot Deck on your GameCrafter account. If you have closed the page that is

(TheGameCrafter.com -> MAKE -> GAME -> select your tarot deck from the list -> select the deck from the following list)

Enable UV Coating, it will make your cards a little more durable. Upload your backing to the BACK selection. Do not change the number of copies in the Tarot Deck. That should always stay at 1. Scroll down and upload the cards. They will appear with the names beside them, hopefully you have been properly naming your cards when exporting them from your software of choice.

You will have to "proof" each card. Make sure everything falls into the provided guidelines and everything looks good and processional. This is a very VERY important step. When you are done, go back to your game page.

Now is time to select the box. You can look to the left and see the "Suggested Box" That will be the box that will most easily and closely fit your deck depending on how-

-many cards are in it. (It may be a different amount if you are making a Oracle deck which doesn't have a set number of cards.)

Click "Add Custom Component" and either search the box that was suggested, or one of the options from the selections offered after searching Tarot. When you select your box, download the PNG template like you did with the card templates.

Use the software and method of your choice to create the box for your cards. Include information you would see on any product. The top should have the title and a main image related to the deck, the sides may include your store name or the creator name, the back should include a blurb about the product that will get people interested and explain the deck.

Go back to your game page and click the SELL tab. From there, follow TheGameCrafter's instructions for filling out product information and images.

You will need to buy a copy of your deck so that they know you are legitimate, as well as for you to take photos of the product to add to the listing page. The better the photos the more likely people will buy the product.

You will need to set a price. Take into consideration the manufacturing fees, and consider the shipping the customer will need to pay for. No matter how beautiful the deck is, the price needs to be reasonable. Even golden edged highly produced decks like the Marigold deck still come in around $50 - $70. Your deck should probably be in the $20 - $40 range.

Online Presence

TheGameCrafter will post your deck to their searchable online marketplace after it goes live, but you absolutely need to sell your deck yourself as well.

Post on FaceBook to your page and get your friends and family involved and interested. If you have a few dollars to spend, you can run a ad campaign for as little as $5

Post the cards on Twitter using hashtags and information that will reel people in.

Post on TikTok. Offer free or paid readings on there and use exclusively your deck. Have a page specifically for that deck or your products if you offer different items or more decks after this.

Create a website. Now this is probably what will usually cost you the most. Luckily if you don't mind having a Wix banner across your screen, Wix offers a free plan for creating your website. Post your products on there, have an official page for people to contact you about it and make sure you have links to the product on TheGameCrafter. A website, with or without the banner, can go a very long way to make your product look professional and with Wix you don't need to learn a word of coding to do it.

Need free advertising? Contact TalesOfTheGods.com and have us write about your deck! We also give away free full page ads in the TalesOfTheGods & Practical Witchcraft Magazine!

If you want to take it one step further, TheGameCrafter allows you to buy your product in bulk. You can contact your local metaphysical shop or book store and see if they allow consignment arrangements to sell your deck. You can take part in festivals and expos to sell them, though that usually requires renting a space and do a lot of personal sales to get your product out there.

Making Tarot decks shouldn't be inaccessible for low income people, and using TheGameCrafter, GIMP, Autodesk Sketchbook, Wix and social media you can absolutely create a beautiful Tarot deck at no cost but time!

- Desirée Goulden

@inkwood_tarot @InkwoodJournal

inkwoodtarot.com

Inkwood Tarot - Readings by Cynthia: tarot reader, empath, certified Reiki practitioner and ordained Pagan clergy.

" I offer tarot readings by phone, video call and seasonally in-person at local events, festivals and shops. With over 20 years of tarot study and experience, I love helping people bring harmony, balance and success to their lives. Join me in exploring your ultimate potential!"

To learn more or schedule a reading visit:
http://inkwoodtarot.com

Modern Terminology In Antiquity

You will often here the claim that XYZ didn't exist in the past and is a modern invention. Now, we all know that people who say things like this aren't looking to have an actual conversation about terminology and identity. That being said, it is a conversation that should be had, particularly during Pride.

Recently I have gotten in the middle of several arguments online about the sexual identity of the Gods and Hero's of old. As a pansexual, non-binary person I don't want to be on the side of "God X is not gay, I'm sorry" but it is the side that I have had to take none the less.

As mentioned in the Hermaphroditus article, the terms we have to describe the GRSM / LGBTQIA2S+ communities did not exist in the past. In this I will be talking specifically about Ancient Greece and Rome sexuality and expression.

Lets get one thing very straight. (Pun intended.) Same sex relationships where not only a thing that happened in antiquity, but was a corner stone of Greek society the bled into the very rearing of children. Trans and intersex people while not common, were common enough to have a deity that represented them among the Erots.

From Zeus to Apollo to Achilles, male and male sexual relationships were as common as the clouds in the sky.

Female and female relationships likely were just as common (probably more considering the limited interactions women were allowed in public and with men) though not written about due to the highly misogynistic society of the time.

With that being said, you can not call these people gay, lesbian, bi or any of the other terms we have to describe sexuality because they did not exist. Not only did they not exist, they did not serve the same functional roll in history as they do today. Were you to go back in time and talk to Patroclus and Achilles and show them the modern GRSM culture and tell them that they were part of that, they would likely get greatly offended.

Femininity was to be looked down upon back then, and sexual relationships where divided into penetrator, and the receiver in a sexual experience. Take for example Julius Caesar. Caesar was the subject of mockery for quite a few things in his sexual and gender expression. He was known for dressing as a woman, and made fun of for his relationship King Nicomedes of Bithynia. While it was normal for men to sleep with men and slaves, he was made a laughing stock for taking the passive roll in the bed with Nicomedes.

Same sex relationships were important to the rearing of children as well. Pederasty was a part of a young boys life in both Rome and Greece and was seen as important sex education. A young boy would sleep with his teacher or tutor in his youth to prepare him for the marital bed and relationships in his adulthood. It was expected to end when he reached adulthood and he would take up the dominant roll in sexual experiences with boys and slaves afterwords.

This is repulsive to modern day sensibilities, and come Christianity, was a source of repulsion as well. People often source a part of the bible saying that "One should not lay with man as one would with women" and the word "homosexual" was deliberately changed in the 30s from "pedophilia" to push a anti gay agenda. The original text was actually commenting that one should not sleep with a man as one would a child. It was condemning the act of pederasty, not homosexuality.

Considering the nature of how homosexual relationships worked, you can see how telling a Ancient Greek that they are gay and all that may entail may not go over so well. Likewise, the modern GRSM would absolutely never want to be considered the same as people who slept with children and groomed them as a hallmark of their society.

Another problem with forcing modern terms on the Gods and Heroes is that it often comes with some problematic connotations.

Take an argument I was in the other day about Artemis. The person I was arguing with said that Artemis was clearly a lesbian, not asexual and claiming that she was is lesbophobic. Now, we will give this person the benefit of the doubt that they truly believe this, and ignore the fact that it sounds like a argument from 2010 Tumblr.

Saying this about virginal Goddesses immediately assumes that because they don't want to get married or sleep with men, that clearly they are lesbian. This is a problematic attitude for many reasons, starting with the fact that it is clearly aphobic. Believe it or not, some people just don't want to have sex. More than that, this represents the same problem as stated above with male on male sexual experiences. While we know nearly nothing about woman on woman relationships due to ancient misogyny and the devaluing of women's relationships and contributions in both history and current archaeology, it is safe-

-to say they most likely had a similar culture of Pederasty as well.

Furthermore this is ignoring the fact that Artemis is a Goddess who is commonly depicted as a child. Artemis is one of 3 virginal Goddesses who all protected their virginity violently. To claim that these Goddesses are lesbians and to worship them in a sexual manor of any sort would likely to draw their ire. Their maidenhood may be linked to their sexual relationships with male Gods and mortals, but you need to respect the ancient and current Greek cultures who state point form that they are virgins.

We often forget that these are living religions that formed the basis of Greek culture, and though Christianity has swept through and majorly taken over they are still important and alive. Imposing western ideals on sexuality and gender and speaking over traditional interpretation of the Greek Gods is activity taking part of the colonization of Hellenismos.

We want to see ourselves in a society that often makes us feel like we aren't normal, and that is understandable. Unfortunately sexuality and gender expression is a deep and complicated topic in modern times, and doubly so for ancient times. It is not bad to see yourself or your identity in the Gods and Heroes of yore, it is however not possible to put our modern terms on them, and can often times be insulting to the time and cultures they come from.

- Desirée Goulden

Lughnasadh 2021

Art By Owen
Witchy poetry & photography

Preserving The Past & Future
Ancient monuments & land

Pagan Activities
Cross words

A New Divination Tool
How to read and use them for $0.00

Influencers
In divination, what are they?

Ethics
In the online pagan and occult world

Sage
Dana explains the magickal background of sage

Restraining Order
Because you're Wiccan? How a mother's life was turned upside down by her neighbour

Tales Of The Gods & - PRACTICAL WITCHCRAFT -

Thank You

By buying this magazine, you support small business owners and small creators!

TalesOfTheGods aims to connect the metaphysical and spiritual communities.

Cover Photo - Owen Lee Heavenhill.

Everything in this magazine belongs to the contributor who submits it, anything that is not will be credited appropriately.

If you would like to write in anonymously, or join our team for the next edition feel free to send a email to TalesOTheGods@gmail.com

TalesOfTheGods, March 2021

TalesOfTheGods.com

- PRACTICAL WITCHCRAFT -

facebook.com/groups/665578877692886

Contributors

Desirée Goulden	Owner, layout design, contributor
Owen Lee Heavenhill	Photographer, Contributor
Dana Lee Beaudreau	Founding member, Contributor
Veronica	Founding member, Contributor

The TalesOfTheGods & Practical Witchcraft magazine is a community project. Our roster of contributors is constantly shifting. Everyone who works on the magazine takes home an equal take of the income from the sales of this magazine.

We aim to bring education and entertainment to people of all levels of experience and paths. If you have a point of view that you would like to share with the world, feel free to reach out to join us. We are currently looking for people of colour to join us. Whether you are a teacher, or just interested in taking part, we have a place for you.

Have a shop or product you want to share with the world? Contact us and we will run a free full page ad for you in the next edition! We release on every day of the wheel of the year, so it's easy to follow release dates!

We understand that there may be some who may not want to support Amazon, so we have made the shift from publishing through Kindle Direct Publishing for our paper back editions to Ingram Spark. This will allow for wider distribution (Chapters, Barns & Noble, indie book shops) for those who want to support us without supporting Amazon and Jeff Bezos.

Please know that all opinions are that of the contributor and may not reflect the team in general.

Contents

About Lughnasadh	PAGE 2
To the exhausted witch - Poem by Owen	PAGE 4
Photography showcase	PAGE 5
Preserving The Past & Future	PAGE 8
All About Sage	PAGE 12
Modern Ethics In The Online Pagan World	PAGE 14
Crosswords	PAGE 20
The Sigils Of Hermes Divination Intro	PAGE 25
Restraining Order Because You're Wiccan *Reprint	PAGE 30

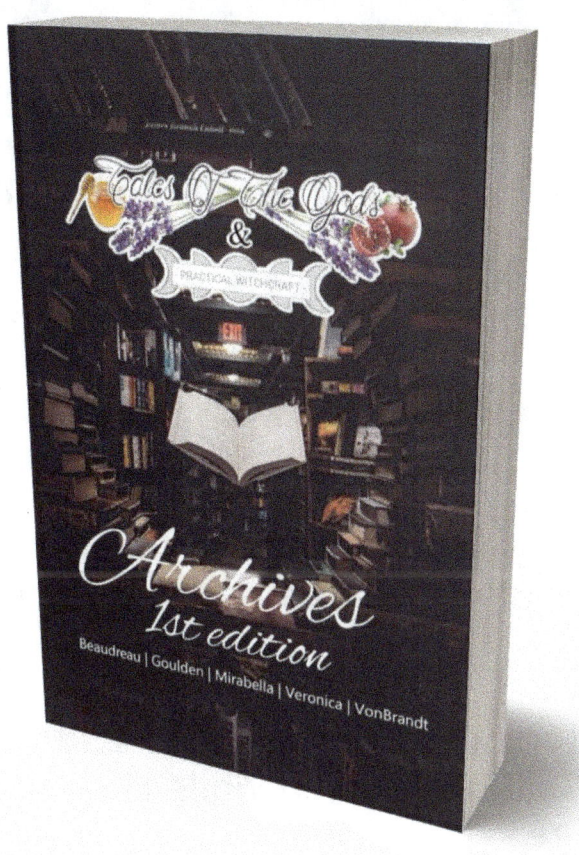

Want to read the articles of the magazine, but have visual setbacks with the magazine format? Want to read without having the budget to buy every magazine?
The Archives are all of our articles in plain text format for your bookcase or digital collection!
Published every 3 magazine editions this has a plethora of knowledge and entertainment!
31 articles, 201 pages of content, all for an affordable price! ($20 cad)
https://www.talesofthegods.com/magazine

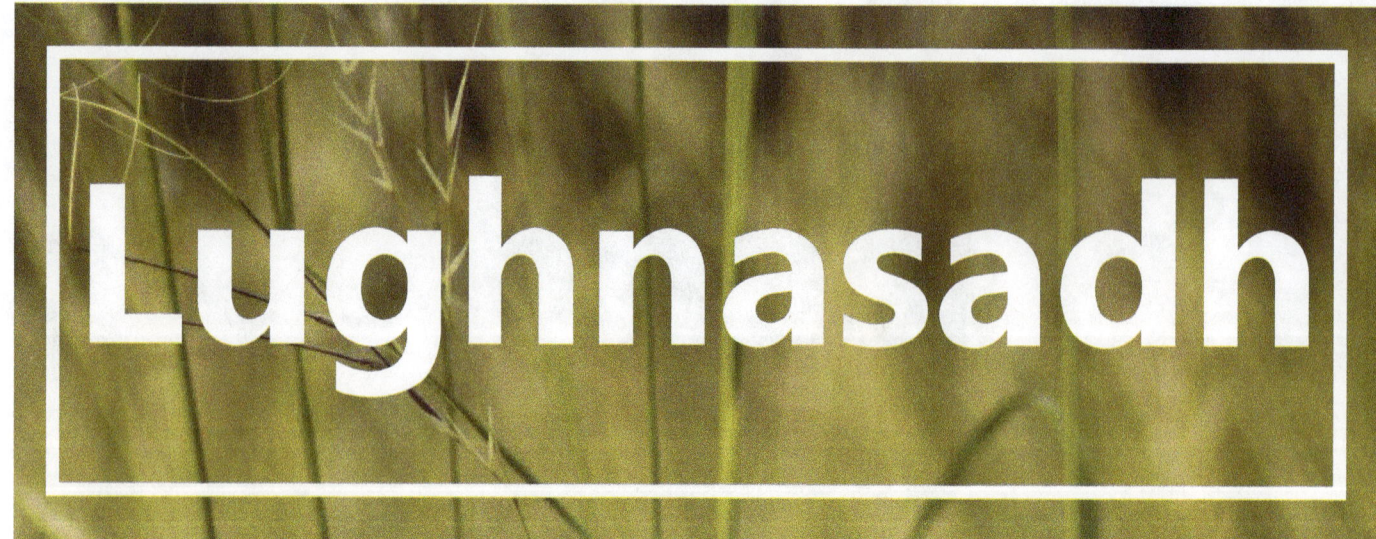

Lughnasadh

Lughnasadh is the 6th day on the Wheel Of The Year. Taken from Irish Gaelic religion, it celebrates the deity Lugh and his foster mother, Tailtiu.

It is an agricultural celebration and is said that Lugh created the holiday his self for Tailtiu who died while clearing the fields of Ireland for agriculture.

I is sometimes also called Lammas in the Anglo-Saxon world, and within medieval England and Scotland and is named for the loaf-mass where the first loaf of bread is consecrated. It also may have become known as the "Feast of the First Fruits" and was a time to give thanks for divine gifts.

Lughnasadh is traditionally celebrated on a hill or mountain top with an alter pointed to the west to represent autumn.

Co-relations and symbology:

Colours

Gold, Yellow, Orange, Brown ,Green

Symbols

Corn, Wheat, Bread, Sun Symbols, Lugh's Spear

 The Underworld Oracle Deck
By Desiree Goulden

25 Full colour cards

Works with reversed cards

Works with other decks

$23.99 Cad

https://www.thegamecrafter.com/games/the-underworld-oracle-deck

-Owen Lee Heavenhill

To the exhausted witch,
As one,
I see you.
The struggle to stay motivated,
In a world that's not for us,
Hasn't been for us.
The struggle to stay afloat,
Within the chaos,
Self created, human created,
It's too easily dismissed.
I see you,
You're not alone.

Owen Lee Heavenhill

Contributor / Photographer

What Are Influencers?

When doing a reading for a client, often you may feel you need further clarification. Whether you use Tarot, Cartomancy, Palmistry, Numerology, Astrology, Phrenology, Kirlian Photography, Runes, Ogham, or any other method, there will be times where what comes to you is not always clear. At such times it may be necessary to consult other reading materials.

An influencer is described as one to three cards from another source that help to explain what is before you in your initial reading. Often the reader will choose to use Angel cards, Oracle cards, Spirit cards, or any other card of choosing, dependant on the reader's background. (As a Christian Witch and a Metis descendant, I often choose to use Spirit cards or Angel cards.)

The idea behind the influencer card is to streamline your reading. From you will meet someone new, you may see that the individual is not all that he seems to be or that he holds ill intent and to give your client a heads up is better than to send a sheep off into the hills alone to face the wolves.
How to use an influencer?

Begin by doing your intended reading. Look over how it all fits together and not just the individual components. What story does this portray? Is there any underlying issue that it appears they are not dealing with or unwilling to face? If so, you may want to look closer. Ask the subject to select an influencer card or three. First examine the card(s) on there own. What do they signify or what is their accepted meaning?

Then look again at how this works if added to the reading. Place the influencer on your spread where you feel it belongs and consider how this changes the reading, in part or in whole.

It is also possible to use an influencer in absence of a reading. Many psychic/intuitive/empathic readers will draw a card at the start of the day to see how their day may be influenced. In this case, everyone has their own preference as to what method speaks most clearly to them.

One of the more common/popular influencer cards is The Crow. This majestic and familiar bird holds great affinity for many of us as friend or familiar. As watchful and resourceful creatures, these birds represent transformation and change. When the crow card appears, know that you need to be more alert to what is going on around you and how the people and circumstances around you are influencing you. You may not be prepared to face the things that are about to arrive on the scene, but you need to know that you are strong enough to face them, to get through them and that, like the crow collects objects into its nest, you have all the tools that you need. All resources you require will be provided, much as the crow is able to forage for all of its life requirements.

(Disclaimer: This card is from the Spirit Animal deck and its reading comes from my grandmother's teaching as a Ojibway descendant.)

—Dana Lee Beaudreau

Preserving The Past & Future

Our legacy is what we leave behind. The art, structures, religion, environment, and culture that we leave behind will be what future generations judge us by.

The Ancients left us their monuments, temples, buried cities, art, and living religions as a reminder of their great civilizations. We can go to the sites of these old places and connect and learn from those who came before. These remains have stood the test of time... until now.

In 2021 many pagan and historical sites have been put in danger by their governments in the name of "development"

Take for example, the many ancient temples and remains in Greece. As a major source of tourism and income in a country that has been dealing with a Government Debt Crisis since the global financial crisis of 2007-8, it is understandable that the Greek government would funnel money into the preservation and renovation of these sites.

The temple of Apollo Epicurius in Bassae was made in 420 BCE and is a a combination of Doric, Ionic, and Corinthian style architecture. The Corinthian style of ancient Greek pillars and architecture being widely lost to history after being looted by British archaeologists and then lost at sea in the 1900s.

It survived for thousands of years before the Greek government in 1986 decided to cover it completely to "preserve it from winds and acid rain" (A thing that surely were it a problem, would have taken its toll in the thousands of years since it's building.) with a large white tarp. The intent was to rebuild and renovate the already well preserved temple but nothing ever came of it and the project was dropped after the recession. Thus, the beauty of the temple was replaced with a eyesore of a tarp that arguably was not needed.

This is not a stand alone problem within Greece either. The Parthenon is a extremely popular tourist spot in Athens and has been under some sort of reconstruction and preservation for some time now, but recently due to "...poor planning, political pressure to hastily complete a dangerous and destructive renovation" (kosmodromio.gr) it has flooded for the first time in 2500 years. The government pushed for an extensive paved road through the premises for "accessibility" and "connivance".

Things like this is not exclusive to Greece, however. Stonehenge, a notorious pagan monument and site, located in Wiltshire, England, is now in danger of losing it's World Heritage Site title. It is in danger of losing it's status, because a $2.3 billion highway tunnel is planned to be built near the site. If the highway is built as planned, and Stonehenge loses it's status, it will also lose it's protection as a World Heritage Site, leaving it open for the government, developers, and the highest bidder to decide what happens to it.

It is not only places from the past that are at risk by the short sighted need for capitol and development, however. It is also the land of the future.

The native Anishinaabe water protectors are fighting against Enbridge pipeline 3. Line 3 cuts through untouched Anishinabbe treaty wetlands, through the Mississippi river, and the shore of Lake Superior. (The largest freshwater source in not only Canada, but the world). The pipeline puts in danger fresh water sources, the majority of wild rice sources, (a major food sourced for the widely disenfranchised native peoples of Turtle Island / Canada, the USA.) and sacred grounds. It is planned to be completed by the

- end of this year, despite the current legal battle and protests against it.

If this sounds familiar, it's because it happens a lot. This happened with the Standing Rock pipeline, which was eventually stopped by President Barack Obama… and then allowed the moment Trump took office. The natives of Standing Rock Sioux Tribe fought against the pipeline, facing extreme violence at the hands of the police. Just like the Anishinaabe are now. They spoke of a destructive entity called the Black Snake that represents destruction and bares a likeness to oil spills. They warned that the Standing Rock Keystone pipeline would leak, and it was a matter of "when" not "if".

They were proven right in October 2019 when the Keystone pipe leaked and caused one of the largest spills in North Dakota, spilling 383,000 gallons of crude oil in the surrounding wetlands.

We as a species need to start to learn to consider time. The unfortunate reality is that money hungry people and leaders refuse to see anything beyond the present. We need to preserve the cultures and structures of the past. We need to acknowledge that they have stood the test of time and that do not always need our modern "improvements". We need to look to and preserve the future as well as the past. We can not allow our wetlands, and native sites and land to be polluted and destroyed by big oil. (A energy source that is quickly being out paced by green energy.)

We stand at a turning point in time. The reality of our actions are now becoming evident and must be addressed. The Parthenon has already been paved, nothing can be done there. The temple of Apollo is fine, even if it is an eyesore now. Stonehenge has recently won their fight against losing it's title and the tunnel being built. The Anishinaabe have had no such luck. Faced with RCMP and private hired police violence, Enbridge ignoring their protests and paying law

The water protectors need your support. The links below are petitions you can sign, and places to donate to protect the water and the native peoples who's food and sacred land is in danger.

https://www.stopline3.org/take-action

https://www.honorearth.org/stop_line_3

https://mn350.org/campaigns/stop-line-3-pipeline/

https://stopthemoneypipeline.com/line3/

—Desirée Goulden

All About Sage

What is Sage?

Also known as Salvia Flower, sage grows in summer to autumn in sunny well-drained areas.
Part of the mint family, these plants grow tall with square flowers and velvety leaves. Good for the planet, they attract hummingbirds, butterflies, and bees to the region. They also work to repel deer, rabbits, small animals, and other garden pests.
While there are many different kinds of sage and every type has its own uses, traditionally, sage is used by many of the arts for cleansing evil or dark chi from the area where practitioners have been assisting their subjects.

Types of Sage

The most commonly types of sage used by witches would be common white sage (used for smudging, sometimes combined with lavender or mint), garden sage is most commonly used for brewing a tea used to enhance memory, Pineapple sage which can be brewed to make an antibacterial medicine, Clary sage is used as an eye bath in order to enforce clarity of vision. According to many sources online, there are potentially over 700 different types of Sage.

The Many Uses of Sage

Over history, sage has been used for many purposes. The most commonly acknowledged these days is that of a purifier, whether through sage sticks, incense, or a tea infusion (when trying to purify the person from the inside). It has also been used in cooking, and while we all believe that this is for the lovely taste it adds to our food, the root of this practice comes from the beliefs that medicinally, when consumed, sage could heal a damaged or sick liver.

Sage was also associated with wealth. The more sage a person grew in their garden the wealthier the household was believed to be. A bath of the leaves infused with lavender was believed to reduce fever, calm anxiety and agitation, and to enhance a person's visionary powers. It is also believed that a person bathing in sage and rosemary would enhance their life and add to their longevity. When stirred in wine, can be used against cramps and side stitches caused by gas.

Harvesting Your Sage

Never use iron or steel tools in harvesting your sage. Also, sage pushes forth best if it is harvested in full moonlight. Some forms of sage are perennials and taking care of your harvesting ensures a good crop from year to year.

Preparations for Sage

Do not limit yourself in the possible applications of sage. Sage can be made into a bath, a tea, a smudge stick, an amulet, a potion, a poultice, a cooking herb, or an essential oil.

Warning: Too much consumption of the sage oil, not essential oil, will lead to a feeling of nausea that can be confused with intoxication.

-Dana Lee Beaudreau

Modern ethics in the online occult & spiritual communities.

(Note, this is from my experience online and contains dark content as well as personal opinions)

The 2020s has brought a wave of social awareness and justice in all walks of life. The occult and spiritual communities in particular.

Many of the magical practices we share today have similarities or are borrowed from other practices. As such, we should all pay attention and be active in the attempt to learn and replace practices and terminology that takes from or negatively effects a minority or closed demographic / practice / religion.

These will be some small explanations for newer notions that many may not know about if they are not present in the online sphere of the occult & paganism. Some may have even been common place in your practices for some time, so here are some practices and terms that may land you in hot water online for doing / saying.

Please note that everyone has their own ethics and views on things and many of these comes down to ones personal values and views. This is by no means a "IF YOU DO THIS YOU ARE EVIL" list, this is only to help people while interacting with the wider occult and pagan communities in a respectful manner.

Blessings Without Permission

While one may think that receiving blessings and beneficial workings would always be good, this is not always the case. It is always best to seek the permission of the person you are blessing. Failing to do so at best can be just uncomfortable.

It's like being told by a Christian that they will pray for you. It may be a kindness in their eyes, but unless you are part of their religion it can be awkward at best. At worst, it can be a notion from a religion your own religion or personal beliefs come in conflict with. This can go for all walks and paths. Not every religion has had a happy past with others.

It can also bring up problems with your deities if you have a close working relationship with them or worship of them. If someone tries to bless you invoking the name of a deity that is in direct conflict with your own deity it could back fire on the person you are trying to bless, or yourself.

Blessings and beneficial workings can be a kindness, but it would be best for you to touch base with the person you're trying to work on so that you don't step on anyone's toes or make things awkward.

Claiming Unearned Titles

Titles can show your experience in situations wherein it is relevant. Unfortunately, many people see them as a way to get clout online.

For most titles, there are years of experience you need, a person to bestow the title upon you, prerequisites to meet, and people to validate that you are who and what you claim to be. You can not just decide that calling yourself a Priestess would look good for your image and proclaim to the world that you are a Priestess, and should be treated as such. That's not how that works, and it's a great way to be laughed at by actual officials of whatever order you are claiming to be clergy for.

This isn't just for the title of Priestess, there are those who are claiming that they are Crones and Elders online because they are older that others in their online or offline social circle... while being 30 with less than 6 years of experience. Being the oldest in your social circle does not a Crone or Elder make. You can not claim these titles arbitrarily whilst having less experience than most 19-year-olds. It takes away from the weight that these titles carry and thus the validity of actual Crones and Elders. To put it in perspective, you wouldn't walk into a retirement home of military vets and demand the same respect they are given because "I'm a 90 year old vet too!" while obviously being a 35 year old librarian.

Closing Open Practices

This seems to be a phenomenon I have seen exclusively online by well meaning younger people trying to be socially aware without really doing much to look into what they are looking at.

People have tried to claim that tarot cards are a closed practice belonging only to the Romani people... Despite the Romani people saying that's false, and that Tarot can be traced back to a card game in Italy and France, known as trionfi, tarocchi, tarock, an eventually tarot. It is said that standard playing cards are based off them originally.

While closed or marginalized practices and peoples may incorporate certain objects, or have similar practices that does not mean that that is the only correct version, and everything else is stolen from them. Humanity and it's cultures are not so unique as we often think and there are many similarities between practices.

You can acknowledge that there are similarities but jumping to claiming that something is stolen without the proper research, while ignoring the people from the practice that you're trying to close saying that you're wrong isn't doing what you think it is. It may actively make people take actual closed practices less seriously as they assume that is just another kid online trying to get social justice brownie points.

Gypsy

This is a term we all know to describe the travelling Romani peoples. There are however a growing population of Romani people within the USA and Canada who have started to speak up against the term "Gypsy".

For a background, the Romani people are a Indo-Aryan peoples who traditionally are nomadic. They live throughout Europe, and the diaspora live within the Americas. A major aspect of their history is their enslavement at the hands of present day Romania which they endured from the years of 1241 to the 1850s. (Roughly 600 years.)

Within Czechoslovakia starting in 1973 forced sterilizations have been forced upon Romani women which while no longer policy, still exists in high levels of coerced sterilization of Romani women.

Throughout the world, the Roma populations deal with their encampments being destroyed, high levels of poverty, low

- levels of education and educational opportunities, and high levels of employment discrimination,

The English word for the Romani people is Gypsy and has become a point of contention in the west. The west has a peculiar relationship with the Roma people.

We in the west still see them as thieves, creating terms like "gypped" to explain if you've been scammed or stolen from. We still see them as uneducated, impoverished, travellers and even though we have not had the history with them that Romania has, they still deal with a lot of prejudice in the west.

While we cast them in this negative life, we somehow still idolize a romanticized version of their life. We promote the "traveller" and "boho" lifestyle, taking influence from Roma traditions, fashions, etc and profiting off the white washed and polished version of them. While we use them to bring in profit in the form of fashion, music, lifestyle blogs and influencers, the actual Roma people deal with the same low quality of life as they have endured elsewhere in the world. We profit from shows like "My Big Fat Gypsy Wedding" and laugh and mock their society while funnelling money into white TV show runners.

We actively equate "Travellers" and "Boho" with whiteness and money, while the people we based and take these notions from as "Gypsy" "Thieves" "Stupid" "Dirty". These are very particular problems within western society that is specific to the Romani experience in Canada and The US. While Gypsy was originally just the English term for Romani, we have turned it into a slur, and the Romani people have seen and voiced that.

There are growing waves of Romani groups who take the term "Gypsy" as a slur and it makes sense, because that's exactly how we have been using the term as. There are people across seas who proclaim that "It's just the English term, and it's not a slur you westerners are insane and obsessed with oppression."... while refusing to acknowledge that a American Romani person faces completely different challenges and realities of oppression than a Romani person from England. There are people who have grown up calling Romani people "Gypsies" and claim that "That's just what they're called" while ignoring the Roma people who try to explain why that word has evolved as words always to in the ever changing English language. There are also Romani people in the west who disagree with the idea that it's a slur.

No matter your ideas of the word, many people are telling you that it is a slur that has negative connotations that harms the people you say it to. When someone tells you something hurts them, it is never your place to say "no it doesn't." Roma people from the west are asking that in western dominated spaces that you use the word "Roma" rather than "Gypsy" and while this segment may seem long and preachy, it's length is only trying to explain why they feel this way. We should all work to make the world a more comfortable place for everyone and attempt to listen to people who we unintentionally hurt without claiming that they are wrong.

Love Spells

Good ol' love spells. One of the first thing people think about when they think of Witches. Love spells have gotten a lot of flack recently with the new waves of young practitioners coming into the craft.

There is the false idea that doing a love spell on someone is exactly the same as drugging and raping them and that consent can never be given under a love spell. This is over estimating the effects of a love spell. People can give consent under them, but there are still very dangerous aspects to love spells.

People under love spells (or at least improperly done love spells where in the other person is not privy to it being done.) have a tenancy for being violently obsessive. These people very quickly turn to stalking, harming others to get the person who they were worked on to love, not being able to think or focus of anything else, obsessive dreams about the person they were made to want for. In some cases if this goes too far it is not uncommon for them to meet violent and deadly ends.

Love spells can be very effective ways to build on a existing relationship between two consenting partners utilizing a experienced practitioner who knows how to properly do the working. People in general look down upon doing love spells in general, but particularly on an unwilling and unknowing partner.

Rule Of Three

You'd be hard pressed to meet a practitioner or pagan who doesn't know about the Rule Of Three. A major tenant of Neo-Wiccan tradition, it states that everything you do will return to you in 3's and "An do as ye wilt if it harms none." Unfortunately this very useful general rule has been weaponized by some people much in the same way as sin and hell has been weaponized by the Christians

- against magical practices they disagree with.

Wicca is very much credited with bringing both the occult and paganism to the west, but that does not make Wicca the moral ruler of all magick. Not every witch is Wiccan, so when you come onto a post of a person doing a baneful working, and comment about how they "need to adhere to the 3 fold law." it doesn't reflect well upon yourself. Your morals are not everyone else's morals. Your religion isn't everyone else's religion. If you would not take well to a Christian telling you you are going to burn in hell for being Wiccan, you should not then turn to people doing baneful workings and tell them to follow the 3 fold law or they will be punished by karma. We get what we give, yes, so by that notion we should give respect for practices that are not our own.

Smudging

Smudging is part of closed native practices. Unless you are a native from the west, you can not and likely have no idea how to properly smudge. You are looking for the term "smoke cleansing."

While smudging is part of native practice (native religion and practices within the west being illegal until 1851 in Canada and 1978 in the USA) and incorporates sacred medicine, prayer, and tools that we have no claim to as the peoples who have made them illegal, and attempted to wipe out through systematic oppression and a attempted cultural genocide.

Smoke cleansing exists across the world in nearly every practice and you can pull from them to smoke cleanse more effectively than attempting to cleanse by smudging without knowing how to do so, and frustrating the native spirits who observe you as you do this.

Speaking For Gods

We have many ways to speak to divinity. Through mediums, divination, observation of the natural world, many are in contact and receive messages from their deities. That being said, you being able to get these messages does not mean you speak for the gods.

If someone is doing something or saying something that you dislike, it will never be your place to claim that "God(dess) XYZ said you're wrong and evil and they hate you!". I is a best distasteful, at worst a bold display of hubris which can put you at odds with your community and the deity in question.

- If a deity dislikes something, they will let the person know directly themselves, not through a strangers tarot, oracle, or runes.

Spirit Animal

Another native term which have very significance religious value exclusive to native people and tribes in the west. While some form of spiritual animal guides have existed in some cultures across time (in Greek; spiritus animalis in Latin, etc) the Spirit Animals of native practice are different and part of a marginalized and previously illegal religious practice.

While some claim that they are practising Italian magic and that's the English word, I personally believe that if they were actually practising Italian magic and referring to Italian spirit animals, they would say the Italian word. People do have animal spirit guides, and if that is to what you are referring to, then they can be called animal guides as not to infringe on the native practices. If you are claiming you are using the native spirit animals while not being native or part of any tribe and have not gone through the proper channels, you are either mistaken or wrongfully practising a closed practice.

Spiritual Bypassing

"The mundane over the magical." No amount of magical prowess, or spiritual belief comes before medical science. If you or (as in most cases) your child are feeling different to others. If you don't connect with people, feel what you perceive to be "too much" or "not enough" then you need to seek out a doctor. Everyone wants to feel special and many are afraid of certain medical labels, but ignoring them and applying spiritual terminology while posting dangerous information online harms yourself and others.

There is no shame in a medical diagnoses. There is shame in ignoring your mental and physical health and actively convincing others to do so because of some magickal or mythical reason with little real evidence.

UPG As Gospel

Unverified personal gnosis is not absolute truth. People experience everything from their particular perspective. We all look to the same sky and see different shades of blue. Just because you see things one way, doesn't make it the only way. I may personally believe that Ares has brown eyes, but it is not my place to attack

- those who would claim that he has blue. Just because you may experience something, it does not mean that you should attack or go after others who have not experience that same thing.

White Sage

White Sage is part of native smudging rituals and is a sacred medicine which is endangered in the Americas. Unless you are part of the native communities, it is destructive to buy White Sage which is sold by white retailers. The herb is endangered and should be available to the natives who's religion it belongs to, and if money is to be made off it, it should be money in the pockets of the natives who are not afforded the same opportunities as the rest of us.

There are about 600 species of sage, and you can buy common sage for less at Bulk Barn, Target, Walmart, and most grocery stores.

-Desirée Goulden

Metaphysical Crossword!

Answers in back of publication.

1- A nature based religion created in the 1900s.
2- The religion of the Ancient Greeks.
3- The people, and religion that is known as the Vikings.
4- A profession, not a people.
5- A non-Abrahamic religion.
6- One who sees the future.
7- An alphabet and divination tool.
8- Answers yes no and maybe questions.
9- God who created the Norse runes.
10- Father of Hermes whose epithet is Xenios

The Future, Regrettably
Coming Fall 2021

The debut urban fantasy novel from Desirée Goulden, prequel to the Aurora Garroway series.

Julian is a man with nothing but a name. Woken from a coma and thrust into a war he does not want to fight, he is the body guard and right hand man of a tyrannical cult leader, Rose. Escape is futile and attempts cause innocent people to be killed to keep him in line. With death as the only escape, he becomes reckless in battle, hoping to be cut down and finally escape the life he is trapped in.

Rose notices and offers him a boon: stay in line and do as she says and he will be able to visit the future in his dreams. He will be able to live a comfortable life and see why the Conduit Hierarchy's war is just, and how it will better the world.

Will this be enough to pacify Julian? Or will this motivate him to tear down the organization that seeks to control him, and find the truth?

Olympian Crossword!

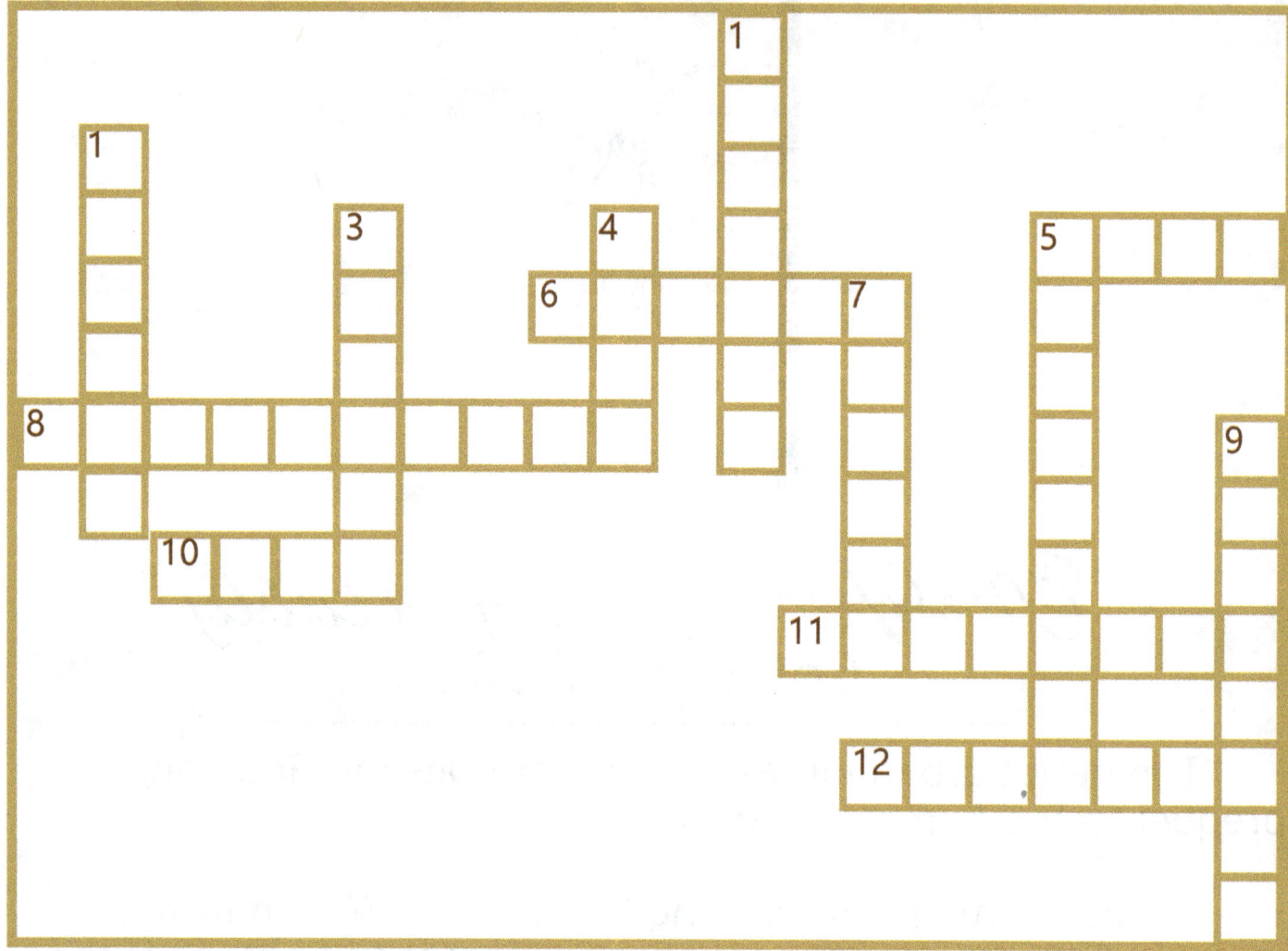

Answers in back of publication.

Across

5. God of civil order and battle lust.
6. A former Olympian
8. Creator of Talos.
10. Competed against Aphrodite and Athena for the golden apple.
11. God of earthquakes
12. Goddess of childbirth protector of girls.

Down

1. Goddess of agriculture.
2. Creator of the lyre.
3. Goddess of good wisdom.
4. God of kings and fate.
5. Loved Adonis.
7. God of archery and plague.
9. Reborn Zagrus.

Crystal Crossword!

Answers in back of publication.

Across
3. range of colours and crystal tends to be highly fluorescent under UV light
5. a set of closely related minerals forming a group whose stone comes in many vibrant colours
7. strontium based crystal
9. A purple variety of quartz
10. commonly associated with malachite and has deep blue colouring

Down
1. dark green, copper-based mineral
2. uncommon stone. vibrant, pink to rose red colored mineral
4. naturally formed as smoky quartz is slowly heated inside the earth
6. most common type of crystal
8. Fools Gold

Introduction To The Sigils Of Hermes

Since finding out I am a medium, there is little I have actually done with the gift beyond personal deity communication. Partially from being socially awkward, and partially because a deep fear of being judged. I've kept my abilities to myself and gone about my life... that was until I released the Underworld Oracle Deck.

The moment I began that project, Hermes (a god I worship and work with closely) took immediate interest. He kept an eye on my progress and made remarks about runes, divination in general, and the affordability of most divination tools. I made a one off comment about how most divination tools are pricey, and those that aren't are not accessible to people living in the brook closet. He told me that I should "figure out a solution to that" and I laughed it off.

Hermes, however, did not. Apparently to Hermes "You should figure out a solution to that." means, "you are going to do intense guided meditation with me to access your akashic records in conjunction with my input and help to create a new divination system, and you're going to like it." While the hand guide and sets are not yet finished, here is a sneak peak of the project and a brief explanation of the sigils.

The sigils of Hermes are 12 sigils connected to the zodiac and created by Hermes with the aid of a human scribe. These sigils can be used in divination, as well as spellwork of all kinds, much like the Norse Eldar Futhark runes. For accessibility the Sigils of Hermes can be created by anybody and come in 3 forms for covert and affordable options. These are made with affordability and people who are in the boom closet in mind, as they were created when I myself was homeless and in a place where divination tools would be looked at poorly.

The first form of the sigils comes in the form of playing dice. Take 2 dice of different colours and on each side of the faces of the die, put a mark to denote the "bottom" of the sigil. Herme's sigils are read in 4s, roll the pair of dice twice get the full reading and record the results. Alterntiavely, if you have a 12 sided die roll it 4 times. (If you have a 12 sided die, we know you are a DnD nerd and have more, you may chose to just roll 4 of them.) If you get a repeat sigil, reroll the last.

The second form are tiles or stones. Take a permanent marker and mark your tiles or stones with the sigils and toss to read them. The 4 that stand apart from the tossed pile are the 4 for your reading.

The third form are playing cards or oracle cards. If you have blank cards of some sort, simply draw the sigils on, shuffle and pull 4. If you have a standard playing deck, remove the king cards and shuffle. Numbers are as ordered with Ace being 1- Movement, Jack being 11- The Summit, and Queen being 12- The Bolt Of Zeus. Shuffle and pull discarding duplicates.

1-Movement.
Action, life, the possibility of growth and new beginnings. Associated with Aries.
Reverse: Stop, stalemate, death, endings.

2-Push.
Movement, force, effort, drive to succeed, initialization. Associated with Taurus.
Reverse: Obstacles, lack of energy, apathy.

3-Block.
Stops, setbacks, blocking, protection. Associated with Gemini.
Reverse: Continuations, breaking down of protections, overstepped boundaries, danger.

4-Lance.
Power, force, action, focused attack, damage. Associated with Cancer.
Reverse: half-hearted, ineffective, weak willed, failed attack or approach.

5-Oar.
Support, guidance, teamwork, leadership. Associated with Leo
Reverse: Working alone, follower mentality, lack of support, stubbornness.

6-Radiance.
Hope, positivity, victory, earned knowledge, self confidence. Associated with Virgo.
Reverse: Self-consciousness, disrepair, depression, ignorance.

7-The Shield.
Protection, safety, community, family. Associated with Libra.
Reverse: Isolation, broken family, broken relationships, vulnerability.

8-The All Seeing Eye.
Divine oversight, being watched, being seen, clarity. Associated with Scorpio.
Reverse: Hidden, Unknown, confusion, sneaky.

9-The Serpent.
Fertility, strength, nature, haste. Associated with Sagittarius.
Reverse: Weakness, barren, sloth.

10-The Spiraling Star
Journey, soul journey, learning, expanding, the spirit, human imperfections, uniqueness. Associated with Capricorn.
Reverse: Artificial perfection, copycat, dead ends, willful ignorance.

11-The Summit.
Peak of power, the highest point, authority, ability, royalty, a steady base. Associated with Aquarius.
Reverse: Rock bottom, no stability, lack of authority, ineptitude.

12-The Bolt Of Zeus.
Destructive power, removing obstacles, destroying what held you back, ascension to power. Associated with Pisces.

Reverse: Held back, fall from grace, self-destruction, obstacles.

Keep an eye out for the official handbook with more in depth information and interpretations, as well as official dice, card, and tile sets! More information to come on TalesOfTheGods.com and the TalesOfTheGods & Practical Witchcraft Magazine. If you use the Sigils of Hermes, let us know! Tag them with #sigilsofhermes on TikTok, Instagram, Twitter, and Tumblr and let us know what you think!

—Desirée Goulden

Jim Two Snakes
Spiritual Advisor

 facebook.com/jimtwosnakes

 instagram.com/jimtwosnakes

 patreon.com/spiritualdad

Many people think the term Spirituality is about religion, but it doesn't have to be. In fact I think most people are Spiritual no matter if they are religious or not! Spirituality is about understanding and exploring your higher purpose, your interconnectedness to all of creation, and living authentically. It is my goal to help you feel inspired and fulfilled.

I do this by asking questions, giving suggestions, and then helping develop ways of marking progress and providing accountability. You don't have to believe the same way I, or anyone else, does. The coaching is centered around your needs and beliefs. I can't do the work for you, but I can help you with motivation and seeing things from a new perspective. Contact me now to schedule a free 15 minute initial consultation.

> Reprint from the Fall 2020 edition*

A Restraining Order Due To Religion

While scrolling on TikTok I came across a rather concerning video with a woman claiming her neighbour took out a restraining order on her, because she's Wiccan. This stuck with me because, in the past few years, the world has become a more safe place for Wiccans, Pagans, and the like. While we do catch some flack now and then for our practice and beliefs, it's far better than even 10 years ago, so I was struck by this video.

Of course, I seem to have an issue keeping my nose to myself, so I had to interview her for the magazine. Note that personal information will be withheld, save for her user name.

When talking to shipwreckshark, hereby known as Shark, the first thing you notice is her warm personality. She's completely sociable, easy to talk to, and kind. Shark does not come off as the kind of person to start drama or enjoy conflict.

She lives in Alaska on base, as her husband is in the military. She lives with him and her young son. She is Wiccan and Puerto Rican and is studying to be an EMT with a 4.0 average in school. By all means, she is the ideal American, yet she found herself at the end of a restraining order based on bigotry.

So what happened? What lead to this? Shark and the neighbour originally started as friends but there were warning signs that the neighbour wasn't what she seemed from the start. Now everyone has at least one witch aesthetic thing, and Shark is no different. She had a Ouija board door mat which was the first thing that made the neighbour seemed uneasy about. Shark claims she's had a pride flag on the outside of her house so she was taken by surprise when the mat was a point of contention.

Alaska is a rather conservative state and Shark claims that the state can be rather unfriendly to both the Native and spiritual communities, so she accepted that the neighbour would likely be uncomfortable with her path, but nothing would prepare her for how the neighbour would act.

From the get-go, the neighbour would be uncomfortable around her house if so much as a tarot deck was out, so she began packing the more notable items away if the neighbour was coming over. That being said, she seemed interested, Shark commented about how the neighbour would ask questions about her beliefs, but no matter what she said, the neighbour would comment about how 'scary' it was.

Shark is a Wiccan and doesn't use magic to harm anyone, not that she could if she wanted to, given the Wiccan Rede which states to harm none and preaches the Rule Of Three. It was enough to make Shark uncomfortable and anyone reading can already see some red flags.

She would begin to show some toxic traits as Shark's husband went through a mental health crisis. Shark supported him through it, as a good partner should. The neighbour seemed to take offence to Shark's approach. Shark alleges that through her husband's difficulties the neighbour was urging her to leave him. The neighbour continued to keep trying to push her way into Shark's life and situation and it came to the point where she had to set up boundaries and tell her that she was no longer comfortable with her actions and that they couldn't be friends any more more.

The neighbour took this setting of boundaries personally and began saying that Shark implied that she hexes everyone she doesn't like.

Eventually, Shark's husband's situation improved and she rekindled her friendship with the neighbour. Yule comes and she has the neighbour over and things seemingly go better as the neighbour doesn't comment on her décor (a hung pentacle with antlers and holly). A few weeks later Shark asked her neighbour if she would babysit her son as she had mentioned she had experience babysitting. The neighbour refused to do it in Shark's house as apparently, her house made the neighbour uncomfortable. It was clear she was on her best behaviour on Yule and she didn't plan on continuing to pretend any more.

The neighbour continued to push to have the kid at her house to the point where Shark began to get nervous, which caused the neighbour to take offence and begin her toxic antics again. Shark decided enough was enough and it became clear they could not be friends any more, despite her attempts.

This is where the neighbour becomes unhinged. She seemed to take Shark's setting of boundaries and not putting up with her toxicity as a personal slight and began a campaign of slander against Shark.

A shortened list of the accusations flung against Shark is as follows: tampering with her car in the middle of winter, smoking weed inside the house (note that marijuana is legal in Alaska, and she never had anything on base or smoked on base.), having and holding drugs on base, walking down the stairs in her home and slamming on the connected wall to disturb the neighbour.

Attached are images submitted by Shark. We have permission to share images from the report that she received. All names are censored to protect the identities of people involved

This went on for about a month before Shark confronted her. The neighbour would begin calling the cops on her numerous times. She noted that the neighbour herself had a smell of weed to her and she felt like she was trying to set her up as part of her little vendetta.

They ended up needing to talk to the military housing company because the neighbour ended up filing a complaint. This in itself is aggravating as Shark had filed a complaint against the neighbour when she began this over a month before, but was ignored.

Shark brought up the neighbour's anti-pagan stance and was ignored. The two left with nothing being done.

Two days later, Shark was woken by the police knocking at her door. Given the stress of her life mixed with the fact that her husband was away on training, this triggered a panic attack. She had assumed the police were there to tell her that her husband was hurt. Luckily when he heard about the incident and talked to the police, it was more of a formality than anything.

This neighbour apparently has a history of being somewhat of a Karen and has harassed and made enemies of many of the people she's met in her life.

The police eventually came back when she was calmer and explained why they were there. Shark had a cinnamon broom attached to her fence in her yard. Cinnamon brooms can be used to "sweep away" obstacles or negativity of people that were brought into your home. Seems like exactly the kind of thing a woman in her position would need, frankly.

Attached to the broom was a spell charm protected by a zip-lock bag with the words "Blessed Be" on it to protect from the constant rainstorms they were dealing with. The neighbour called the cops because she got the idea in her head that the bag had her name in it and it was a hex or curse against her.

The neighbour took it upon herself to bring her to court to get a restraining order on her shortly after. This is where things get... tricky. It is no secret that the military is usually pretty conservative, on top of the fact that she lives in a very conservative state, as she mentioned earlier.

Not only was the neighbour awarded the restraining order against Shark, but the judge also said that Shark's "religion can instill fear". The neighbour had a lawyer and Shark, as a mother and student did not so there wasn't a lot she could do aside from just dealing with it.

So to recap: an angry ex-friend who tried to get her [Shark] to leave her husband when he went through a mental health crisis harassed and lied and wasted police and military resources to get back at Shark for not putting up with her toxic and domineering attitude. The military refused to take Shark, the Puerto Rican Wiccan's harassment complaint, yet dealt with the white Christian's complaint quickly despite the obvious lies. Despite the right to religious freedom on which the United States Of America is founded on, a judge looked her in the eyes and told her that because of her religion, people fear her to the point where restraining orders are an appropriate course of action.

It baffles the mind to think about the hypocrisy of this situation. This is not something that would ever happen if we turned the tables. You would not see months of harassment, fake phone calls to the police, and restraining orders because you saw a bible once at your friend's house, and then she hung a cross outside. Why is it that we bend over backward to cater to Christians whenever we can, from removing their kids from sex ed to literally forming the bank and work cycles of the country around their practices and religion but all a non-Christian has to do to get BROUGHT TO ACTUAL COURT is to hang a good luck charm?

Shark is preparing to fight back however, she will be appealing and doing whatever she can to make this right. She is not laying down and taking this crap. She is building her appeal, but no longer feels safe in her own home. Her husband leaves again soon and she doesn't leave the house without her family or friends on video call as now the neighbour has installed cameras focused on her cars to watch her. She fears that the moment her husband leaves, the neighbour will begin again, as she has been doing this when her husband is gone.

I wish there was a resolution to the situation, but unfortunately, this has only just begun. Who knows how long the appeal will take or if she will even win the appeal. Shark makes it very clear that she does not think that this sort of thing would happen in other states, and I'd have to agree.

-Desirée Goulden

Metaphysical Crossword Answers!

1- Thor
2- Odin
3- Oracle
4- Deosil
5- Zeus
6- Wicca
7- Minotaur
8- Hellenismos
9- Futharkn
10- Pagan
11- Norse

Olympian Crossworsd Answers!

1- Demeter
2- Hemes
3- Athena
4- Zeus
5- Aphrodite
6- Hestia
7- Apollo
8- Hephaestus
9- Dionysus
10- Hera
11- Poseidon
12- Artemis

Olympian Crossworsd Answers!

1- malachite
2- rhodochrosite
3- fluorite
4- citrine
5- garnet
6- quartz
7- celestite
8- pyrite
9- amethyst
10- azurite

Have news?

Have a story to share or a cause to fight for?

Let us know!

Email us at TalesOTheGods@gmail.com and we will cover your story!

Enjoyed this edition? Rate us on GoodReads.com or Amazon!
Keep an eye on TalesOfTheGods.com or the Practical Witchcraft group for updates on free giveaways like our Litha & Pride edition!

Photo Credits

Owen Lee Heavenhill - Cover, pg 2, 4, 5

Soulful Stock - pg 6

Roberto Barbara - pg 8

Paulina H - 12

Joshua Rawson Harris - pg 14

"Short and jam packed with useful knowledge. Great for avid readers of the craft and metaphysical. Great way to stay in touch with the the pagan community!"
-GoodReads reviewer

A publication printed on every day of the wheel of the year. From an ever-changing group of writers and contributors that bring education, entertainment, and spiritual and occult news for people of all paths and expertise. Read the Lughnasadh edition and learn about the holiday, sage, modern ethics in the online sphere, the Sigils Of Hermes, a restraining order against a person for being Wiccan. Have fun with our crosswords and take in the poetry and photography from Owen!

With every purchase of the TalesOfTheGods & Practical Witchcraft magazine, you support small creators! Income for this magazine is split equally between all contributors, and we are always welcoming new people to our team!

Want to join? Have a story, news, or a skill to share? Write in to TalesOTheGods@gmail.com!

Feel free to drop us a review on GoodReads or Amazon and keep an eye out on TalesOfTheGods.com or in the Practical Witchcraft and Paganism FaceBook group for freebies and updates! Thank you for reading and we can't wait to see you in the Mabon edition!

-to say they most likely had a similar culture of Pederasty as well.

Furthermore this is ignoring the fact that Artemis is a Goddess who is commonly depicted as a child. Artemis is one of 3 virginal Goddesses who all protected their virginity violently. To claim that these Goddesses are lesbians and to worship them in a sexual manor of any sort would likely to draw their ire. Their maidenhood may be linked to their sexual relationships with male Gods and mortals, but you need to respect the ancient and current Greek cultures who state point form that they are virgins.

We often forget that these are living religions that formed the basis of Greek culture, and though Christianity has swept through and majorly taken over they are still important and alive. Imposing western ideals on sexuality and gender and speaking over traditional interpretation of the Greek Gods is activity taking part of the colonization of Hellenismos.

We want to see ourselves in a society that often makes us feel like we aren't normal, and that is understandable. Unfortunately sexuality and gender expression is a deep and complicated topic in modern times, and doubly so for ancient times. It is not bad to see yourself or your identity in the Gods and Heroes of yore, it is however not possible to put our modern terms on them, and can often times be insulting to the time and cultures they come from.

— Desirée Goulden

Autumn Equinox

Book Review
The Great Work

Ogham
An introduction

Karens
They're witches too apparently

Music
Can it influence magic?

Reddit Witches
Curse the Taliban?

Witch Shop
A cult in disguise?

Altar Art
And more...

Tales Of The Gods & - PRACTICAL WITCHCRAFT -

Thank You

By buying this magazine, you support small business owners and small creators!

TalesOfTheGods aims to connect the metaphysical and spiritual communities.

Cover Photo - Matteo Spagnolo.

If you would like to write in anonymously, or join our team for the next edition feel free to send a email to TalesOTheGods@gmail.com

TalesOfTheGods, September 2021

facebook.com/groups/665578877692886

Contributors

Desirée Goulden	Owner, layout design, contributor
Owen Lee Heavenhill	Photographer, Contributor
Dana Lee Beaudreau	Founding member, Contributor

The TalesOfTheGods & Practical Witchcraft magazine is a community project. Our roster of contributors is constantly shifting. Everyone who works on the magazine takes home an equal take of the income from the sales of this magazine.

We aim to bring education and entertainment to people of all levels of experience and paths. If you have a point of view that you would like to share with the world, feel free to reach out to join us. We are currently looking for people of colour to join us. Whether you are a teacher, or just interested in taking part, we have a place for you.

Have a shop or product you want to share with the world? Contact us and we will run a free full page ad for you in the next edition! We release on every day of the wheel of the year, so it's easy to follow release dates!

We understand that there may be some who may not want to support Amazon, so we have made the shift from publishing through Kindle Direct Publishing for our paper back editions to Ingram Spark. This will allow for wider distribution (Chapters, Barns & Noble, indie book shops) for those who want to support us without supporting Amazon and Jeff Bezos.

Please know that all opinions are that of the contributor and may not reflect the team in general.

Contents

Reflections From Owen On Religion	PAGE 2
Can Music Influence Your Magic?	PAGE 6
Tiffany Lazic's "The Great Work": a Review	PAGE 10
An Introduction to Ogham	PAGE 15
A Witch Called Karen	PAGE 18
Witch shop new illegal owner running a cult?	PAGE 20
Reddit Witches "Hex" The Taliban	PAGE 27
Altar Art	PAGE 34

 The Underworld Oracle Deck
By Desiree Goulden

25 Full colour cards

Works with reversed cards

Works with other decks

$23.99 Cad

https://www.thegamecrafter.com/games/the-underworld-oracle-deck

Reflections From Owen On Religion

Before I started working with the other gods, I was at one point a christian. I was raised in the church. I have since gone back to church, and let me tell you, when the pagan goes back to church and starts working with Jesus again, things get a little weird. Questions like, "If I wanted to do communion again, but with the rest of my deities and guides instead, how would that work?" That question was after I decided I needed to make it an entire ritual, complete with baking the bread from scratch, with intention, picking out the wine.

So, to answer that question, how would one? The answer is easy, you pour for them, when you would pour for the disciples.

The day that I actually made it, I was actually surprisingly nervous. This was my first time doing communion in probably about 5 years, and to be honest, I wasn't sure if I could at first either. Meditation and reflection, and the knowledge that I don't worship any gods, I only work with them, so therefore none of them are before any of them, led me to realize that yes, I still could.

I went out that day and picked out a bottle of red wine, I don't have any advice on what I picked. I picked out a petite sirah, but really, whatever you want to drink is fine. (And, yes, grape juice, or cranberry juice, will always be a good substitute if you don't want to drink.) And when I went home, I started the bread so it could rise. As I started kneading it, I put my intentions in it.

Once the bread was rise, I put it in the oven. I kept the basics of communion (from a Methodist stand point.) the same, and added in a few of my own touches and changed a few small things to just better suit me and my spiritual path.

This all leads up a broader point though, of, part of why christianity never quite felt right to me, was because something always felt missing, like there could be something more. Piecing everything for communion together into one big ritual, like I would do with my other dieties, it didn't feel like anything was missing anymore. I do think the intention and thought I put into it really helped with what was missing.

-Owen Lee Heavenhill

Jim Two Snakes
Spiritual Advisor

 jimtwosnakes.net

 facebook.com/jimtwosnakes

 instagram.com/jimtwosnakes

 patreon.com/spiritualdad

Many people think the term Spirituality is about religion, but it doesn't have to be. In fact I think most people are Spiritual no matter if they are religious or not! Spirituality is about understanding and exploring your higher purpose, your interconnectedness to all of creation, and living authentically. It is my goal to help you feel inspired and fulfilled.

I do this by asking questions, giving suggestions, and then helping develop ways of marking progress and providing accountability. You don't have to believe the same way I, or anyone else, does. The coaching is centered around your needs and beliefs. I can't do the work for you, but I can help you with motivation and seeing things from a new perspective. Contact me now to schedule a free 15 minute initial consultation.

CONSULTATION PACKAGE

A call, a game plan, and a follow up.
One initial hour long call via Zoom, Skype or Discord
A recording of the call you can refer back to later
20 minute follow up / accountability call two weeks later

$150

TAROT READING

Divination to help guide you.
1-3 questions, submitted by email
Photos, a written report, and an audio report of your reading sent via email
48 hour turn around

$60

FIRE CEREMONY

A POWERFUL ceremony of change performed on your behalf.

You will receive instructions how to prepare for the ceremony
I will conduct the Fire Ceremony at an arranged time
You will receive a video of your ceremony, and any insights I have

$60

A POWERFUL ceremony of change performed in person for you or a group.
For individuals or groups up to ten
I will bring all needed supplies, teach you about the history of the Q'ero and
the ceremony, how to participate, and then perform the ceremony
Please contact us about larger groups and gatherings

$250

SPIRITUAL CLEANSINGS

Removal of heavy energy and negativity.
For individuals, homes, or businesses.
I will bring all needed supplies.
Home cleansings can include help sorting and tidying
Rates will vary depending on number of people and/or size of house or
business. Contact us for more information

The Best Value For Jim's Services visit
www.jimtwosnakes.net or
www.patreon.com/spiritualdad for more
information

Can Music Influence Your Magic?

　　According to psychological research, infants are able to detect music even in the womb. It stands to reason then that music, which is found in almost every culture, has a large impact on almost every creature on the planet. Music alters our moods, influences our actions, and even plays with our creativity and imagination. If music be the food of our souls, one can take the stance that music serves as one of the more important tools when we are learning to expand and grow our abilities and our craft. (In my own opinion)

　　There are many ways music can be used when we are training ourselves up to the greater beings that we promise to be. Be it an Indigo Child or a Priest/Priestess or simply a Lightworker, music is a key tool that in many respects might be overlooked simply because it is so commonly used.

　　Music sets a mood for ceremony but depending on the type of music and its resonance it can also become a key to open doors that might otherwise be closed to us.

　　In meditation, the right music, uncluttered by someone else's words, can lead us to a clearer image seen through the third eye, opening us to messages that might otherwise be mistaken for daydreaming or outside noise.

　　In Reiki and healing practices, music is often used to mellow out the patient and unblock any doors or pipes that they may have shuttered in defense which might otherwise prevent the necessary healing that their chakra or their spirit may be barred against.

In potion making, music is often used like a stir stick to help combine and glue together the elements creating a more effective salve, tonic, or elixir.

Music has a wide base of styles and uses, and any practitioner can use it anyway they feel like using it.

We are not limited in how we call our guides or how we use our tools. Everyone's craft is different and so is everyone's skill/talent/gift. I invite you to experiment with how music might help you improve your magic and share with others what you discover there..

— Dana Lee Beaudreau

The Future, Regrettably
Coming Fall 2021

The debut urban fantasy novel from Desirée Goulden, prequel to the Aurora Garroway series.

Julian is a man with nothing but a name. Woken from a coma and thrust into a war he does not want to fight, he is the body guard and right hand man of a tyrannical cult leader, Rose. Escape is futile and attempts cause innocent people to be killed to keep him in line. With death as the only escape, he becomes reckless in battle, hoping to be cut down and finally escape the life he is trapped in.

Rose notices and offers him a boon: stay in line and do as she says and he will be able to visit the future in his dreams. He will be able to live a comfortable life and see why the Conduit Hierarchy's war is just, and how it will better the world.

Will this be enough to pacify Julian? Or will this motivate him to tear down the organization that seeks to control him, and find the truth?

@inkwood_tarot   @InkwoodJournal

inkwoodtarot.com

Inkwood Tarot - Readings by Cynthia: tarot reader, empath, certified Reiki practitioner and ordained Pagan clergy.

" I offer tarot readings by phone, video call and seasonally in-person at local events, festivals and shops. With over 20 years of tarot study and experience, I love helping people bring harmony, balance and success to their lives. Join me in exploring your ultimate potential!"

To learn more or schedule a reading visit:
http://inkwoodtarot.com

Tiffany Lazic's "The Great Work": a Review

For many of you who are just starting out on your journey or who are looking for a way to expand you base, The Great Work by Tiffany Lazic is a great place to start. The Great Work is a day by day growing experience which provides the reader with daily exercises to help them grow in their craft and enables them to explore or discover new areas of the arts without needing to invest large amounts of time or expense to find out if it's a good fit. Written without any particular spirit guide or deity in mind, the information and daily assignment help you simply and slowly explore different areas of yourself and you craft. Exploring a number of fields including Reiki, healing, tarot, rune reading, and meditation, the reader can choose to discover whether the skills involved are of an interest, calling or fit for them. If you have only recently discovered your gift or are unsure about your gift and how to use it, this book provides many small bits of homework to be done each day that have been designed to help you become more acquainted with yourself and your gift. It is also divided into sections dedicated to many of the skills, or gifts that you may want to explore going so far as to explain many of the crafts that some may not even be aware of. This book, designed to be a year long journey of learning, growing and exploration, makes it easy to try out new things or dig a little deeper into those abilities that you have only scratched the surface into opening. I highly recommend reading this if you are just starting out or looking for a way to expand your craft base.

Tiffany Lazic is the owner of The Hive and Grove Centre for Holistic Wellness and a graduate of Transformational Arts College of Spiritual Healing as a Spiritual Psychotherapist.

— *Dana Lee Beaudreau*

(Lazic, 2015)

References

Lazic, T. (2015). the Great Work: Self-Knowledge and Healing Through the Wheel of the Year. In T. Lazic, the Great Work: Self-Knowledge and Healing Through the Wheel of the Year. Woodbury, MN: Llewellyn Publication, Llewellyn Worldwide Ltd.

"Fusing ancient Western spirituality, energy work, and psychology, The Great Work is a practical guide to personal transformation season by season. Learn to be truly holistic by incorporating key physical, emotional, and energetic practices into your life at times when the natural tides are in harmony with your process.

The Great Work captures the core essence of each festival with eight key themes that span the annual cycle—a cycle that reflects human development and experience. Discover how Yule can alleviate a painful childhood, how Beltane can facilitate conscious relationships, and how Mabon can assist with determining your life's purpose. Find guidance through daily journal questions, elemental meditations, and the author's unique energy-healing technique of Hynni. With this invaluable resource for your journey of inner alchemy, you'll develop an intimate connection with the earth's impulse to create balance and harmony." - Amazon store page.

Paperback: $32.26
Kindle: $ 28.71
Purchase:
https://amzn.to/39ahtQi

TOTG Merch!

We have new additions to the TalesOfTheGods.com merch page!

This is a back and white illustration of Achilles and Patroclus with a rainbow background and a inscription that reads: "No dude, they were totally just really good friends!" -Very Smart People.

Buy at **https://tales-of-the-gods-2.creator-spring.com/listing/achilles-and-patroclus-being-b**

$44.17 $6.20 $31.54

Christina & Martin

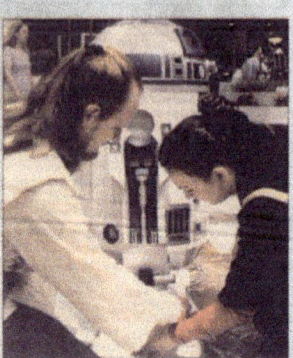
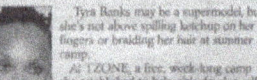

✉ carrhunger@carrhunger.com

📷 www.instagram.com/Carrhunger/

f www.facebook.com/carrhunger/

Meeting at a Dr Who convention in Toronto in 1987, Christina and Martin have, combined, over 62 years experience in the entertainment industry.
Accumulating such titles as Camera, Editing, Tape Operator, Director, Actor, Writer, Costumes, Props Builders, AD, Fight Coordinator, etc and so on... their experiences are broad and diverse BUT they still, to this day, love bringing the joy of building props, education on the industry and the popular process of Cosplay to conventions and events. X-Men, Cody Banks, Total Recall 2070, Scooby Doo, Stargate, Star Trek, FX The Series, EFC, Flash, Arrow, Legends of Tomorrow, are only a few of the productions on their list of experiences.
Stage, Live Performances, Characters at Festivals, add to their range of talents. Come experience their love of sharing knowledge, their skills and stories of their experiences.

An Introduction to Ogham

A long time ago Druids used a secret language to communicate and perform their ceremonies. This language was so secret that rather than write it down, it was passed along from generation to generation by word of mouth. It was many centuries later before it was first written down on stones (we call these runes) and wooden sticks, called staves (known as Ogham).

Consisting of twenty letters in four sets of five letters or symbols, these are inscribed on trees native to Ireland. The first three sets consist of consonants and the last set is made up of vowels. These were arranged to communicate in a secret language used only by those trained up to this purpose.

These days, students of ogham are taught instead how to respectfully use these runic inscriptions to decipher situations and read the energies effecting a person's predestined path.

How to read Ogham:
The staves are gathered together and stored in a velvet or specially prepared bag. The reader calls upon their guide to lead the client or subject to reveal themselves in the staves. The individual (or the reader on their behalf) reaches into the bag and withdraws three staves. These staves are inscribed with symbols that relate to various trees. Trees much like flowers each have their own meaning and thus are able to communicate with us.

The first stave drawn is the Ray of Knowledge. This is the influence that the past has on the subject. It may represent the events surrounding the subject and how they are manipulating or being manipulated by the subject.

The second stave is the Ray of Peace. This stave represents the foundation of the present or what is influencing the subject now. This position represents intelligence. Here we see what is the undercurrent of the events that are unfolding. What is at the root of things.

The final stave drawn is the Ray of Power. This stave speaks to the future of events as they are unfolding. It represents the potential for change and the movement of energy in the subject's pilgrimage. Our third position is the magic box. The gift or message which is being bestowed on us in order to step into the answers or quest we are now encountering.

There are two spreads that we are familiar with.

The Awen which is used to examine knowledge, peace, and power. It speaks with the Land/Sea/Sky or Earth/Water/Air.
The Welsh Triad which mainly focuses on the event, intelligence, and the god's influence. You begin with a Bridge which carries down to a vine and follows into the event line of thinking and examination.

Either spread will answer the same basic questions.

While I could go into what all the trees, runes and symbols are holding in significance, I think it would be better if you are interested in further study into Ogham reading that you seek out books that are more in depth than this basic introduction.
I will leave you with this one taste. Mistletoe is a parasite and therefore it is all powerful. Should mistletoe appear in your reading be very cautious. Its influence may be more than you can handle.

— *Dana Lee Beaudreau*

Simply Magical Audio!

Want something magical to listen to? Here are a selection of some of out favourite practicioner made podcast and music! From good jams to great podcasts, these creators give hours of education and art!

The Guide Your Soul podcast is a new podcast with great potential! Mary Fellows talks about anything and everything through a spiritualist point of view.

She is a respected healer and spiritual teacher who you should keep your eye on.

A great podcast lead by two experienced practitioners. You will always learn something new from this podcast and is great to listen to throughout your day.

Grab some tea and curl up with your favourite knitted blanket and give this a listen!

Selki Girl brings the nostalgic vibes of the 2000s with a hint of magic. Her album "For The Profane" gained some traction with some scandalous tales of it causing one to astral project. People seemed to make up tall tales about this album and from listening to it, it's not hard to see why. While it wont make you astral project, it is a experience that shouldn't be missed!

An oldie but a goody. Some of my favourite songs from my teen years where written by him.

This bard weaves magic in his words and story telling and music and will forever be an adored musician in the Pagan world.

A Witch Called Karen

The internet has shed light on no small number of obnoxious, racist, older, white women in recent years. With everyone having a phone on them at all times, it is becoming increasingly difficult for people to act like a fool in public and get away with it. While the name "Karen" usually denotes an entitled, older, white, Christian conservative throwing a hissy fit over people just existing around her, entitledness is as always: intersectional.

We have seen Karens of all shapes, sizes, ages, and colours and has seemed to move from the stereotypical bottle blonde churchgoer to anyone with an entitled attitude, loud mouth, and arrogant disposition. It seems now, that one of our own has been bestowed the title of "Karen."

On August 24th I came across a video from the TikTok creator tizzyent who duetted a video of a woman being harassed by a screaming harpy on an electric scooter. The woman on the scooter rides around in frantic and rapid movements while screaming "Ugly Packie fuck get out of my path!" as she blocks the road for the woman trying to cross it.

As the video stated, this took place at Port Perry Waterfront, Ontario Canada. According to IBTimes she continues on to harass people who intervene and stop her from attacking the family. The original post was made by @_rabioli on TikTok who was the victim of the hate. Apparently, the woman disliked her race, as well as her clothes.

When the woman called her a witch in a derogatory but less rude version of "bitch", she turns and states that she is in fact a witch, and the girl "knows nothing about witches". Apparently, this is a common theme with the Witch Of The Wheelchair, and this is not the first time she has caused trouble in the neighborhood. Although we have not been able to dig up her name, we have found out the stores in the area have nearly all banned her from shopping there, so it is unlikely that she will be causing trouble there for a while.

    By her admission, she is a witch and the victim has "no idea what that means." She claiming to be one of us, leaves a bad taste in many in the communities mouths, as well as a stain on our name. While I do not condone harassment, doxing, or anything of the sort, accountability must be held. Our community is small and any bad apple can ruin the bunch. If you have any information about this woman, please contact us at TalesOTheGods@gmail.com, or through our CONTACT page. If she is in any circle, gathering, group, or moot of yours, it may be worthwhile to have a chat about her conduct and how it affects the entire community. Remember, much of western spirituality and magical practice is influenced or comes from people that have different races, clothes, religions, and practices. Our differences strengthen us and build the community. There is no place for racism here.

-*Desirée Gouldem*

A SHOP OR A CULT?

Metaphysical and Witch shops are the cornerstone for the occult and spiritual communities. They give us tools, knowledge, and services as well as a sense of community where we are usually surrounded by people who don't share our religious and magical beliefs. They can make or break the local community, especially if they are the only one in a certain area. I would say if there is one thing that almost all of us hold sacred it is the local Witch shop.

(Please know that all claims are allegations until proven true in a court of law. Much of what comes from this article is first-hand experiences from people in and around the business, customers, and that which is public information.)

This is why I was dismayed to see that one such Witch shop has become more a thinly veiled cult than a servant of the community. While interacting in one of the many Witchy groups I am a part of on FaceBook, I came across a post asking for more metaphysical shops in South Carolina because the store has gone downhill since new management. She claims that the new owner has admitted to selling "defective merchandise" and blaming the customer for the product. She also claims that they knowingly stock and sell white supremacist content there, and bullied one of the workers until he quit because he was gay.

Hey I'm looking for some good places to buy supplies from. My local shop (Canterbury Emporium) has just completely gone down hill under their new management. The new owner has admitted to knowingly sell defective merchandise and when people would call and ask about what was wrong with their products the owner would tell them that is wasn't the product, something must have gone wrong with the spell and sell more of the defective item to them KNOWING what was truly wrong. Not to mention all the lies she's been telling customers to get them to buy more stuff. AND knowingly being affiliated/ stocking white supremacy merchandise. She even bullied my friend until he was fired because he's gay. I can't support this. They're the only local store that sells occult supplies and I would hate to have to order off Amazon. So if anyone has any good online suppliers, please help a girl out. This woman does NOT deserve to stay in business let alone take my money.

All names will be protected for the protection of the people who have brought it to light, so let's call the person who brought this up, Anon. When I saw Anon's post, I was intrigued and approached them to ask if she would give me a bit more information for a new article for the website. What I expected was to find someone with little to no actual proof, and to walk away with some gossip and nothing to write about. What I found was the beginnings of a cult, a woman who legally should not be in charge of a business, a business that is in decline, and so many red flags that even rose coloured glasses could stop you from seeing them.

So what is going on with Canterbury Emporium?

Canterbury Emporium LLC was Canterbury Cloak and Dagger until January 1st, 2021. We don't know why but from what we understand, the original owner (Christina Crider) wanted to either lessen the load of the shop on her or get a business partner. We don't know why, but considering Covid has affected us all, and especially small businesses, that is not surprising. Unfortunately, the person who heard the call for help had less than charitable motives.

Enter Elizabeth Donovan and the beginning of the downfall of Canterbury Emporium. Elizabeth, 36 was allegedly brought on to co-own the store, but from get-go there was trouble in paradise when Christina found out she would not be the owner on paper. Why would that be?

Because Elizabeth has charges for a DUS (driving under suspension), a simple possession charge (Marijuana), and a DUI wherein she allegedly hit a police car. Anon tells us that because of this that she can not have a business license... which is problematic as the reason she was brought on was specifically to be the new owner so that Christina could bow out of the store.

So concerned was Christina in finding someone that she did not perform a background check on Elizabeth and it managed to bite her in the butt almost immediately. On top of Elizabeth not being able to have a business license because of her charges, her credit is apparently so terrible she can't even be put on any of the business accounts. They agreed on a 50/50 partnership and things started going downhill.

Anon paints a picture of a schoolyard bully made a boss. From day one, Elizabeth would harass and bully Christina to get her way. At one point, Christina wanted to install cameras for the protection of her staff from Elizabeth. Apparently, Elizabeth had a nasty habit of ignoring her duties.

She would ask if she could help customers then walk off and ignore them on a constant basis, as well as apparently being rather judgmental to anyone who was obviously new to the craft. This can be backed up by some of the negative reviews you can find on Google (All within the last year and sullying the nearly 5 star rating it once had, mind you.)

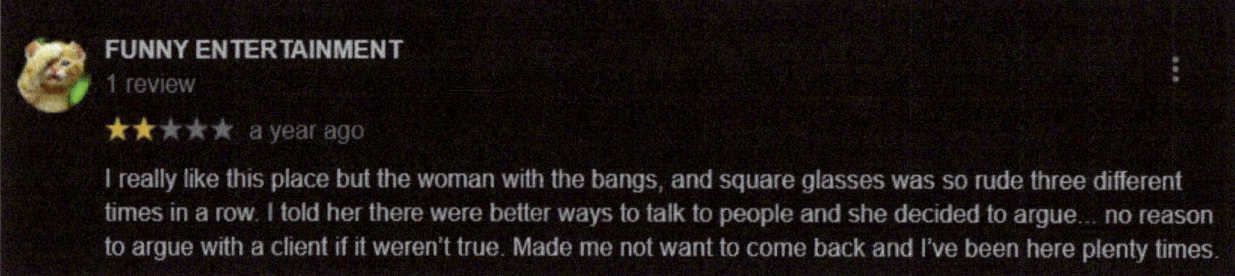

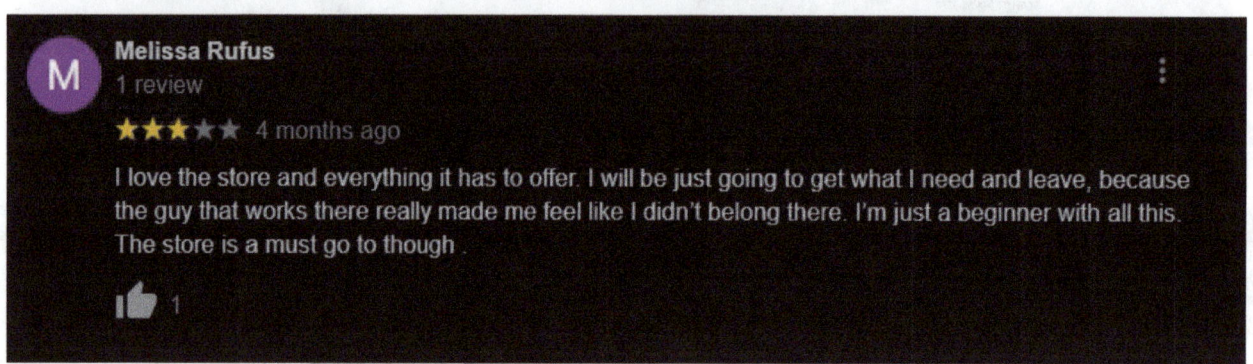

Anon explains that Elizabeth constantly is at odds with workers who were there before she got involved because they would constantly correct her false information regarding the craft. It's not that she is new to her craft either, as she allegedly brags about constantly using manipulation spells on people around her including her significant other. She has apparently said she asks your big 3 zodiac signs not out of curiosity, but so that she can assess how easily she can control you based on them.

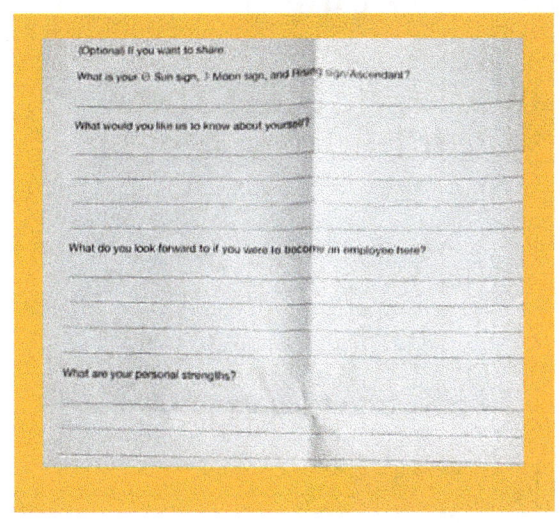

These manipulation spells and need for control has caused more than a few people to make sure to not leave any personal items at the store, lest the woman uses them in a spell which she allegedly admitted to doing before. Our sources claim that Canterbury Emporium is the only metaphysical shop in the town, meaning they ought to play an important part in the local community. Unfortunately, our sources have given us the image of the beginnings of a cult.

One of the key points on the BITE model (a way to identify cult mentality and abusive religious structures) is information control, and Elizabeth has an iron grip on the magical information coming in and going out of the Emporium. Anon tells us that Elizabeth purposely does not hire priestesses or people of authority within the magical community, and goes out of her way to hire "Baby Witches" (extremely new practitioners) so that she can continue to lie to the customers about the products they offer. The workers that are there from before she took over and are knowledgeable are constantly getting in trouble for "disrespecting" Elizabeth when they were correcting the misinformation Elizabeth gave to the clientele. Workers who have no history of problems under Christina are now coming under constant fire by Elizabeth as she attempts to push her own narrative, though what that narrative is we have no idea yet.

Our sources say that Elizabeth has admitted to only being in it for the money, but seems to be unenthused in actually putting the real effort into it. Allegedly, one of Elizabeth's duties is to control the social media accounts and all things online, however, when the reviews were shown to our sources, they reagreed that the responses sound more like Christina than Elizabeth. They have a Instagram, TikTok, and FaceBook but they seem half-assed

- at best which is is sad considering if you have a strong media presence, you can take your shop from just a shop to a full-on media icon. Witch shops on TikTok have thousands of followers and fans from across the world, not just their local community. Take, for example, Catland Books in New York.

    Run by Bee Hollywood, br00klynwitch is the TikTok about Bee and their Witch shop, Catland Books. They have 188 thousand followers and over 2 million collective likes on their videos, and their social media presence has made them a very well-known name in the witchy community.

    While not uploading every day, they bring flavor and entertainment to their video series "Wild ass phone calls while working at a witch shop". These videos bring an approachable, funny, and interesting look into the day-to-day workings of the shop, and give the vibe of a sitcom taking place in a metaphysical store.

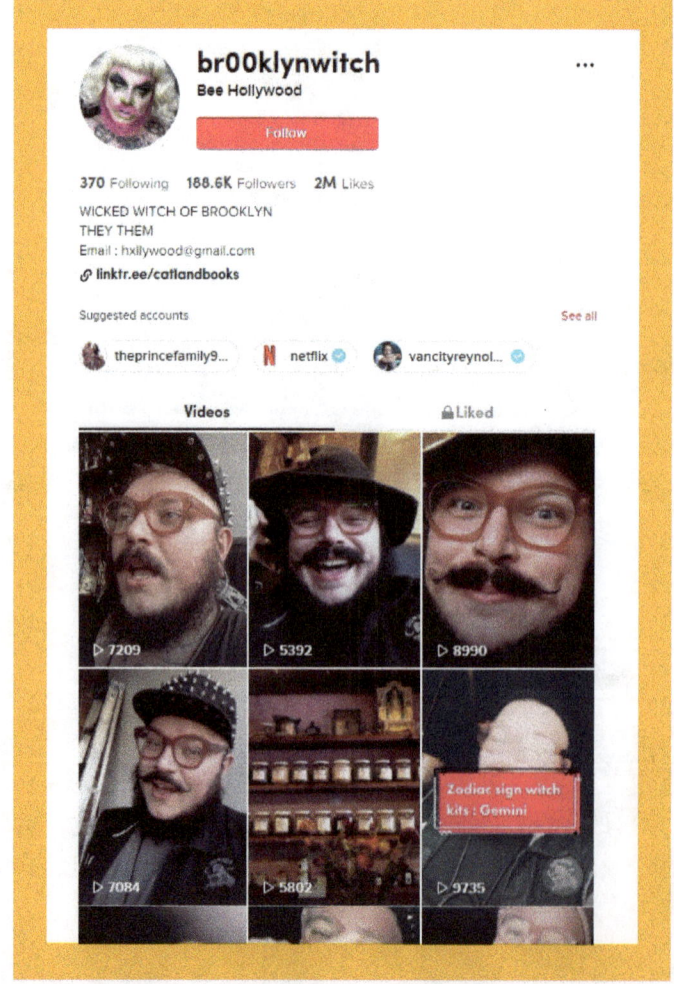

This is to say, it is not terribly difficult to create a relevant social media presence, and you would think that Elizabeth would be able to do more than a video kissing an amethyst geode. Maybe this is just me nitpicking, but if you are going to try to manipulate an entire community, and especially the young practitioners therein, you'd think a bit more effort would be put into it.

Because no shit show is complete without white supremacy, of course, she has begun stocking the shelves with content by known white supremacists. Until they were called out for it. For a time they stocked the book Futhark, a handbook of rune magic by Edred Thorsson, an alias for Stephen E. Flowers. MrFlowers is a renowned white supremacist and is part of the Asatru Folk Assembly, a white supremacist heathen organization. He is known for distorting the information in his books with a neo-satanic ideals and philosophy, and his publishing house closed and he was sued by his business partner.

While they did take the book out of the shop, but you have to wonder how they didn't catch that as Flowers is a decently well-known person for his problematic tendencies. I feel like if Christina was in charge completely that would have never happened. If Elizabeth wasn't so retaliatory against people correcting her information, she would have been told about this. I want to give her the benefit of the doubt that Elizabeth just didn't know, but considering that she doesn't seem to be new to her craft, as well as the fact that there are 838 tracked hate groups in the US, 20 of them being in South Carolina, I am doubtful that it was not an intentional push to see what the community would allow. There are 2 white supremacist organizations in Summerville alone, those being Renaissance Horizon and Patriotic Flag, both being white supremacist organizations. That is of course only personal opinion, so take that with a grain of salt, but it seems in conjunction with everything else to be a little too fishy for me.

We can't get confirmation of the claims of homophobic harassment, for obvious reasons many within the shop refuse to answer questions and put their jobs on the line, but considering these sort of supremacist organizations very often have homophobic sentiment as well, I would personally take Anon's claims at her word.

Elizabeth is coasting off the reputation of Canterbury Cloak and Dagger, actively ruining the store, manipulating and hurting people who work under her, is only in it for the money, giving faulty products and spells, and when they doing work as advertised, she blames the customer. Canterbury Emporium as it is is starting to go majorly downhill, and I believe that unless they get rid of Christina, it is going to devolve into a local cult and is going to actively hurt the local community,

If you are in Summerville and are looking for a new shop, here are some local shops, and some online to help you get what you need without supporting a white supremacist, alleged homophobe, and subpar and faulty products and spells.

Summerville Metaphysical Stores

Botanica De La Gitana - 106 E Doty Ave, Summerville, SC 29483

Online Metaphysical Stores

Grove and Grotto - Affordable metaphysical and Witchy supplies

The Quirky Cup Collective - Books, tarot decks, journals, misc

All That Shimmerzz - Crystals

-Desirée Gouldem

A Witch Called Karen

WitchTok is by far the laughing stock of the online witching world at this point. Between their creators attempting to claim Tarot cards are a closed Romani practice, to hexing the moon, fae, Artemis, Apollo, etc. From the "hex" videos from Fluffy Bunnies and "Baby Witches" sticking random things into lemons to the song Bottom Of The River by Delta Ray, to the forming of the "Reality Shifting" into anime, causing hundreds of kids to fall into maladaptive daydreaming, nobody is surprised they have played into the hands of the Reddit trolls.

R/BewitchTheTaliban is a forum on the website, Reddit, a message board website, and self-proclaimed "Front page of the internet". Reddit has come into the limelight and gained popularity over the years, drawing in a wide range of people because of it's community-generated and shared content. As it appeals to such a large amount of people, it does tend to attract Trolls and people who just want to start chaos in other parts of the internet. It is unclear whether R/BewitchTheTaliban was originally a Troll board or not. The first signs of this board was inside the R/Witchcraft forum via a post made by u/Cogito_Ergo_Sum1

Cogito_Ergo_Sum1 has an interesting history of posting. Their account was made on November 25th, 2020. Reddit allows you to scroll through people's posts and comments and it is obvious this person has been somewhat of a Troll since they opened their account. They moderate 2 groups those being R/BewitchTheTaliban and R/HexTheTaliban.

Many of their posts that aren't related to the two groups are flagged and deleted. Some of these posts include: Israel and Covid-19 (Removed for "A variety of reasons") in R/ConspiracyTheories, and A Prophecy of Hermes in the Asclepius (Removed for spam) in R/Occult. They post at length about their drug use, in both R/Psychedelics and other unrelated forums. They ask about "how much blood makes you native" and if they can do sacred native practices. They ask about working with Isis, while also claiming to work with Paimon, and claims to be a new witch.

While I have no doubt Cogito_Ergo_Sum1 is a Troll account, with anti-Islamic sentiment, and the R/HexTheTaliban containing the first post of a naked man offering up his... orifice, a hybrid human-washing machine, and a post just saying "AAAAAAAAAAAAAAAAA", the same can not be said for those who have fallen into their R/BewitchTheTaliban forum.

In the original post, you can see people in the comments saying things like:

"I'm perfectly willing to join in but I think the word you're looking for is curse lol… I may be wrong but hexes are generally considered less severe, and since it's the Taliban we're talking about…."

"You will need to summon and gain the favor of a God of War for this one"

"I work with Freyja, sounds like a cause she would definitely get behind."

"Athena for sure. Definitely not Ares"

There are paragraphs upon paragraphs about protections, how to curse, who to curse, who to protect, who to invoke, how to invoke them and while reading I can't help but think... this sounds a lot like prayer warriors who don't actually donate or help or do anything in times of crisis, but say platitudes of "I'll pray for you".

But what is the actual forum in question like? Well... let these screenshots speak for themselves.

Posted by u/Castlefree43 5 days ago

You'd be surprised what could be done if Israel just put 5% of their energy into bringing peace to the Middle East -- All they need to do is begin talks of it in the region and you'll see what can get done when it's done right

If you don't believe me, that's fine but I know it's time for Israel's leaders to begin the process.

It will be rocky at first but it has to start somewhere, and if they do try it, please be supportive of them as this is a huge step for humanity, should it happen.

When Israel's leaders (whether this generation's, the next's, or one in the future) put their energy and consciousness into bringing peace in that region, you will see great change. It's just that their current leadership wants to continue warring, hating, etc - just like the Middle Easterners - but the Israeli's have a far greater ability within them to begin the peace making process.

I know people don't think it's possible because of what we've seen in the past, but that is exactly the kind of thinking that stops this from going forward. This idea that things will always remain the same, so they have to just clamp down and win, but that's not working so it's time to try for something else.

The younger generation of Israeli's (and their children, and so on) will understand this intuitively but it would still help to get Israel's current leadership to consider it at least as a possibility.

89 Comments   Award   Share   Save   Hide   Report   72% Upvoted

There are some posts I can't track down, likely they were deleted after TikTok got a hold of them.

Some of these include warning people against fighting Allah in the Astral alone, generally just hexing Hallah, and warnings to be careful when hexing the Taliban.

There is a concerning mix of people in this group, both Trolls and young practitioners who actually want to do this. Unfortunately what was contained to Reddit, was spread like a wildfire by people on TikTok who lack critical thinking skills and know to just ignore the small group of fools and racists. Witchtokers spread screenshots across the app which currently hosts the largest online group of witches, pagans, and practitioners.

"Baby Witches" (A new more derogatory infantilizing term for new practitioners, usually similar to Fluffy Bunnies) saw a way to show how "powerful" they are to their audiences on TikTok and while most people decried the stupidity of the group, some Baby Witches joined the "fight" to "hex the Taliban".

There has been a constant buzz since this started on August 17th and has left a bad taste in my, and many other's mouths. The Trolls aside, the underlying feeling of racism, islamophobia, and xenophobia is obvious.

Let's get something very clear for the younger audiences who may not remember 9/11. This want to get back at the Taliban for what happened in Afghanistan does:

1) Absolutely nothing. Your spellwork will do nothing, you can barely cast a circle let alone "hex" a giant group of extremists whom you don't know anything of.

2) Spread blatant and harmful islamophobia by "Attempting to kill/hex/curse Allah."

3) Shows that you don't actually want to do anything to help by donations and pushing your government officials to allow and help refugees into your country to seek refuge.

4) Shows your obvious performative activism at best, and your islamophobia at worse.

There are many Muslim countries, peoples, and traditions, some of which hold the title of "Witch" themselves. Islam is the 2nd most popular religion in the world with 1.907 Muslims around the world. (24.9% of the world's religion.) The idea that you would want to kill Allah is hateful of the people that follow him. You're looking at a tragedy that sets back women's rights in the middle east by 20 years, marks the loss of the long battle between the people of Afghanistan, and the Taliban. This is a terrible situation which we will be dealing with the fallout of for decades to come.

People are suffering, and rather than helping, some people in the Witch community are taking the piss, or actively using the conflict for clout and to spread hate.

While the Trolls started this, Baby Witches and in particular WitchTok has managed to spread a wave of hate and are actively making fools of Witches worldwide by their constant spreading of something that should have lived and died on Reddit. I understand that this will lead to this spreading of this, but I feel like people need to know how this started, and how illegitimate of a movement this is.

If you want to ACTUALLY help, and not contribute to the performative activism of "Hex the Taliban and kill Allah" Here are some links you can donate to.

https://give.unhcr.ca/page/86611/donate/1?ea.tracking.id=SEM21_AFG&utm_campaign=CA_PS_EN_AFS&gclid=CjwKCAjw64eJBhAGEiwABr9o2AC-VeuMiVPa3GeNjGa7MgUNc4UWUUEa2ooXcwpVPOrblPHB0ufv7hoCIYUQAvD_BwE&gclsrc=aw.ds

https://secure.unicef.ca/page/88400/donate/1?ea.tracking.id=21DIEM11GSE&gclid=CjwKCAjw64eJBhAGEiwABr9o2F5_J98FYM7DrSoJRi9Yqo_2uuHBAWcrpqjlMKzhgnGC_H6qzSCpnRoCdsQQAvD_BwE

https://www.savethechildren.org/us/where-we-work/afghanistan

https://donate.unhcr.org/int/en/afghanistan-situation

https://help.rescue.org/donate-ca/afghanistan

-Desirée Gouldem

The Law Of Hospitality
Xenia - ξενία

Do not turn away your guests, be it strangers or friends.

Welcome your guest warmly into your house, invite them to stay, show them the house.

Allow to use the bath and change into clean cloths.

Ask how you may help your guest.

Provide them with a good meal, gifts, and aid to reach their next destination if needed.

Do not ask invasive questions until they are clean and have eaten.

Guests may not be a burden to their hosts, do not threaten, harm nor steal from them.

Guests are to provide the hose with stories and news of the wider world and welcome them into their own home in the future.

Follow these rules and honour the gods for Zeus, Xenios, watches over and protects travellers near and far.

"Short and jam packed with useful knowledge. Great for avid readers of the craft and metaphysical. Great way to stay in touch with the the pagan community!"
-GoodReads reviewer

A publication printed on every day of the wheel of the year. From an ever-changing group of writers and contributors that bring education, entertainment, and spiritual and occult news for people of all paths and expertise. Read the Lughnasadh edition and learn about the holiday, sage, modern ethics in the online sphere, the Sigils Of Hermes, a restraining order against a person for being Wiccan. Have fun with our crosswords and take in the poetry and photography from Owen!

With every purchase of the TalesOfTheGods & Practical Witchcraft magazine, you support small creators! Income for this magazine is split equally between all contributors, and we are always welcoming new people to our team!

Want to join? Have a story, news, or a skill to share? Write in to TalesOTheGods@gmail.com!

Feel free to drop us a review on GoodReads or Amazon and keep an eye out on TalesOfTheGods.com or in the Practical Witchcraft and Paganism FaceBook group for freebies and updates! Thank you for reading and we can't wait to see you in the Mabon edition!

Samhain 2021

Understanding
Soul Contracts

Death Rituals
Around The World

Grief & Cookies

Misconceptions
About Ouija Boards

And more!

Tales Of The Gods & Practical Witchcraft

Thank You

By buying this magazine, you support small business owners and small creators!

TalesOfTheGods aims to connect the metaphysical and spiritual communities.

Cover Photo - Coincidence on Unsplash.

If you would like to write in anonymously, or join our team for the next edition feel free to send a email to TalesOTheGods@gmail.com

TalesOfTheGods, September 2021

facebook.com/groups/665578877692886

Contributors

Desirée Goulden	Owner, layout design, contributor
Owen Lee Heavenhill	Photographer, Contributor
Dana Lee Beaudreau	Founding member, Contributor

The TalesOfTheGods & Practical Witchcraft magazine is a community project. Our roster of contributors is constantly shifting. Everyone who works on the magazine takes home an equal take of the income from the sales of this magazine.

We aim to bring education and entertainment to people of all levels of experience and paths. If you have a point of view that you would like to share with the world, feel free to reach out to join us. We are currently looking for people of colour to join us. Whether you are a teacher, or just interested in taking part, we have a place for you.

Have a shop or product you want to share with the world? Contact us and we will run a free full page ad for you in the next edition! We release on every day of the wheel of the year, so it's easy to follow release dates!

We understand that there may be some who may not want to support Amazon, so we have made the shift from publishing through Kindle Direct Publishing for our paper back editions to Ingram Spark. This will allow for wider distribution (Chapters, Barns & Noble, indie book shops) for those who want to support us without supporting Amazon and Jeff Bezos.

Please know that all opinions are that of the contributor and may not reflect the team in general.

Contents

About Samhain	PAGE 2
Understanding Soul Contracts	PAGE 4
Death Rituals Around The World	PAGE 6
Grief & Cookies	PAGE 10
The Misconceptions About Ouija Boards	PAGE 12
Grief	PAGE 16
For This I am Ever Thankful	PAGE 18
What Is A Death Witch?	PAGE 20
Book Of Shadows Pages	PAGE 25
Pagans & Cremation	PAGE 30
Magazine Updates	PAGE 36

 **The Underworld Oracle Deck By Desiree Goulden**

25 Full colour cards

Works with reversed cards

Works with other decks

$23.99 Cad

https://www.thegamecrafter.com/games/the-underworld-oracle-deck

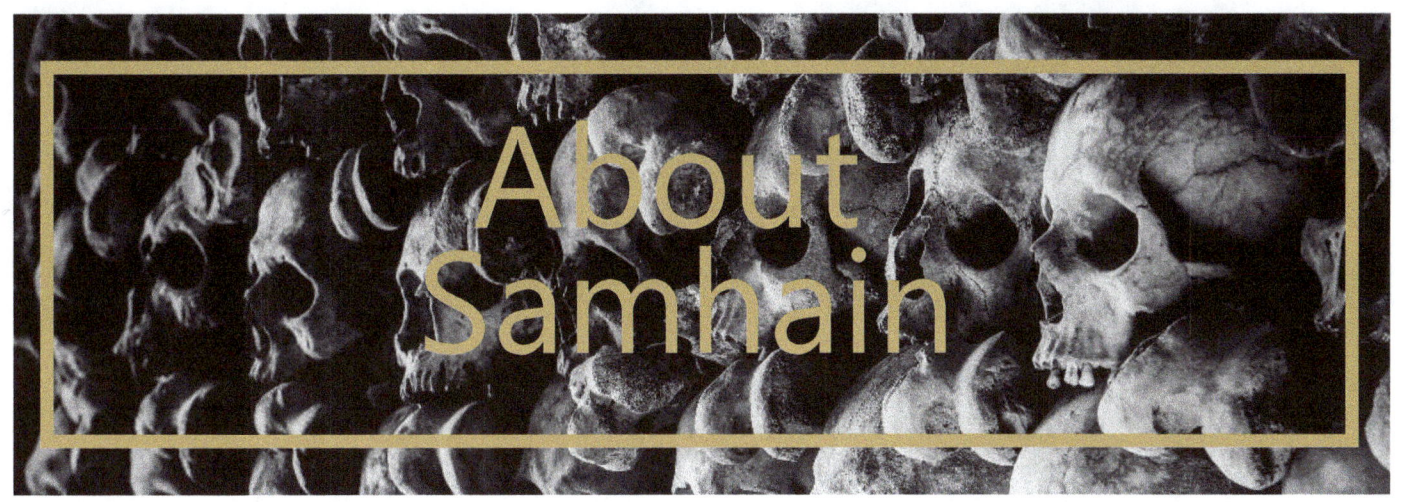

About Samhain

Samhain is the second last day on the wheel of the year. It takes from the Celtic day of the same name. Samhain is when the veil between worlds is at it's thinnest and is the time to celebrate and honor the dead. In Celtic traditions they wouldn't speak after a certain hour, held a dummy dinner for the dead, and put out carved turnips to avoid being taken as the souls of the dead are collected.

Modern Wiccan and witchy traditions in the west celebrate it on the same day as Halloween and is a little more relaxed and festive. You can dress up your altar to honor those you've lost. You can host a dummy dinner, and take part of wider cultural festivities of Halloween.

Some people regard this as the time that Persephone returns to the Underworld to reunite with Hades, so some Hellenic Pagans take this time to celebrate the two.

The colours of Samhain are: yellow, brown, and gold.

The symbols of Samhain are: mulled whine, leaves, nuts, acorns, dark loaves of bread, corn, scarecrows, scythes, and skulls.

Jim Two Snakes
Spiritual Advisor

 jimtwosnakes.net

 facebook.com/jimtwosnakes

 instagram.com/jimtwosnakes

 patreon.com/spiritualdad

Many people think the term Spirituality is about religion, but it doesn't have to be. In fact I think most people are Spiritual no matter if they are religious or not! Spirituality is about understanding and exploring your higher purpose, your interconnectedness to all of creation, and living authentically. It is my goal to help you feel inspired and fulfilled.

I do this by asking questions, giving suggestions, and then helping develop ways of marking progress and providing accountability. You don't have to believe the same way I, or anyone else, does. The coaching is centered around your needs and beliefs. I can't do the work for you, but I can help you with motivation and seeing things from a new perspective. Contact me now to schedule a free 15 minute initial consultation.

Understanding Soul Contracts

Soul contracts sound ominous and risky. They bring to mind images of Faust and Pictures of Dorian Grey. Books and plays have been written about them and tales and rumours abound about what they are. It's fun to think in terms of television magic and immortality and becoming omnipotent all through a simple negotiation and signing on the bottom line, fine print and all, but soul contracts actually have nothing to do with the wonderful world of filmation. Now don't get me wrong, I'm not suggesting that those kind of soul contracts don't exist, rather I am talking about a different kind of soul contract, the kind the universe brings to your door at the moment of your existence.

Let me start at the beginning, the kind of soul contract (and yes, that is the correct term) that I am talking about is your fate or destiny according to the universe. To quote Shakespeare, "a rose by any other name would smell as sweet" is completely a misnomer. Your name in reality is the simplified "terms" of your soul contract. If your life is a book, your soul contract as defined by your name is the Coles' Notes version. When we are born, most of us are given a name by our parents or some other respected authority. In many cultures or religions, this name choosing is considered a great privilege. But is the name we receive really just luck or chance? I don't know how many times I've heard other parents in the mall yelling out their child's name and it always seems to be the same three names. The name you were given can actually define your character, personality, talents, and even give you a heads up about major life events or shapers that you will encounter. No, I'm not saying your name can predict your future.

But in reading a soul contract for a client, I can see the events or influencers that their life has or may encounter.

How do you read a soul contract? I'm only going to say that through a series of mathematical computations, the underlying story is readable. It's like a word problem in algebra though more that a basic BEDMAS equation. The one right answer can be manipulated to show you different aspects such as problem-solving strengths, life events, talents, character, even where your hidden threats may come from. Calculating a soul contract is very much like the study of numerology. Your birthdate and time however cannot be altered. Your name can.

What do I mean? The name you are given at birth does show all these details of your life. But that name is not the be all and end all. In many cultures, when the child seems to suffer an "unlucky" life, that family may go to visit the wise person, a shaman, or a psychic to help them alter the "luck". They choose another name at the suggestion of someone who understands how the letters and numbers change our path. Even in North America, the changing of one's name is fairly common. Not just in the changing of your last name to that of your partner. On occasion, the name is changed for work, or for ease, or for impulse. The changed name will change and influence your story/your fate. Nicknames, pet names, gender change names. All of these speak volumes as to who you are over and above how they make you sound. So next time you are trying to decide what to call your child, your pet, yourself, see if you can get some help and a heads up for what's to come.

-Dana Lee Beaudreau

Death Rituals Around The World

In Canada, we are really only familiar with two different kinds of funeral: the traditional burial, and the cremation, but there are hundreds of funeral rites and rituals across the world. Each culture has their own traditions that reflect the cultures and religions they come from and reflect how said culture deals with grief. Here are a small selection of lesser known death rituals for Samhain / Halloween.

Sky Burials (bya gtor)

Sky burials are a Tibetan practice specifically among Buddhists. They believe in sending their soul towards heaven, and the Tibetan name, bya gtor means "bird-scattered". It is practiced in Chinese provinces and autonomous regions of Tibet, Qinghai, Sichuan and Inner Mongolia, and Mongolia, Bhutan and parts of India like Sikkim and Zanskar. A body is placed on a sacred place called the charnel grounds. Charnel grounds are sacred sites that are elevated and are for the decomposition or putrefaction of human remains.

The body would be left at the charnel grounds uncovered for wildlife (usually birds) to eat it as it decays. For Tibetan Buddhists, sky burials and cremations were important and showed the impermanence of life. Sky burial in particular was seen as a act of generosity as it fed the animals around the charnel grounds and gave back to nature. Unlike western cultures, they feel no need to preserve the body, as once the soul is gone, it's only an empty vessel.

Unfortunately due to religious marginalization, urbanization, and it being considered a relic of "the old cultures" within China, and the closure of many charnal grounds, it's popularity has waned but it is still practiced in the more remote regions.

Famadihana (the turning of the bones)

A funeral tradition from the native Malagasy people of Madagascar. The turning of the bones is a more recent tradition likely originating around the 17th century. It is likely influenced by southern Asian traditions that believe the soul can only move on after full decomposition. 7 years after the death and burial, the family comes together and exhumes the body and rewraps it in new silks. They proceed to dance to live music while holding the body over their heads. They dance around the tomb before returning it to the family crypt. This is a celebration of the life the person had, rather than a tearful event and was known to reunite families even if there is tension between them.

Famadihana is beginning to decline in popularity due to how expensive it is to buy the silks required to do the ritual. The practice was also decried by missionaries and the church who were trying to stomp out the practice as they colonize- I mean "convert" the native peoples. The Catholic church in modern times claims to no longer have a problem with the practice because it is "cultural, not religious." as if the two can be separated. The practice was linked to the transmission of the pneumonic plague and the Malagasy government put in restrictions on the ritual upon those who have died of the plague, which may have aided to the decline in the practice.

Korean Death Beads

South Korea is a very densely populated area and because of that, cremation was the most logical solution to burial. As the population grows the traditional cremation-

-urns and family crypts also have become a space issue as well so they came up with a new tradition: death beads.

They take the cremains of the deceased and make them into tiny luminescent beads that are kept in glass jars and bowls in the house. This is a newer tradition that costs around $900 to do. The death beads have drawn some criticism with critics saying that it is essentially a soulless cash grab, but worse things were said about cremation in the west when it was introduced.

Funeral Strippers

In Taiwan and some parts of China, it was common to have funeral strippers. They were a sign of wealth and social status. Business men, government officials, and important social figures were known to have them. There were spiritual significance of course. Having the strippers was said to "appease wandering spirits" and give one last hurrah to the departed. They would dance and strip on non lit stages but with music, and DJ's, though they rarely undressed completely.

In Chinese and Taiwanese tradition, the more people that showed up to a funeral, the better one's trip to the afterlife would be. The funeral strippers served a dual purpose as a display of social status, and as a tactic to draw people in to the funeral processions. The Chinese government disapproves of the practice, and is trying to end it but it survives in rural areas.

Personally, I wouldn't mind strippers at my own funeral, but I doubt that's allowed in Canada.

Natural Burials

A return to basic traditions after the standardization of embalming in the west. Natural burials are exactly what they sound like. You wrap the body in a shroud that will -

-decompose with the body. You place the body in a biodegradable coffin, and bury them in a shallow grave to allow for natural decomposition without the pollution of the water table associated with an embalmed corpse.

You can have home viewings with natural burials or a traditional viewing depending on the laws in your province, territory, or state. Despite what the funeral industry will tell you, they were never illegal. As long as you can follow local laws around the handling of a corpse as well as find a funeral house that will work with you, natural burials are a cheaper and more green alternative to traditional funerals.

-Desirée Goulden

Grief & Cookies

It's been almost a year since I've lost my great grandmother, the woman who was my rock. I thought by now that I would know what to say, how to process it, something more clever to say than, I still want to scream, it's not fair and I miss her. Is it bad enough that I have the object permanence of a goldfish, so I forget that she's gone. So it's been almost a year of it hitting me, over and over again like it was the first time. That's something that's not talked about enough when it comes to grieving.

Someone at my church, which was my nanna's church, asked me what she was like. And I blanked, so I mentioned her baking and her divinity. Yes, she was known for her divinity at the church bake sales, but she was so much more than that. Yes, she spent a lot of time in that church, but she was more than that church. She was a mother, a grandmother, and eventually great grandmother to 3. She was a wife. She loved to garden. I could talk about how she was president of the garden club and was well known for her roses. There was always coffee on the pot for guest and always cookies..

I could talk about the fact that she grew up in the great depression as the honorary boy for her dad after he lost his arm in a tractor accident. I could tell stories she doesn't know I know about her sneaking out and drinking, and probably on a few nights, almost dying behind a barn.

I wish I could tell you her pigs name. I long forgot that before I could even think to ask her.

Yet, it all feels shallow, because I can remember these things, but it still doesn't feel right. Because, yes, absolutely for a moment she can live on in stories, but I still can't hug her. I can't sit down and watch Lawrence Welk with her. She'll never curl my hair again, even though it never needed the curler. I can't go to a movie with her just for her to nap through it, she always said she had some of the best naps then.

I also kicked myself, because I had so much time I could have asked her and written everything down. But, when you're young, you don't realize how real that loss will be when it happens. You think, "Oh, I want to remember, they're good memories, of course I'll always have them." But, no, if there's one fact about anything I've learned is, you can't always rely on your memories.

I watched my nanna start to lose hers due to dementia, and I still didn't think to ask her to write them down. I watched her slip away from us all while she was still here, but I can't change the past. I can only start to write down the memories I have and the lessons she taught me while I still have them in my head.

So, maybe I can't hug her again, but I still remember the smell of peanut butter cookies made on the spot because the guests wanted cookies. She assured them all, it was no big deal. And it wasn't, it's simply:

1 egg, 1 cup of sugar, and 1 cup of peanut butter. Bake at 350 for 7-10 minutes. And maybe the grief isn't such a big deal either, maybe I can deal with it like she made cookies, as she needed them. I long forgot that before I could even think to ask her.

-Owen Lee Heavenhill

The Misconceptions About Ouija Boards

Ouija boards are dangerous.

This is what we are told constantly. Not only from Christians, but from people within the pagan and witchy spheres as well. We are taught that they are inherently dangerous and you need to be a very experienced witch to use them, and you need to use a lot of protection while using them. They can usher in demons, trickster spirits, and can get you possessed.

It is actually rather comical to hear these same comments come from both sides. Especially considering that they're talking about a children's board game that was created for and sold at Walmart.

Let's talk for a moment about the origins of the Ouija board because there seems to be a lot of misinformation circulating about them.

The Ouija board is also known as the spirit board or the talking board and was created on July 1st 1980 by Elijah Bond. It was originally intended to be a normal board game but unfortunately it was created during the Victorian spiritualist movement. The spiritualist movement was a occult movement in the 1900's that consisted of the idea that anyone could communicate with the dead and spirits through crystal gazing and other forms of divination. One might say that the spiritualist movement helped pave the way for modern occult practices. There may have been many ligament mediums, psychics, and people with clairsenses within the spiritualist movement, there were also way more frauds. The frauds were usually the ones that got all the media attention. You may recall the Cottingley Fairies photographs taken by the spiritualist's Elsie Wright and Frances Griffiths, which would go on to spread en mass a of misinformation and culturally appropriative narratives about the fae.

One of these spiritualists was Pearl Curran, who brought fame to the Ouija board by allegedly contacting the dead. "Many moons ago I lived. Again, I come. Patience Worth, my name." was the first message she got through the board, and over the months Pearl would build an entire narrative and character around "Patience". By 1915 Pearl and Patience were having sessions where Patience would give her from 500 to 3000 words in a single sitting. This is... Ridiculous and as a medium myself, I can say with absolute certainty that it was nothing more that Pearl being an excellent saleswoman and con-artist.

None the less, the Ouija board would go on to gain fame and infamy in the occult world and beyond. In recent years the dramatic and over the top travel channel show, Ghost Adventures, had an entire episode based around a Ouija board demon named Zozo. Apparently this is a demon of destruction that is summoned through the Ouija board and can possess people and has followed people through generations and... the story can be tracked back to a bare bones 2000s website called "true ghost tales". People claim that Zozo is no less than 3 different entities, all of which are tricksters and most of them have "African" heritage, dispite the closet mention of the entity being from a 1818 French book called Le Dictionnaire Infernal.

If you are starting to see a trend here, you're not alone. It seems the majority of scary stories surrounding the Ouija board are all from less than reputable sources likely looking for media attention. Now I am not saying that spirit communication is not possible, but I am saying that you are not going to get possessed and have your house haunted because you bought a Ouija board from Walmart. (Which you can do by the way. It was $20 last time I checked.)

Ouija boards can be used for divination just like tarot, automatic writing, pendulums, and the like. Some may indeed use them to contact the dead, but the danger of doing that is only the same danger that is associated with anyone who preforms necromancy. Necromancy is any magic or practice that is related to contacting the dead. From ancestor work to speaking to lost family, necromancy is more common than people seem to think. Depending on what you're doing with the dead, you're going to deal with a certain amount of danger. There is a reason why more advanced practitioners get frustrated when we see younger practitioners saying that they are doing automatic writing with their deity or ancestor. Any form of divination that involves any spirit physically manipulating your body, like the Ouija board does, is dangerous and can open you up to possession.

The thing is; when practitioners do these things, we know what we're doing. We know how to invite spirits in, and banish them after. We know how to protect ourselves against possession and we know how to handle these things if they do happen. We know and accept the risks associated with necromancy and low tier possession and physical manipulation. We go in to these settings with the tools to handle them.

The problem is as always, the non occult practitioner "spooky people" who get their shits and giggles from messing with the dead.

These people don't seem to realize that there is a danger to these things inherently. The will use the Spirit Box communication method constantly, get just as haunted and because they looked at a Ouija board once, they'll blame the Ouija board. Obviously you are going to get harassed and haunted if you constantly antagonize and bother the dead, and it is silly to blame the Ouija board rather than accepting that this is the result of your own actions.

Ouija boards are not dangerous. Necromancy is. Necromancy is the act of contacting the dead. If you do not know how to safely do that, don't do it. If you do... don't blame the Ouija board.

-Desirée Goulden

Candles

What's more witchy than a good candle? Here are a selection of TalesOfTheGods approved candles for you to buy the next time you're looking for one!

The original creator of the crystal pyramid candles is back at it with her new business and pyramids!

Made with quality wax and scents and with over 65 hours of burn time, these candles are a must have. Each candle has crystals inside waiting for you as you burn the candle down making it a wonderful gift!

https://selaluzcandles.com

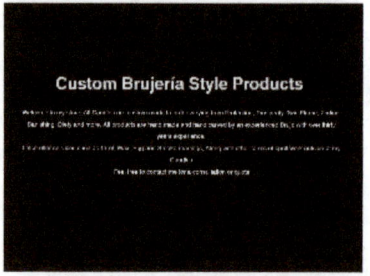

Need a spell? Look no further than ThugBrujo from TikTok! His spell candles are amazingly effective and aesthetically pleasing to boot! Hand carved and worth every penny!

https://www.candlelitglow.com

Need candles for your altar or for your own spells? Grove and Grotto as usual, has your back. Pick up a 20 pack of multi coloured chime candles and whatever else you may need!

https://www.groveandgrotto.com

Do you have a product or service you offer? Are you looking for free advertisement? Contact us at TalesOTheGods@gmail.com and we will run your add in the next edition of the TalesOfTheGods & Practical Witchcraft magazine!

Grief

Griefs talked about a lot, I feel like I've talked about it a lot. But, it's also not talked about enough. There's a weird catch 22, where it's talked about, but from a neurotypical, usually christian stand point. Grief looks different for everybody though and so let me share a couple of lessons I've learned in the almost year since my great grandmother has passed.

The first lesson being, object permanence can absolutely effect the grieving process. For me personally, I either completely forgot about her existence for a moment, which is heartbreaking, or I'll forget that she's passed and I can't call her. They both have their issues, and they both feel like they cause hurdles in whatever the grieving process is supposed to be.

Number two, I don't think there really is a specific process. We can try and lay out a roadmp and say you may deal with grief, denail, anger, etc, but I've seen some people completely accept the death and seem to never go through any of that. It all depends on so much, and not to sound crude, but having already started grieving them for whatever reason in their life, doesn't make a difference. It just, extends your grieving process.

Not everyone will grieve. Some people, literally do just accept that they're dead and move on. I thought that was going to be me, seeing as I knew I would still be able to contact her and death is an inevitabltly. And yes, while I did fully accept her death even before she'd actually passed, what hurt me was not being able to call her up and ask her for advice on cooking, household things. It was the little things. Yes, in all seriousness, I could use my mediumship abilities to try and ask her still, and believe me, I have, but it's not the same.

While most spirits and most of your ancestors will still have some of their human memories, they will lose some of them immediately upon passing. They'll remember some of the most basic mundane things, like their microwave chocolate fudge recipe, but if you want to ask them what the name of their pig was growing up, it's crickets.

Some people have said that grief comes in waves, but maybe this is also tied to my object permanence causing issues, mine likes to hit me like a deer flying across the interstate with not a care in the world. I don't like the wave analogy because that implies that you can see it coming. And, yes, that might ring true for some, but others may have different analogies. I think, it doesn't matter what analogy you're going to use, just make sure you use one that feels right to the way it works for you. If you ever have to describe your grief and how it effects you, it needs to be an accurate analogy.

Some days the analogies don't fit and I just want to burn everything down because all I need. Is to hear her voice one more time and just sit and have dinner with her. But I can't, either one, so instead on those days, I'll scream, cry, throw a pillow if I need, drink coffee, maybe a glass of wine to her, and maybe do something in honor of her, usually cleaning something if I'm going to be honest. Are there days where all it does is make the whole feel bigger? Yes. And on those days, I give mysef the grace to wallow in memories if I need to.

The biggest thing I've learned about grief though, is sometimes its a month by month basis, sometimes its week to week, and sometimes its second to second. It's been almost a year, and I won't say I feel like I've gotten through it. I will say that I've better learned how to live with it. And if I never make it past that point, that's a fine point to have made it to.

-Owen Lee Heavenhill

For This I am Ever Thankful

I am writing this even though the idea is fairly commonplace. How do we show gratitude to our guides, gods, and goddesses? I know that we all have our own way of acknowledging the help we receive in performing our craft. For some of us we glean help from our ancestors, or spirit guides. For others of us we receive our help from our god(s) or goddess(es). For others of us the help comes from the fairy realm or the Others. But I know that even in my case, it can be really easy to forget to say thank you.

At this time of year, I feel like we/I should take some time to re-evaluate my own habits and place some new ones into my routine to show the gratitude that I own to the one who guides me. As a Christian witch, I do lean most on God. But as an Ojibwe descendant, I also have called upon my spirit guides or ancestors to assist on occasion. So, to be clear, I am not telling you who you need to be aligned with, I'm merely opening up a discussion. gratitude. And I'd welcome anyone else out there to share with me what their routine, ceremony, or habits are in showing thanks to their guides or helpers.

Gratitude for me involves both ceremony and habits. I do make offerings of blessed or moon water to the earth on a full moon or a special occasion and on occasion I may even offer a toast of wine or spirits. I try to keep a gratitude journal, where I record three things that have been a joy or a blessing (even if it is small or insignificant) that happened that day and say a word of thanks before sleep. I light my candles in ceremony before I kneel in prayer in the new moon.

My routine? (order in which I light my candles – yes colour is involved)

First set: Earth, Air, Fire Water Spirit - red

Second set: sun, moon, stars - blue

Third set: North, south, east, west - green

Fourth set: Father, Son, Holy ghost. - white

Final candle: Amen - white

I know that meant nothing to most of you. It wasn't meant to. Ceremony is very personal. Each and every person has their own way and their own call to heart. Each person has their own ritual and strength. I want to invite you all to take a moment and think about what yours is and know that gratitude, that thankful heart that you are sharing with your guide, in my mind strengthens the positive energy that feeds the Earth and the Universe. Let's keep the power growing.

-Dana Lee Beaudreau

What Is A Death Witch?

There are many closed and secretive practices within paganism, the religions, paths, and the occult. One of these paths is the path of the Death Witch, but what is that?

Death Witch may be both a singular path, or an umbrella term for many similar paths that are oriented around the ushering of souls across the veil. Death Witchery is a very secretive path that can be handed down through families and traditions and what one Death Witch does may be completely different than what another does. What is common however are a few things:

1) They usher the souls of the dead across to their respective afterlife, whether they are a soul that's trapped or whether they are hired to help someone across the moment they pass.

2) The work they do is dangerous to themselves, and has physical repercussions making it a very specialized skill set that is not a path for most people.

3) They need to have a mentor, and the initiation process is dangerous and mandatory for the Death Witch in question to complete to earn their title.

I myself am a subsect of Death Witch known as a Psychopomp. I have been in training for just over a year, and would still consider to be new as the training for a Death Witch can be as long as 10 years.

Many won't talk about their paths due to the darker nature of it and how personal it is, but I don't mind dipping into some of my own practice, which more or less the same as many others who claim to be Psychopomps. Please note, that while we fall under the umbrella term of "Death Witch" it does follow a Hellenic Pagan path and other paths may conflict or be different to my own.

I started my path via a justice working. I was doing a working to sway a court case in 2020 and had to pay a price for their aid: use my mediumship skills to become a messenger for the gods and humans, and to help Hermes in the moving of souls as a Psychopomp. This was long before I had even herd of Death Witches.

That night was the first night I did any sort of Psychopompary. He lead me via the the astral to several of the dead and I got the first glimpse of what would be expected of me and why it was important. I was brought to a old man who died alone in his study with nobody close to notice his passing. I was brought to a house where a child committed suicide as his parents found him. Hermes ended up dealing with that spirit personally due to its aggression and emotional distress. I was brought to many lost and hurt souls that night in order to test to see what I was personally able to handle emotionally.

I would come to understand a few things as I continued on my training with him. (I am still in training, and likely will be for years) The first of which was that Psychopomp entities, deities, and spirits from many pantheons and beliefs help other religions and paths in regards to helping the dead to were they ought to be. Because of that, I would have to learn of and accept many path's beliefs and deities, even those (Christianity) that I have personally been harmed by or disagree with. The second was that no matter how many Psychopomps there are in the world, there are always going to be outnumbered by millions of dead souls due to the population of the earth. This is one of the many reasons why we have lost and wandering souls.

The third is that in most cases where I personally am involved, it will be to guide souls who have died in terrible ways and are in major emotional distress.

There are a few souls that just need some guidance, but they are always going to be outnumbered by the distressed ones. People need Psychopomps and Death Witches in order to to help move these souls that can not be handled by the common folk. There is always a physical toll to this. Some people have body aches, I personally become mentally drained and tired but am unable to make my body sleep for days. Dealing this personally with the dead and the magical energy needed to move them will draw from you just as normal magical workings do. Unlike magical workings, however, these can last hours and drain you very fast. There is a notion going around that Death Witches don't live long lives due to this, but I personally live off of spite so I don't plan on dying before 97 no matter how tired I am. (I can practically hear the Fates laughing at me)

Psychopompary is a very interesting practice, and a very needed one. I have only met one other Psychopomp aside from myself. They were also put on this path and trained by Hermes. I can't tell people to get into it or seek it out, as it takes someone who is able to see the worst of the worse and still hold themselves together. If you are meant for this path a teacher will reach out to you for your respective path, whether it be a deity or other initiated practitioner.

If you have been contacted about starting on that path I urge you to consider it. If you want to help the dead and dying without being a Death Witch, look into death positivity. There is a lot of jobs in death work and the death positivity movement is a growing one that always needs more people. End of life care may be working as a mortician, death doula, end of life councillor and planning, grief counseling, and more. You can visit your local graveyard and tend to and clean the graves, set up altars for your lost loved ones, and educate yourself on local and foreign death rituals.

If you know any kind of Death Witch, ask them about their practice if they are okay with sharing. We are a secretive and often misunderstood bunch that can seem scary by the name alone. Our job is to help, and we don't bite.

Unless you ask.

—Desirée Goulden

The Future, Regrettably
Coming soon!

The debut urban fantasy novel from Desirée Goulden, prequel to the Aurora Garroway series.

Julian is a man with nothing but a name. Woken from a coma and thrust into a war he does not want to fight, he is the body guard and right hand man of a tyrannical cult leader, Rose. Escape is futile and attempts cause innocent people to be killed to keep him in line. With death as the only escape, he becomes reckless in battle, hoping to be cut down and finally escape the life he is trapped in.

Rose notices and offers him a boon: stay in line and do as she says and he will be able to visit the future in his dreams. He will be able to live a comfortable life and see why the Conduit Hierarchy's war is just, and how it will better the world.

Will this be enough to pacify Julian? Or will this motivate him to tear down the organization that seeks to control him, and find the truth?

(Crystals)

Crystals have become a mainstay in new age practice. Crystals contain and can help move and transform energy that we can use in out practice and lives. While many more traditional paths do not often involve crystals, and certainly not in the way new age practitioners use them, they are very common in many paths now-a-days

(Agate)

Prosperity, health, abundance, ward against negativity

(Amber)

Purification, ease of pain, ward against negativity, grieving, protection, illness recovery, beauty, fertility

(Amethyst)
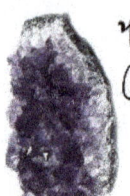
Royalty, intuition, sobriety, peace, calm, creativity

(Bloodstone)

Renewal, presentness, self-confidence, victory over enemies, breaking down of others defenses, unselfishness, intuition

(Clear quartz)

Clarity, focus, cleansing, healing, purify energy, calmness, inner peace

(Hematite)

Grounding, money, decisions, manifestations, money, focus, stability, balance, divination, problem solving, communication, strength

(Jade)

Clarity, focus, cleansing, healing, purify energy, calmness, inner peace

(Jasper)

Grounding, money, decisions, manifestations, money, focus, stability, balance, divination, problem solving, communication, strength

(Crystals)

(Lapis Lazuli)
Opens minds, self awareness, self esteem, peace, harmony, morality

(Moonstone)
Connecting to feminine energy, fertility, calming, the moon, intuition, remove negativity, protection when travelling at night, balance

(Obsidian)
Scrying, protection, ward against negativity, blocks psychic attacks, clarity, past life healing

(Opal)
Love, passion, desire, freedom, independence, realizing potential, creativity, good luck

(Rose quartz)
Strengthening love, sex, passion, blocks nightmares, calms conflict, emotional healing

(Selenite)
The moon, protection, cleansing, purity, innocence, spiritual growth

(Tiger's Eye)
Fearlessness, certanty, courage, grace, action, wisdom, understanding beyond emotional interference

(Turquoise)
Dream work, fertility, wards against negativity, happiness, compassion, manifestation, creativity, clear communication, intuition

(Plant & herbs)

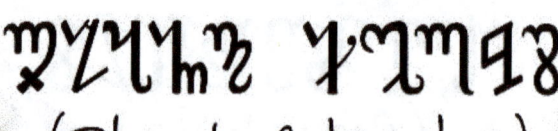

(Apple)
Love, healing, fertility, immortality, beauty. The wood is prime for wand making.

(Basil)
Happiness, peace, love, money attraction, protection.

(Black Pepper)
Protection, healing.

(Chamomile)
Money, peace, love, tranquility, purification, aids in meditation.

(Cinnamon)
Love, happiness, money.

(Clove)
Luck, prosperity, friendship, stops gossip.

(Garlic)
Repel unwanted advances, used in love magic, used in baneful workings, repels the evil eye and thieves, luck, love, aphrodisiac, exorcisms, strength, spell breaking.

(Lavender)
Purification, clarity, fertility, love

(Lemon)
Purification, cleansing, love, repel or break spells against you, turns away the evil eye.

(Oregano)
Happiness, joy tranquility, luck, health, protection, letting go, strengthen love.
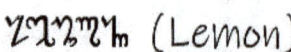

(Plant & herbs)

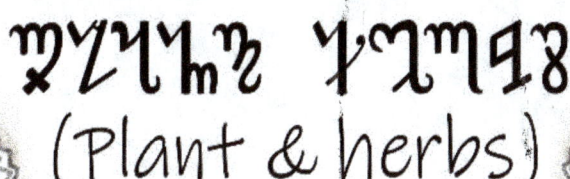

(Parsley)

Necromancy, strength, passion, vitality, sobriety.

(Rosemary)

Fidelity, the removal of jealousy, memory, recollection of dreams, money, cleansing of negativity.

(Sage (Not white))

Cleansing, immortality, protection, grant wishes, wisdom, easing pain from the death of a loved one.

(Star Anise)

Youth, repel nightmares, lust, blessings, exorcisms, aids divination, attracts spirits.

(Thyme)
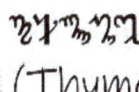

Strength, courage, positivity, remove negativity, remove sadness, happy dreams, repel nightmares.

pagans & cremation.

In 2014 47% of people within the USA chose cremation over traditional burial, but how many people know that without Pagans, you would most likely not be able to have that option?

While cremation was always around in some form (There are records of burning bodies as funeral processes as far back as Ancient Athens ((1100 BC))) across the world, American Christian grievers were taken aback at the thought of them. American at the time of the first cremation (1876) were very concerned with the preservation of one's self after death and referred to cremation as dehumanizing and disgusting. Caitlin Doughty, Mortician, owner of Clarity Funerals and Cremation of Los Angeles, author, and YouTuber, reports that one of the reviewers of the first cremation called it "Another exemplification of the wickedness of the metropolis" which should give you an idea as to how the general populous thought of cremation.

Cremation wouldn't really shake its stigma and become popular until the 1980's, but if it wasn't for the Theosophical Society Of America, I have my doubts that it ever would be as popular as what it is now. But what is the Theosophical Society and what happened during the first cremation?

The Theosophical Society Of America was formed in 1875 by Helena Petrovna Blavatsky, noblewoman, Colonel Henry Steel Olcott and William Quan Judge, attorneys and 16 others.

This religious movement hand amongst its members noblemen and women and influential people of status, including Thomas Edison and William Butler Yeats.

The Society states its beliefs as follows from it's website, https://www.theosophical.org/ "Ever since its founding in 1875, the Theosophical Society has stood for freedom of thought and respect for all people regardless of race, class, caste, sex, or religion. To join the Theosophical Society, you are required to have no specific beliefs. You need only to state your agreement with the Society's Three Objects:

1. To form a nucleus of the universal brotherhood of humanity, without distinction of race, creed, sex, caste, or color.

2. To encourage the comparative study of religion, philosophy, and science.

3. To investigate unexplained laws of nature and the powers latent in humanity."
It draws it's belief system from Vedānta, Mahāyāna Buddhism, Qabbalah, and Sufism and wants to unite Eastern and Western practices to show the commonality of human culture.

Given this rather progressive thinking (particularly for the 1870's) it is easy to see how this group would straddle the line of what was acceptable and what was obscene for the time. It seems people could not come to a conclusion as to what to think of the group as they either loved or hated the idea. None the less, regardless of the public opinion, they made it a goal to push forward with presenting cremation to the western world. A move allowed only by their titles, and class, and money, no doubt.

The first cremation was the cremation of Baron Joseph Henry Louis Charles, Baron de Palm, who died after battling with an illness that effected many of his organs.

He left his body and much of his estate to Olcott for his kindness to him in life. He also requested in his will that no clergyman or priest should officiate at his funeral.

His funeral was held as the Masonic Temple in New York on the corner of 23rd Street and 6th Avenue on May 20, 1876. His funeral was a grand spectacle that many "reviewers" showed up to report upon for local news papers. There was roughly 2000 guests for the Baron's funeral. It was due to this media presence that we know what happened during the funerary ceremonies. One of re reporters from The New York Times called the ceremony "a hodge-podge of notions, a mixture of guess-work and jugglery, of elixirs and pentagons, of charms and conjurations"

The ceremonies consisted of "a home-brewed liturgy of Hindu scriptures, passages from Charles Darwin's writings, scraps of spiritualism and transcendentalism, references to fire worship, and invocations of the Nile goddess Isis" and were called "Folly," "farce," "weird," "objectionable," "repulsive," "revolting," "a desecration" "one might have supposed that the company had been assembled to have a good time over roast pig." (via https://www.questia.com/) To the common Christen citizen of the day, this may very well have seemed to be a barbaric display of glee over the death of the Baron. To modern practitioners, this may seem to be a appropriation of many cultures and religions with no real acknowledgement of the fact that if anyone of the cultures of which the Theosophical Society took from tried this, the already abysmal reception would have been far worse.

So they had their ceremony and weather they had wanted the negative press or not, they caught the attention of the United States Of America. Did this allow for them to cremate the body? No. In fact it would be 6 months before the Baron could be cremated. Dr. Francis Julius LeMoyne designed the crematorium that would eventually cremate De Palm.

LeMoyne had the plans for his crematorium for some time, as he began to worry about pollution from the decomposing bodies after traditional burial (a thought process that at the time were unfounded but if he lived today with the commonplace of embalming would have been a valid concern) but was bound by his own money for the project and hindered by protests every step of the way. All while De Palm waited for his body to be tended to. You can't really blame people at the time for disliking the process. I imagine that this would be extremely macabre to the common folk, especially when you consider that they lost the body of De Palm amongst the cargo on the train carrying him to the crematory. You can't blame them from being struck with fear when he was put into the machine finally and his arm stuck up and apparently raising 3 fingers (it is a normal part of the crematory process for the limbs to curl up and contort as the body burns and the liquid vaporizes out of the body).

Despite the spectacle and outrage, the LeMoyne crematory would continue to cremate bodies after that. It closed in 1901 after cremating 42 bodies, LeMoyne included. His ashes were buried on the property and a headstone stands over them to this day.

As for De Palm, his remains were put into a "Hindu-style urn" and spectators took with them some of his ashes. LeMoyne took some of his bones to keep on his desk and there were rumours that some of the Theosophical Society kept some of De Palm's ashes in snuff boxes which they carried on them, although that may have just been a fanciful rumour.

Since then, cremations became more and more common until today where they account for around half of funerals in America. We may never know if cremation would have become acceptable if it weren't for LeMoyne, De Palm and The Theosophical Society, I for one doubt it would have, but none the less we have them to thank for cremation.

I can't help but to think that one could make a interesting historical comedy based off these events. If you want to know more, head to AskAMortician on YouTube, or watch the connected video beneath this.

It's always interesting to see where Pagan influence lies in modern society, and this shows that we can all make positive change in the world. Even if you're a penniless faux Baron, a strange old man with dreams of burning corpses, or a person who thinks cremation is the only way to stop vampires (listen it was the 1800's it was a valid concern back in the day) never doubt that you as a Pagan can bring about change.

-Desirée Goulden

Tales Of The Gods

Free shops & services listings

Have a shop or service and want to extend your reach without speding some coin? Contact us! We will set up your shop in our public database including a explination of your business and a landing page to display your wares!

We will post you on our online shops and services for free! Just contact us at our contact page on TalesOfTheGods.com or send us a email at TalesOTheGods@gmail.com or at our social medias! We can be found on Facebook, Twitter, and Instagram!

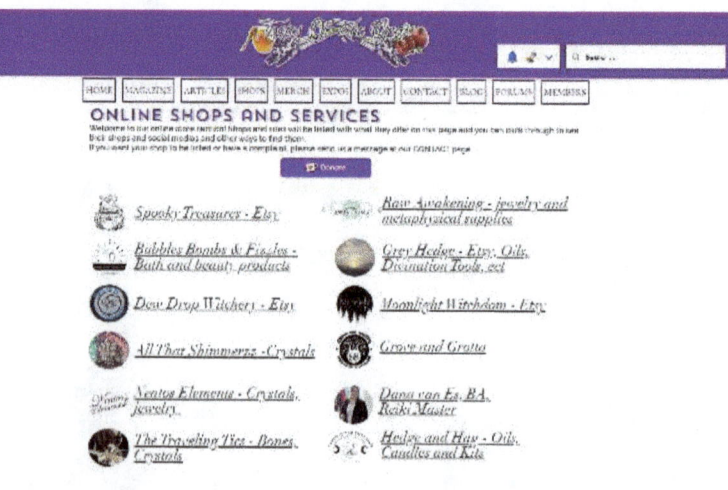

Magazine Updates

The Yule edition marks the one year anniversary of the TalesOfTheGods & Practical Witchcraft magazine! Since the beginning this magazine has gone through many changes. Staff changes, publisher changes, format changes, and more! Not all of these changes have come without growing pains.

You may have noticed the last 3 editions were not released on the day of the wheel of the year for which they are named. Recently we have changed to a new publisher, IngramSpark. As IngramSpark distributes to hundreds of book stores across the world both online and off, it takes time for sellers to get the copies of the magazine. On top of this, there is also a fee of about $60 cad that has to be paid to publish the magazine. As this is a small group of creators, and is made with a budget of $0, that money comes out of pocket on my end and thus if a publication date falls in the middle of the month I may not be able to pay said fee.

We are working on changing this but it takes time as it requires shifting the entire production time back a month. The Yule edition will come out on time, and likely earlier as we finally hit a part of the wheel of the year where we aren't essentially publishing month after month back to back.

We also have finally figured out the problems regarding the digital editions, and from now on out there should be no problem with the Kindle print reproduction of the magazine.

People have been contacting us about creating a subscription for the magazine, and we are working on it. It is likely that a digital edition subscription will be implemented but it is a work in process and will likely result in PDF's being distributed rather than Kindle editions. Like I said, this is a work in process and the details are being ironed out. A physical subscription will be created in time, but that will most likely be done in mid to late 2022.

We decided to axe the TalesOfTheGods & Practical Witchcraft Archives due to a lack of interest, and settled on a once yearly collection of all the magazines in that said year. After Yule you will be able to find the 2021 compilation which will be a single hardback book containing the full colour editions of all the magazines within it. It will also contain contributor bios and information about the magazine. You will be able to see the improvements over the year, and the journey from a small KDP publication to a more professional and constant witchy magazine.

We thank you for your patience and for sticking with us through our journey. We look forward to the coming years, and to bringing you pagan and occult entertainment, education, and news for people of all paths and levels of experience.

www.ingramcontent.com/pod-product-compliance
Lightning Source LLC
Chambersburg PA
CBHW080628170426
43209CB00007B/1538